Y0-BZG-002

Game Work

Game Work

Language, Power, and Computer Game Culture

Ken S. McAllister

The University of Alabama Press
Tuscaloosa

Manufactured in the United States of America

Typeface: Minion and Goudy Sans

∞
The paper on which this book is printed meets the minimum requirements of American National Standard for Information Science—Permanence of Paper for Printed Library Materials, ANSI Z39.48-1984.

Library of Congress Cataloging-in-Publication Data

McAllister, Ken S., 1966–
Game work : language, power, and computer game culture / Ken S. McAllister.
p. cm. — (Rhetoric, culture, and social critique)
Includes bibliographical references and index.
ISBN 0-8173-1418-0 (cloth : alk. paper) — ISBN 0-8173-5125-6 (pbk. : alk. paper)
1. Computer games—Social aspects. 2. Electronic games industry. I. Title. II. Series.
GV1469.17.S63M33 2005
794.8—dc22
2004010252

Contents

Preface vii
Acknowledgments xiii

PART 1
INTRODUCTION TO PART 1
1. Studying the Computer Game Complex 5
Computer Games as Mass Culture 9
Computer Games as Mass Media 13
Computer Games as Psychophysiological Force 14
Computer Games as Economic Force 18
Computer Games as Instructional Force 24
So, Why Study Computer Games? 25

2. A Grammar of Gamework 27
Rhetoric and Dialectic 29
Propositions of the Gamework 31
The Problematic of Play 34
The Grammar of Gameworks: Analyzing the Computer Game Complex 41

PART 2
INTRODUCTION TO PART 2
3. Capturing Imaginations: Rhetoric in the Art of Computer Game Development 71
Rhetorical Functions Revisited 78
Rhetoric in the Discourse of Game Developers 80
Working Through the Grammar of Gameworks: Agents, Influences, Manifestations, and Transformative Locales 114

4. Making Meanings Out of Contradictions: The Work of Computer Game Reviewing 118
Computer Game Reviewing Online 120

Computer Game Reviewing in Print 126
Playing Up Influence to Influence Play 129
Reviewing the Meanings of the Computer Game Complex 139

5. The Economies of *Black & White* 140
Defining Economies 144
The "Purchase" of Natural Resources 149
The "Purchase" of Spiritual Resources 154
The "Purchase" of Temporal Resources 156
The Work of *Black & White* 157
Transformative Locales: Economic Force as Game Work 166

Epilogue 169

Appendices 171

Notes 205

Works Cited 219

Index 227

Preface

Technically speaking, computer games—the term I use to designate any game that requires a computer to work, including those for desktop machines, console and coin-op systems, and handheld devices—are software applications, just like word processors, image editors, and database programs.[1] Anyone who plays computer games seriously, however, will tell you that games are *not* essentially the same as Microsoft Word, Photoshop, or Oracle, but rather are much more: they are works of art. Using unique combinations of image, sound, and interactivity, computer games draw players in, getting them to think and act, to use their imaginations to solve problems, and to have fun in make-believe worlds. Not all games succeed equally as artworks, of course, but these rough criteria indicate how gamers can quite reasonably lay claim to that designation.

But computer games are really "works" in the broadest sense of that term. They require work to create; they require players to work to engage with them; they are themselves both works of art and industrial works; and finally, they *do* work, particularly rhetorical and cultural work. Computer games are always condensates of all this work, yet they often seem to stand estranged from it. *Splinter Cell,* for example, is just another game to most consumers, perhaps at most associated with spy novelist Tom Clancy. But *Splinter Cell* required the work and labor of hundreds—perhaps even thousands—of people, and in an important way changed the computer game industry by advancing the art of computer game writing—not writing code but rather writing skillfully crafted language around plot twists, scene descriptions, and dialogue. So why aren't the names and faces of *Splinter Cell*'s writers—Clint Hocking and J. T. Petty—noted prominently on the packaging? The simplest answer is that where games are concerned, looks are more compelling to most shoppers than promises of "good storytelling" or "sharp dialogue."

So, does the art of the sale ultimately trump the musical, graphical, and verbal arts in the computer game industry? Often—many would say too often—the answer is yes. But the game industry is highly competitive, and a good sales pitch or celebrity eye candy will go only so far if the game itself doesn't deliver. The game *Daikatana*, for instance, received massive media hype and had very well respected developers behind the project, but when it was endlessly delayed and then failed to impress (or even entertain) critics and gamers, *Daikatana* became the poster product for how good work can go bad. To those who study computer games, then, the work that makes games what they are in a sociocultural context is dynamic, multidisciplinary, and frequently rendered invisible. Computer games are, in a word, complicated.

As artifacts, computer games are extraordinarily difficult to study because they are so socially complex; recollections of how they were inspired and of the myriad collective and negotiated decisions that gave them their final form, as well as explanations of how and in what contexts they are eventually to be experienced, are difficult to identify and reconstruct. To paraphrase Sigmund Freud (who was actually writing about "dream work," not the gamework): the game is meager, paltry, and laconic in comparison with the range and copiousness of the influences that made it what it is. The analyst's work, then, is to try to "recollect" some of these influences in order to see other meanings of the game and its contexts.[2] This book sets out a method for doing just this sort of recollection and does so (I hope) without sacrificing too much of the complexity that makes computer games so unique as a medium of expression, instruction, entertainment, and moneymaking.

I should confess here to having mixed feelings about computer games. According to a recently developed survey instrument that types game players from "Non-player/Ultra Casual" to "Obsessive/Ultra Hardcore," I fall well within the latter category. I am, however, probably unlike most other "ultra hardcore" gamers in that much of the time (though not all) I spend playing, researching, and thinking about games is from a critical perspective. I puzzle over the ways ideology is coded into games, follow the ways legislators and industry lobbyists dance uncomfortably around issues like media violence and censorship, and study the ways that game developers describe the work they do. I admit that I derive a vicarious thrill from all of this. Should anyone in the computer gaming industry read this book, they will no doubt say to themselves: "Now here is a wannabe game designer if ever there was one."

And they will be right. Like many of the people described in the pages that follow, I have spent many hours—hours that by now have run into months—not only playing games but also reading gaming magazines, building "mods" (post-release add-ons to commercially developed games), and customizing various home-built computers to get games like *Quake* and *Wing Commander* to run as smoothly as possible. I've even written a couple of games, the best of which—"Cave-In"—made me famous among my other TI-99-using friends for at least two weeks back in the summer of 1982. I wasn't out to get rich. I was simply fascinated by the surprising things that could be done with programming languages. And I was amazed that so many people laughed, got scared, and lost an obscene amount of sleep because of certain configurations of GOTO statements and variable arrays.

In retrospect I see what was so compelling to me about the art of computer game design was that the professionals who practiced this art were thinking hard about how language, images, gestures, and sound could influence and grip people, an art that I now associate with the fields of rhetoric, communication, and media arts. Among the things I discovered in the course of writing *Game Work* is that, by and large, game studies scholars—whether they're engineers, historians, or specialists in media, communication, or rhetorical theory—recognize and are trying to document the ways computer games exert influence on individuals, communities, cultures, and societies. They are all—academics and game developers alike—working to understand the manifold powers of influence that coalesce in and around computer games and to wield that influence in critical and compelling ways.

Like other forms of media, computer games can work to build up, maintain, or reject what players (among others) believe about a wide range of subjects, from the constitution of truth and goodness to understandings of social mores and global politics. Like poetry, fiction, journalism, and film, computer games can work to maintain the status quo, celebrate liberation, tolerate enslavement, and conjure feelings of hope and despair, assent and dissent, clarity and confusion. They can play equally well on emotion and rationality, pervade radical discourse and common sense alike, and exist comfortably at all points on a semiotic continuum that spans the idiosyncratic to the universal. In short, a good deal of the work of computer games is that they are always making and managing meanings, sometimes by demonstration and sometimes through interpretation. Such work is always simultaneously, then, the work of power negotiation.

Game Work examines these processes of meaning-making and power negotiation both in computer games themselves and in the industry that surrounds them. It is written for people who, like me, are interested in and concerned about the influences of and on computer games, gamers, and the computer game industry, an amalgam I call the "computer game complex." Such people are interested in trying to understand this influence in ways that extend beyond easy moralism and casual commercialism. In addition to scholars of the technologies of influence—people who try to understand how discourse changes people and the world in which they live—this book is also for game developers, game reviewers, and game players, all of whom live every day in and among these discourses and have as much (if not more) responsibility as scholars for thinking about the power of the meaning-making processes with which they work and play.

In part 1 of *Game Work* I offer a glimpse into the efforts that have gone into building the computer game complex over the past fifty years and provide a fairly comprehensive overview of the English-language scholarship that concerns games. I focus in particular on the ways that balances of power inside and outside the computer game complex have shifted in response to factors such as a fluctuating U.S. economy and emerging trends in other media industries. The critical method I put forward in the second chapter and explicate in subsequent ones is specifically designed to facilitate the investigation of the computer game complex, and takes into consideration the necessity that such a method be what Doug Kellner calls "multiperspectival."

Part 2 of *Game Work* demonstrates the critical method described in part 1 in three different contexts. Chapter 3 looks at how computer game designers communicate with each other about the work they do and examines how they cope with some of the contradictory positions within which they often find themselves working. Chapter 4 turns to game reviewing, which, like other kinds of rudimentary media analysis, both evaluates its subject according to certain criteria and establishes those criteria as valuable. Here, I specifically use the grammar of gameworks to show how influences like the mass media, mass culture, and psychophysiological, economic, and instructional force are brought to bear by consumers to shape the market for computer games and to negotiate the contradictions of computer gaming that are so apparent in popular journalism. *Game Work* concludes with an analysis of a single game, the remarkable *Black & White.* Using a relational (i.e., Marxist) rather than monetary understanding of "economy," I show how understanding a complex set of virtual economies can facilitate an understanding (not necessarily a good one) of the infinitely more complex economies of life under global capitalism. This chapter is the most pedagogically oriented one of the book, suggesting as it does that undertaking such analyses is an educational experience itself, one that is particularly well suited for students in cultures in which games have a considerable role in shaping interpretive frameworks.

Readers will find at the back of the book several appendices that may prove useful. Appendices A and B are diagrams of different aspects of the grammar of gameworks. For visual thinkers, or for readers who are dipping into the book here and there, these diagrams may help to clarify the conceptual relationships outlined in detail throughout the book. Appendix C is a listing of all the games that are mentioned in the book, along with their publishers and release dates. Appendix D is a brief description of "How to Run a Game Night," a hands-on application of some of what this book is about, and which my colleagues David Menchaca, Judd Ruggill, Lonni Pearce, Jeffrey Reed, and I have developed over the past several years. Finally, appendix E is a glossary that contains not only brief definitions of the rhetorical concepts described here but also of game-related technical terms that occasionally appear throughout the book. These terms appear italicized when they are first discussed in detail.

The ultimate goal of gamework analyses is to help scholars actively engage the rhetoric and dialectic of computer games with a clearer understanding of how the computer game complex has effected individual, communal, and social transformations in the past. It also works to understand how these processes are continuing and changing here at the dawn of the third millennium. To begin, chapter 1 briefly surveys the computer game complex from a research perspective and sets the stage for the grammar of gameworks outlined in chapter 2.

Acknowledgments

Most academic projects, I imagine, seem a little bit strange—abstract yet highly focused—to the communities of which their authors are a part. For example, as an avid caver I was often acutely aware that my friends in the local chapter of the National Speleological Society were being remarkably supportive of me even though they didn't entirely understand why studying computer games was an important scholarly undertaking. Similarly, many of my academic colleagues—Theresa Enos, Tom Miller, Ed White, Roxanne Mountford, and Amy Kimme-Hae in particular—were very gracious about the fact that while their work took them to illustrious manuscript archives around the world, required them to pore over Latin, Greek, German, and French texts, and to untangle the knots inherent in the history of rhetoric and composition, my research took me to video arcades around the world, required me to learn the languages of the PlayStation, Xbox, GameCube, and Dreamcast, and to untangle the knots inherent in the design of games like *Oddworld, Halo,* and *Dance, Dance, Revolution.*

I could not have written *Game Work* without the help and support of many people, some of whom worked with me on my ideas and prose, while others helped me to stay engaged with the world beyond my research. Among the former group, first and foremost were Judd Ruggill, David Menchaca, Ron Scott, Lonni Pearce, Ryan Moeller, Jeffrey Reed, and Bryan Pearce. These friends spent innumerable hours talking with me, helping me to refine my analyses of the computer game complex, and offering ruthless critiques of my writing (to paraphrase Marx). It is no exaggeration to say that without their help you would not be reading this book today.

I was fortunate, too, to have friends who despite their own very busy research schedules made time to listen and support me in mine: John Warnock,

Tilly Warnock, Larry Evers, M. J. Braun, Cathy Chaput, Jill McCracken, Hale Thomas, Alison Miller, Lourdes Canto, Stephanie Pearman, Susan Bouldin, Danika Brown, Jim Sosnoski, Bryan Carter, Marcelo Milrad, Barry Brummett, Chuck Tatum, Reeve Huston, Jerry Gill, Mari Sori, Nina and Sam Dellaria, and all of the graduate students with whom I've worked. John Lucaites, Daniel Waterman, and Jill Hughes also offered immeasurably helpful suggestions for refining my argument and prose. Without exception, these friends and colleagues helped me clarify my objectives and, in the midst of a subject that threatens to overwhelm at every turn, to keep my focus.

I'm also grateful to the people who, while they may not have read drafts of the manuscript or helped me "research" the classic games subculture, did help keep my life balanced between work and play. Andy McCune, Scott Street, Marshal Vest, and Randy Mayer were the best banjo buddies I could hope for, always knowing just when to insist that I get away from the computer screen and pick up my five-string. I'm grateful as well to Dennis and Rebecca O'Sullivan, Steve Smith, Lang Brod, Ron and Kathy Dehn, Judy and Marion Vittetoe, Jean-Paul Jorquera, Joanne Staley, Henry Truebe, Joe and Mike Gallardo, Brett Cook, Dave and Phyllis Hamer, Sue McCready, Jerry Orcutt, and all the rest of the gang in the Escabrosa Grotto who asked that I use some of my energies to help nurture southern Arizona caves and the caving community.

I'm grateful, too, for all the love and support of my near and extended family: Susan Reggin; Amanda, Rich, and Jacob Paige; Amiee Reggin; Cheryl and Will Rennick; Don and Dianne Nisbett; Jennifer, Bob, Madison, and Michael James; Kim, Charlie, Josh, and Ashley Woods; Alice and John Srubas; Jon Srubas; Amy Srubas; Michael Giammanco; Ellis and Kendall Srubas-Giammanco; Mike Perkovich; Ralph Johnson; Sam and Joel Pearce; Julie, Jacob, and Noah Moeller; Rose Taul; Jean Bronson; Melanie Sethney; and all the monks at the Benedictine Monastery of the Sisters of Perpetual Adoration (Tucson, Arizona) and at Christ in the Desert Monastery (Abiquiu, New Mexico). Thanks to you all for believing in me.

Finally, I want to thank my wife, Rachel Srubas. Even though she'd never played a computer game in her life, she had the vision to see the importance of studying them as cultural artifacts with transformative potential. Such clear vision, coupled with her perception of the relationships among language, politics, and play, has been a great gift to me, both as a scholar and as a human being. With all that I have, Rachel, and all that I am, I dedicate this book to you.

Game Work

PART I
Introduction to Part I

In order to set the scene for this multiperspectival approach, I begin by surveying the themes and contradictory findings of computer game research. In subsections titled "Games as Mass Culture," "Games as Mass Media," "Games as Psychophysiological Force," "Games as Economic Force," and "Games as Instructional Force," I examine the areas in culture where computer games have both catalyzed transformative effects and have themselves been transformed by these cultural forces. Clearly the contradictory nature of the research indicates an important site of discursive and cultural struggle, but the stakes of this struggle are often ambiguous: Is it merely dominance over a lucrative market niche or the prestige of industry awards like "Best Game" or "Top Gamer"? Or is this struggle about something more profound, perhaps about the importance of equitable human relationships or the balancing of technological advancement against a meaningful ethical framework?

The method I detail offers a way to investigate such questions and is modeled on Kenneth Burke's concept of a "grammar," though it also draws on a Marxist understanding of the dialectic. This "grammar of gameworks" proposes that one way to make meaning out of an artifact like a computer game is to see how it "works" in five integral areas of power: agents (who have the power to catalyze transformative effects); functions (the purported and actual purposes of these effects); influences (the external forces that impinge upon agents and functions and that inevitably change the transformative effects of historically situated artifacts); manifestations (the ways in which transformative efforts are realized in particular contexts); and transformative locales (the spatiotemporal instances in which ideologies—individual, communal, or societal—have *specific* transformative effects). This grammar affords computer game scholars a flexible framework by which they may arrange their examinations of particular struggles they see playing out in computer games and in the electronic entertainment industry.

This flexibility has its costs. The grammar of gameworks dictates that examinations undertaken according to its protocols necessarily consider dominant discourses, suasory techniques, sociopolitical interests, and the points and conditions under which transformations are possible in given cases and contexts. The breadth of this method can seem overwhelming at first, but in practice the grammar of gameworks usually presents scholars with only a few notable challenges. First, one must decide where among the five areas of power their research and critical attention will be focused: on agents and their influences, perhaps, or on functions, manifestations, and transformative locales? While it is possible and even ideal for the computer game scholar to address in equal depth all five of the areas of power, practically speaking it would be exceedingly difficult. More likely is that the scholar would initially conduct research into all five areas as they relate to a chosen subject but would then select only two or three to investigate in depth. The advantage of proceeding in this way is that the preliminary process of investigating all the general areas of power allows one to develop an overall perspective of the ways a particular subject mediates and is mediated by a variety of forces. This perspective helps prevent the scholar from seeing a subject too narrowly, even after he or she has drilled down into a particular aspect of it.

Another challenge that the grammar of gameworks raises is that attending even briefly to the multiple ways power is negotiated in the computer game complex inevitably requires the scholar to discuss some of the complex's most technical aspects. In chapter 3 of *Game Work,* for example, I examine the discourse of game developers in order to show how the agents of game production negotiate the contradictions that prevail in their work. Because developers' language tends to be highly technical—peppered with mathematical, programming, and industry jargon—the analyst must be mindful of the fact that explications of such discourse will sometimes begin to seem indistinguishable from it. The upshot of such tight analytical integration can be that some readers will sense a shift in the critique's audience from interested bystander to native speaker of the cant.

This audience dilemma, I propose, is inherent to all multiperspectival projects, because at some point the analyst undertaking it will have to explain the suasory mechanisms of the subject's most technical elements. Film scholars, for example, may spend most of their time considering such elements as plot, dialogue, and symbol, but eventually they must also come to terms (literally) with auteurship, that is, the art of filmmaking: camera angles, optical and digital lens characteristics, tracking techniques, blocking, Foley effects, lighting, and so on. The same is true of game work; discussing the impact of virtual violence on young minds, the importance of genre tropes in making a game a best seller, and the ubiquity of racist and sexist imagery are all vital ways of approaching computer game criticism, but at some point, scholars must also interrogate developers' knowledge of hardware acceleration techniques, data-set bone manipulation, and MIP mapping if their investigations are going to be truly multiperspectival and encompass the elements of production as well as those of marketing and consumption.[1]

In his essay "Critical Theory and British Cultural Studies," Doug Kellner summarizes well the requirements of "multiperspectival cultural studies":

> I am proposing that cultural studies develop a multiperspectival approach which includes investigation of a wide range of artifacts interrogating relationships within the three dimensions of: (1) the production and political economy of culture; (2) textual analysis and critique of its artifacts; and (3) study of audience reception and the uses of media/cultural products. This proposal involves suggesting, first, that cultural studies itself be multiperspectival, getting at culture from the perspectives of political economy and production, text analysis and audience reception. I would also propose that textual analysis and audience reception studies utilize a multiplicity of perspectives, or critical methods, when engaging in textual analysis, and in delineating the multiplicity of subject positions, or perspectives, through which audiences appropriate culture. Moreover, I would argue that the results of such studies need to be interpreted and contextualized within critical social theory to adequately delineate their meanings and effects. (25)

Game Work is just such a multiperspectival project, and it addresses the audience dilemma by being sensitive to its potentially disorienting effects. Kellner suggests that readers must learn to see and interpret the results of multiperspectival studies with eyes and minds as similarly dynamic as those of the scholars who developed them. In the many workshops and talks I've given about gamework analysis, I've learned that such vision does not always come readily, and so I provide as many orienting markers as seem necessary to help readers critically assimilate production-side technicalities.

1
Studying the Computer Game Complex

Steve, a happily married forty-four-year-old man with two kids, sits before a nineteen-inch flat-screen computer monitor, a joystick in his hand. And not just any joystick. Steve grips the award-winning Logitech Wingman Force, a game controller modeled after the joysticks in the latest fighter jets. It has nine buttons, a throttle mechanism, and a "POV" hat switch that allows him to look sideways, above, and behind his simulated "Warthog," a U.S. Air Force A-10 Thunderbolt II. The Intel Pentium 4 processor (3.2 GHz) and NVIDIA GeForce Ultra 5950 video card with 256 MB of onboard RAM render the ground below the aircraft with amazing realism, and because Steve has activated the simulator's "weather effects," the joystick shakes in his hand when he flies through turbulence. The stick also gives him a jolt when he kicks in the afterburners and vibrates when he pulls the trigger. The vibrations are rapid but dull in his palm, just how Steve expects it would feel to fire off thirty-millimeter rounds loaded into a real nose-mounted General Electric GAU-8/A Avenger seven-barrel cannon. And though Steve is only a casual player of Jane's USAF*—five to ten hours a week—he has already played this simulation for more than fifty hours (and he's still working on the training missions). Tonight he plans to focus his training on air-to-ground attacks, especially moving targets like tanks and supply convoys. Lieutenant Colonel "Scooter" Davis, the simulator's training persona, warns Steve that today's practice is going to be a tough one but wishes him "Happy Flying" just the same. Steve smiles and tightens his grip on the joystick. "Bring it on," he says, and moments later he loses touch with the real world as he works the sluggish virtual Warthog down runway 22R of Nellis Air Force Base and takes to the sky.*

~

In the media wake of the Littleton, Colorado, high school shooting in 1999, news coverage quickly turned to finger-pointing as people struggled to understand what could have motivated such youth violence. Within twenty-four hours, national TV news programs were reporting that the young men who had walked into their school and shot thirteen classmates to death had two unsavory pastimes: listening to Goth music and playing computer games. Within forty-eight hours, dozens of newspapers had printed stories specifically on these two elements of this tragic event.

Nothing about these stories, which seemed most interested in scapegoating the band Marilyn Manson and computer games like *Doom,* was very revealing. Music has been blamed for corrupting youth for centuries. And despite the fact that at the beginning of the twenty-first century they are arguably little more than a hybrid medium extending the genres of film, TV, fiction, and comic books, *computer games* have a similarly troubled—if shorter—past. Stories about both were formulaic: music and games are popular, engaging, and filled with disturbing images of rage, despair, supernaturalism, and death. It is to be expected then, the stories suggested, that those who are exposed to such material are going to be changed, made somehow more amenable to acting out in their own lives these supposedly artistic expressions of others' profound frustration with the world. This narrative formula generally continues with a bit of scientism noting the considerable research that purportedly establishes a link between media exposure and violent tendencies in youth, offers several semi-shocking excerpts from a song or a violent screenshot from a game, and concludes by advising people—parents especially—to attend to their children (and to themselves) lest they be further exposed to such deleterious effects.

Newspaper headlines demonstrated this formula as well. After the Littleton shooting, the Reuters newswire service distributed a story headlined "Colorado Teen Gunmen Liked Computers, War Games" (Reuters). Appreciation is enough to warrant claims of causality in this early "report." *USA Today* took the liberty of explicitly expressing the implied generalizations of earlier computer game–blaming stories by running a piece headlined "Kids, Online and Off, Feast on Violence" (Thomas). This story summarized in broad and affirming strokes the various claims that have been made about how TV, movies, and computer games breed real violence in children by exposing them to its simulated two-dimensional representation. The Littleton assassins, like everyone else but more so, were made psychopathic by their gluttonous consumption of simulated, interactive violence, argues this piece. Three days after the shooting, the *Los Angeles Times* strengthened this accusation—actually a strongly contested one in social science circles—by bolstering it with a remark made by the president in a public address expressing his sorrow about the Littleton shooting: "Clinton Sees Violent Influence in 3 Video Games" (Gerstenzang). Here, in what could reasonably be considered an ironic statement made by the political and military leader of one of the most heavily armed and historically violent countries in the world, Bill Clinton pronounced judgment on violent video games, more or less effectively diverting attention away from the politically sensitive subject of gun control that was concurrently dogging his administration.

Those who are sensitive to media spin-doctoring likely saw this scapegoating of computer games for what it was and dismissed it. Computer game players, however, responded more protectively, arguing in both print and online that one can't blame a technology or its designers for what consumers do after they've had exposure to the technology. Chief among their evidence was the simple fact that millions of people play computer games, but very few of them turn their play into acts of real and sociopathic violence. In the same year as the Littleton shooting, for instance, the Fairfield Research Group conducted a national survey of computer users and determined that there were more than fifty million households with at least one regular computer game player (Eddy). Game players and gaming industry insiders were quick to point out such statistics and to observe further that very few of these households included homicidal maniacs. Instead of blaming *Doom* and *Duke Nukem,* this community tended to blame poor parenting, neurochemical imbalances, and societal values for such random acts of violence.

Andy Eddy, the West Coast editor for *Game Weekly,* articulates this view most succinctly:

> On the surface, it makes sense to take games like *Doom, Quake,* or *Duke Nukem*—[full of] what many would call violence-inspiring activities—and say that they're destroying our youth's ability to discern right from wrong. Of course, it would be great to find a concrete connection between a heinous event and the activities of the ones who committed it, but pointing such a finger at electronic games or other entertainments is at best a knee-jerk reaction.
>
> However, millions of people get enjoyment out of such games every day and don't become deranged murderers. And that's because 99.99% of those gaming enthusiasts see electronic games—and movies and

> TV—for what they are: entertainment sources that inspire the imagination and delve the participant into a diversionary fantasy world for a period of time.

For Eddy and millions of other computer gamers, games are mere diversions, virtual toys that harmlessly entertain the mind, despite their powerfully charged emotional themes.

This position, though, is as untenable as the one held by the scapegoaters. The claim that spending dozens and sometimes hundreds of hours immersed in a simulated interactive environment—exploring, communicating, deciphering, planning, stalking, hiding, and killing—has no significant effect on players is naive at best and malicious at worst. Eddy claims that those who point fingers at electronic games are having a "knee-jerk reaction." While I don't dispute this possibility, in this book I take up the probability that such reactions take place on all sides of the gaming debates and are often equally misinformed. Such a situation results in a rhetorical stalemate that artificially stabilizes the dialectical struggle within which arguments and analyses concerning computer games take place. In the next chapter I will discuss in greater detail what I mean by "dialectical struggle." For now, suffice it to say that it is generative argumentation over irreconcilable viewpoints. A central struggle that was frequently engaged in the stories about the Littleton shooting, for example, was generally reduced to one of the following claims:

1. Computer games affect players only temporarily, that is, only while they are being played. They activate players' imaginations, but for most people, engagement in such fantasy play has little or no effect in their real lives, except perhaps to relieve tension;
2. Computer games incline players to change their behaviors long-term in the real world. They may make players more violent, more selfish, and less patient, but they may also improve their abilities to think logically and strategically and may improve certain psychomotor skills.

These two positions do not, of course, represent the fullness of the struggle concerning the value(s) of computer games but rather reveal a particular subset of the struggle—a struggle that is itself linked to other struggles in society. Despite the media's oversimplification of this antagonism, however, even this subset can give scholars interested in critiquing the *computer game complex* a gross starting point away from which they can work toward developing a more informed understanding of computer games, the gaming industry, and all the people whose lives are touched by computer games. Working toward just such an understanding is a major purpose of this book.

As is always the case with struggles about power, those involving computer games reside at a nexus of forces that, in their interaction, directs how the struggles evolve. The fact that a struggle, a contradiction, or an antagonism—three varieties of ideological and material conflict—can exhibit movement and change is what characterizes it as "dialectical." By identifying the rhetorical forces at this nexus and observing the moments when and the ways in which each of them is sometimes privileged over the others, computer game scholars (professional or not) can develop an understanding of the forces' scopes and ranges of influence. Consequently, we may begin to see more broadly the cultural and psychological complexity of particular struggles —in the case of computer gaming, this broader view would encompass the entertainment industry—and fashion the beginnings of a critical framework that can help us to see new alternatives for working with the struggles in their cultural contexts. Such alternatives may reveal previously unrecognized opportunities for redirecting particular struggles toward more desirable ends; this is the praxis that follows critique. In the sections that follow, I characterize the most influential of these rhetorical forces and describe how they are made to work in and through the computer game complex to construct meanings that shape minds, bodies, and cultures.

Computer Games as Mass Culture

Few people would challenge the assertion that computer games are popular. Games are installed and played on millions of personal computers and console systems like GameCube, PlayStation, Dreamcast, and Xbox. Millions more are loaded into Game Boys, N-Gages, Zodiacs, WonderSwans, and Neo-Geos, handheld computer games that use memory cards and cartridges about the size of a book of matches. Virtually every mall, bar, bowling alley, and movie theater has a sizable video arcade, many of which—unbeknownst to most players—are test beds for the popularity of future PC and console games; if a coin-operated arcade game is popular, *developers* have learned, so too will be the home version.

Another sign of the popularity of computer gaming is the level of celebrity attained by game characters. Many such characters have become household names, from such 1980s classics as Pac-Man and Mario, to the 1990s game stars like Sonic the Hedgehog, Duke Nukem, and Lara Croft.[2] Recent games facilitate this trend by periodically crossing over into other media genres. Dozens of games in stores today include digital movies starring famous (or once-famous) actors: *Wing Commander* (Mark Hamill, John Rhys-Davies, Malcolm McDowell, Ginger Lynn Allen), *Star Trek: Starfleet Academy* (William Shatner, Walter Koenig, and George Takei), and *P.Y.S.T.*—a parody of the extremely popular *Myst*—which stars John Goodman. In addition, more than a dozen games have been turned into feature-length movies, including *Wing Commander, Mortal Kombat, Street Fighter, Tomb Raider,* and *Resident Evil.*

All of these markers of popularity suggest that computer games do become manifest in culture, but in what way does popularity constitute a "force," that is, a power capable of effecting or resisting change? Cultural studies scholars generally agree that there are actually two kinds of popularity: one that emerges naturally and another that is imposed. Donal Carbaugh, for instance, offers three criteria for determining whether or not something is "popular": it must be "(a) deeply felt, (b) commonly intelligible, and (c) widely accessible" (38). This definition reflects a more emergent conception of "popular," one that fits such cultural phenomena as folk music and mythology. On the other hand, Barry Brummett's citation of Raymond Williams's "venerable" definition of "popular" as "work deliberately setting out to win favor" suggests how contrived popularity can be (Brummett xxi). Carbaugh's definition, which is an amalgam of many similar understandings of the term "popular" used by pop culture scholars, discerns that a popular artifact affects a wide audience's emotions ("deeply felt") and minds ("commonly intelligible") and is readily available ("widely accessible"). Unlike Williams's definition, which clearly points out the agency behind popular artifacts, Carbaugh's "popular" provides only the merest hint of the people behind the artifact, the popularity makers.

Richard Ohmann takes up this very distinction, renaming it the difference between "popular" and "mass" culture. He writes that "mass culture"

> signals the homogenization, the overriding of local and subcultural distinctions, that has accompanied the expansion of media in our century, and rightly implies the power of the culture industries to shape audiences and groups of consumers. It wrongly implies a passivity and a static uniformity of audiences, and connotes a snobbish disparagement of popular tastes, or at worst of the people themselves. "Popular culture" restores the respect withdrawn by the other term; it credits popularity as authentic (not cynically imposed from above), and rightly implies a more active role for audiences in choosing and interpreting entertainments. But it erases the stark inequality inherent in late-

> twentieth-century cultural production, and often implies a politically mystifying celebration of marketplace democracy. (14)

In the end, writes Ohmann, "[n]either term is adequate," but he opts for "mass culture" as the ruling one for his subject—early-twentieth-century popular magazines—because he wants "to keep questions of production and power in the foreground" (14).

I share this desire, and I find that Ohmann's definition of "mass culture" works particularly well for describing the role of computer games and gaming in industrialized societies where they are most popular: the United States, Canada, Western Europe, Scandinavia, Japan, and several urban areas in Korea and China. For Ohmann, "mass culture . . . includes voluntary experiences, produced by a relatively small number of specialists, for millions across the nation to share, in similar or identical form, either simultaneously or nearly so, with dependable frequency; mass culture shapes habitual audiences, around common needs or interests, and it is made for profit" (14).

Each phrase in Ohmann's definition has significance for computer game scholars. By "voluntary experiences," for example, Ohmann means those experiences we elect to participate in that are not directly related to the fulfillment of real needs (i.e., food, clothing, shelter). By making this distinction, Ohmann excludes experiences that we might otherwise consider voluntary, such as eating at Taco Bell or buying Tommy Hilfiger pants. In short, Ohmann restricts "mass culture" to a category of entertainment. Computer gaming is clearly a voluntary experience; regardless of venue (arcade, console, portable, or PC), players pay to pass their time on an engaging electronic challenge. Players gain little from this experience—as some researchers have noted—either mentally or physically. Rather, they do it for "fun."

By recognizing that computer games exert a mass culture force on particular social antagonisms, the critic's vision of that antagonism is clarified, allowing her or him to see the *agents* involved in a game's development (agents who are usually invisible) and consequently to see the interests that might be at stake for those agents as they design a "popular" product. Consider the fact that some computer games come about as the result of just three or four game designers and programmers.[3] This is what Ohmann means by "produced by a relatively small number of specialists." The "*relatively* small" qualification here is crucial: even if the entertainment were created by a team of dozens (as are sophisticated computer games) or hundreds (like most general release movies), it would still fall into the category of "mass culture" because, as Ohmann observes, "[m]ass culture comes at us from a distance, produced by strangers" (15).[4] Mass culture is intended "for millions across the nation to share," Ohmann notes, and in the case of computer games, it is often intended for international reception. The scholar who is able to articulate how a computer game exerts mass culture force on an antagonism like the one concerning representations of violence, then, will be able to see how a game does not simply encourage or mitigate violent behavior but will also be able to explain how such rhetoric functions as an integral mechanism in the culture from which it emerges and into which it is received.

The international direction of mass culture noted above is also important to take into account because not all games translate well into the conventions and mores of cultures other than the one in which it was designed. Such challenges give rise to corporate strategies designed to make computer games appealing to gamers across a variety of cultures and nations. This phenomenon directs us to consider the globalizing and homogenizing effects of computer games, effects that are also revealed when one considers computer games as a mass culture force. These effects are magnified by the fact that, as Ohmann argues, mass culture occurs "in similar or identical form, either simultaneously or nearly so" and with "dependable frequency." Here, Ohmann draws our attention to the crucial importance of repetition and exposure for maximizing the popularity of an artifact destined for mass culture. In computer gaming this means firmly establishing game genres and provoking and maintaining interest through other media, for example, fan magazines, strategy Web sites, and TV and magazine advertising. In some cases it even means blurring the boundaries between games and these other media, as when we see computer games based on TV shows (e.g., *Jeopardy, Survivor, Star Trek*). When computer games enter the international market, their mass culture force can align with other hegemonic forces to diminish local culture and embed a foreign one.

Finally, Ohmann tells us how and why mass culture works: to produce and reproduce desire for particular products in the audience ("mass culture shapes habitual audiences") so that they will go out and purchase them ("it is made for profit"). In gaming circles these last two points become most apparent when we look at how games are designed to look and feel the way they do—the strategic decisions that are made about content, interfaces, and players' expectations, habits, and technology. They also become apparent in how games are presented to potential consumers.[5] By recognizing how computer games act as (and are themselves influenced by) a mass—not popular—culture force, scholars gain a perspective on them that reveals the human agents hidden behind the software and are led to question how certain struggles are influenced.

Computer Games as Mass Media

While computer games, gamers, and the gaming industry contribute significantly to the evolution of mass culture (and vice versa), this is not the only force that constellates around them. The discourse of computer gamers, for instance, reveals another force, one that represents real-world information and recasts computer games as sources for news and commentary on society and world events. In this role, computer games become a mass media force, and—sometimes intentionally, sometimes not—developers parlay their access to millions of gamers to promote certain real-life agendas or comment on real-life events. In the game *Duke Nukem,* which takes place in Los Angeles in the year 2012, players work amid the flippant implication that rampant police brutality exists because police officers are inhabited by aliens. It was surely no coincidence that the game's alien-cops were given pig heads and made to congregate in adult bookstores, strip clubs, and bars (where they watch O. J. Simpson endlessly flee police in his white Ford Bronco). *Wing Commander IV: The Price of Freedom,* a space flight/battle simulation in which gamers play war hero and ace pilot Colonel Blair, communicates to players the state of the game's battle campaigns using simulated TV news coverage clearly designed in the style of reportage developed during the Vietnam War and refined in the Gulf War: frontline battle footage, interviews with wounded soldiers and military strategists, and shots of microphone-clogged podiums behind which stand politicians and generals during press conferences. Games like *Railroad Tycoon* and *Imperialism* actually require players to gain control of the media in order to achieve particular ends, not the least of which is getting rich and gaining monopoly power over certain enterprises and resources. In 2001 two computer games were released that directly raised questions about the increasing militarization of real-life international bureaucracies: *Deus Ex* and *State of Emergency.* In the former, the United Nations is in league with an international pharmaceutical company to infect the world population with a deadly virus of its own design so that it can then sell its antidote to the nations of the world for huge profits. The latter game is described by its makers as an "urban riot game set in the near future, where the oppressive American Trade Organization has declared a state of emergency . . . it is up to you to smash up everything and everyone in order to destabilize the ATO" (Rockstar).[6]

The idea that computer games are a form of mass media is one that has not been explored in much detail, perhaps because researchers are only beginning to understand the psychological effects of games on those who play them. It also seems to be the case that until recently researchers assumed that the number of computer gamers was small and so did not imagine that computer games could justifiably be considered "mass media." The likelihood that they are, however, now certainly warrants further investigation, for while computer games may not have the circulation of *Reader's Digest* or the established reputation for investigative reporting of the *New York Times*, they do have the advantage of relatively free access to millions of expectant minds waiting to be taught about this alternative environment they've just loaded into their computers and that bears a striking resemblance to players' own real world. And since computer games rely heavily on visual metonymy—oversimplification for the purposes of understanding complex phenomena, a common trope in TV and print journalism—players do this learning very rapidly, in part because for most people, sight is the sense that the brain processes most quickly.[7] Done well, visual (and audio and tactile, for that matter) metonymies result in immersive and interactive mass media, a form of communication that teaches players a host of behaviors, attitudes, and concepts quickly, albeit grossly. Such realistic—or at least sensorily rich—simulations suggest to players that they *really* understand phenomena like battle, city planning, and detective work when in fact they understand only one version, one very reductive model, of the phenomenon. This model, designed with principles in mind that include engaging players quickly and keeping their attention for long periods of time, is necessarily highly selective. To observe, then, that computer games operate with the force of mass media is also to observe that computer games operate with the force of propaganda.[8] Scholars who recognize how computer games are both influenced by other mass media and how they exert their own mass media force on broader social antagonisms will be able to ask after the ways that computer games metonymize complex issues for a broad demographic. Such scholars will also be in an excellent position to ask about the interests being served by such metonymies, particularly when those metonymies are interactive.

Computer Games as Psychophysiological Force

Unlike the other four forces that work in and through the computer game complex, the rhetorical force that addresses how games affect the human body and mind is the most tangible from a scholarly perspective. Almost since their creation, computer games have been both condemned and celebrated for their ability to surreptitiously alter the people who play them, and considerable research has been done to document these psychological and physiological effects. Not surprisingly, the research is as contradictory as the anecdotal perceptions of players and parents. Regardless of physical and social scientists' lack of agreement, however, the fact that there are over two hundred scholarly essays concerned with the corporal and mental effects of computer games testifies to their captivating power for players and scholars alike. Researchers see that players are caught up in the games, adopting new, sometimes repulsive behaviors, mastering game strategies and tactics more quickly and willingly than those necessary for daily life, and ignoring the economic, social, and physical consequences that often accompany game playing. Researchers also see that some players dispose of their real and limited incomes too casually on game-related material, obsess over a game to the exclusion of primary social relations with friends and intimates, and ignore various tendon-related disorders such as carpal tunnel syndrome, tendonitis, and repetitive motion disorder. And while researchers recognize that not all computer game players behave so addictively, they also recognize that all players experience some variety of effects on their bodies and minds when they sit before the screen, solving puzzles, shooting zombies, or driving souped-up autos they've carjacked in Miami.

These studies that find in computer games a variety of harmful effects also suggest that computer games exert specific kinds of force on players. According to the "bad effects" camp, this force is powerful enough to negatively influence how players live their lives outside of the games they play, sometimes intentionally but more often inadvertently. In fact, an undercurrent of the research showing the negative effects of computer games is that it is because the games work at a subconscious level to engage players that they are so insidious. This is an important concern because it highlights an unspoken anxiety about the scope and power of covert influences, or what I will later refer to (following Brummett) as the "implicative" function of computer game rhetoric. When games exert force in this way—and I believe they sometimes do—the nongame antagonisms with which players struggle in their daily lives are likely sometimes influenced by the psychophysiological effects that computer games can and do inflict.

On the other hand, nearly as many researchers document games' positive (or at least harmless) effects as those who do so with negative ones. Reputable studies show, for instance, that computer games cheer players up, make them more sociable, improve their ability to think strategically and transfer abstract concepts to concrete situations, and even take certain kinds of tests better. Other studies have shown that gamers are better able to judge the relative velocities of objects, the likelihood that two objects moving toward each other will collide, and quickly evaluate the physical layout of a room more rapidly than nongamers. Several studies have also shown that computer games can effectively help gamers express emotions that they might otherwise mask or repress, and that they can be used to effectively treat a variety of brainwave-related diseases, including epilepsy, attention deficit disorder, and post-traumatic stress disorder. Finally, it is worth noting that there are roughly a dozen studies that indicate that computer games have no significant behavioral or mental effects on players at all. With the exception of those that conclude there is "no significant difference," all of these studies clearly suggest that computer games do constitute a psychophysiological force powerful enough to influence how players live their daily routines outside of the games affecting them. In some cases this force is intentionally called upon by the guardians or medical professionals who have a stake in the well-being of the players, while in other cases the psychophysiological force is inadvertently applied. In either case, however, researchers took note of this force and were at pains to explain its effects.

The fact that the scholarly research on the psychophysiological effects of computer games is contradictory, coupled with the fact that games always teach players *something*, makes for a conundrum: How does one comprehend the role rhetoric plays within the computer game complex when rhetoric seems to simultaneously fail and succeed in the same context? How is it, in other words, that both anecdotal wisdom and scientific investigation conclude that computer games are both healthful and harmful? The answer—one that I will elaborate on toward the end of the chapter—is that the computer game complex is dialectical, a complicated and ever-changing system constructed out of innumerable relationships among people, things, and symbols, all of which are in turn connected to other vast dialectical systems: the entertainment industry, the high-tech business, capitalism, articulations of democracy and freedom, and so on. By recognizing that the computer game complex is dialectical, those who set out to make sense of how meanings are constructed within and about it—that is, people who are investigating the computer game complex's rhetorics—will necessarily do this work mindful of the fact that their perspectives may be very different than others'. This does not mean that all perspectives are equally valid; some people are better informed than others. As scholar of dialectics Bertell Ollman reminds us, some people enjoy "a privileged position from which to view and make sense out of the developmental character of the [dialectical] system" (14). Such privilege comes both from proximity to the system—in this instance, proximity to some aspect of the computer game complex—and from breadth and depth of knowledge about it.

There is no better place than amid the wealth of scholarship on the psychophysiological effects of computer games to gain some of this analytical privilege. While it will not provide much proximal authority—one may read all about games without ever playing with or building them—it will offer the privilege accorded by familiarity with the academic rhetoric surrounding the computer game complex. This privilege is authoritative because it prepares the game scholar for discerning the complex's dialectical nature through academic *discourse,* one of the most apparent forms of rhetoric: scholars, whether scientists or humanists, see and interpret the world in particular ways, ultimately making an argument about how things mean. Reviewing how scholars in a variety of disciplines articulate how games mean in the context of the forces they exert on human minds and bodies makes clear how the computer game complex is profoundly dialectical—multiperspectival, contradictory, and transforming. It also has the practical consequence of revealing the range of psychophysiological research that has been done over the years on computer games.

Together these understandings illustrate how the scholarly rhetorics of the computer game complex have contributed to the formation of the computer game complex itself. It is primarily through popular reportage that the scholarship on the psychophysiological effects of computer games gains the power to have formative cultural effects on the complex. The rhetoric of the academy, which generally tries to appear unbiased and is constrained by specific research parameters limiting the conclusions that can be logically drawn, gives way in the popular press to simplifications that often exceed these limits. Typically, this reportage advises readers that computer games are harmful, healthful, or simply innocuous, and more often than not it is just such popular coverage of technical research projects that gives rise to public debate about particular games or the computer game industry generally. That computer games have *particular* psychophysiological effects is clearly a matter of some dispute; that they exert *some* influence on people and culture in *some* way, and that the discourse surrounding these claims exerts a powerful influence on the gaming industry and on cultural understandings about this recreation, however, is beyond question. The scholar who is aware of the details of this debate—arguably a complex struggle in its own right—will be better equipped to examine the role computer games play in influencing other nongame struggles such as those that involve censorship, definitions of "quality time," concerns about the digital divide, mass media ownership and control, and even more local debates like those engaged by parents and amateur coaches who struggle to weigh the possibility of young people's physical injury against the potential cognitive and behavioral advantages of team sports for them.

Another advantage of becoming familiar with computer game research is that, taken as a whole, it provides a rather rare opportunity to see how new research influences subsequent policies, policies that regiment industry practices, government interventions, and familial patterns. Computer game research affords this opportunity more efficiently than most other research into cultural artifacts because the cultural value of computer games is so strongly contested. This potential for spurring debate and discussion is compelling—especially to journalists—and thus computer game research often finds its way into mainstream media outlets with notable rapidity. As the popularizations of the research are dispersed and concerns and criticisms are raised, policies too—from federally mandated advertising guidelines to parental restrictions on their child's PlayStation use—are drawn up and sanctioned. Scholars familiar with the history and contentiousness of computer game research—that is, with the rhetoric of the computer game complex's psychophysiological force—will be in a unique place to comment on and critique such policies.

Computer Games as Economic Force

So far I've discussed three primary rhetorical forces that are commonly found to be driving the struggles related to the computer game complex: mass culture, mass media, and psychophysiological effects. I have also briefly described how each of these forces is made manifest in various real-world processes with distinct material consequences. I will discuss this phenomenon in more detail in the next chapter, but first two additional forces remain to be examined. The one I turn to now, economic force, is especially important because it overlaps all the others. Since 1992, according to some studies, the computer game industry has outgrossed the Hollywood movie industry on a regular basis.[9] Billions of dollars every year are spent on the development, marketing, and playing of games, and game companies have become a necessary fixture of nearly every transnational media conglomerate today. Time-Warner, Simon & Schuster, Viacom, and Disney all have divisions that specialize in computer game development, as do many toy manufacturers, including Hasbro and Mattel. There are several computer game stock market portfolios that have been designed, and one in particular—the *GameWEEK* Retailer/Distributor Index—often outpaces the NASDAQ Composite Index. In 1998 alone almost seven million copies of the top ten video fighting games were sold, each copy selling for an average price of $44.40 ("Fighting Game"). Many games carry licensing agreements with professional sports organizations such as the NBA, NFL, NHL, and WWF, agreements that, while expensive, are also eventually lucrative; the professional sports organizations' endorsements lure customers who might not otherwise buy games, and the contract agreements also often provide access to otherwise difficult-to-obtain TV advertising slots before, during, and after professional games and matches.

It's clear enough, then, that computer games have become an important part of the entertainment industry, and the plethora of business literature that addresses it as such is a testament to computer gaming as a powerful economic force. Books such as *Game Architecture and Design, Game Design: Secrets of the Sages,* and *Game Over* (a history of Nintendo) give game industry novices an inside look into how to build and maintain a corporate empire constructed out of the work of a few creative programmers and artists. At least half a dozen "kits" were for sale at the end of 2003, each promising to teach novices how to design and build their own computer games. These kits usually include a book of generic game design advice ("a good game can only be made by someone who is also a game player") and a CD with a few programming tools. Mostly these kits are gimmicks designed to appeal to game players-cum-designers and are positioned on store shelves to appeal to players rather than to experienced computer programmers. I call this a "gimmick" because computer game production for the twenty-first-century market is incredibly complex and difficult, requiring a thorough understanding not only of several computer languages but also of graphic design, three-dimensional modeling, audio engineering, and a wealth of business savvy. According to the *Gaming 2001* report, an ongoing survey begun in 1999 to study the future of the computer gaming market, all of this technical expertise, in addition to being able to tell a good story, is required to make a successful game.

The software that comprises what most people think of as computer games, however, is actually only one part of the economic force of the computer gaming industry. On the whole, the computer gaming industry spends most of its research and production money on hardware: cabinets, circuit boards, microchips, wiring harnesses, and CRTs for arcade-style games; injection-molded plastic casings and specialized cables and game controllers for console games; dozens of models of specialized video and audio cards, joysticks, mice, steering wheels, rudder pedals, and throttle controls for desktop systems; and several varieties of handheld devices for game playing that require state-of-the-art low-power color LCD screens and microcircuitry housed in rugged and ergonomically designed cases. Memory cards, *RFU adapters,* and wireless game controllers are among the best-selling video game accessories, each of which costs between ten and fifty dollars. PC gamers often need bigger, faster hard drives on which to run their games, which are sometimes stored on five or more CD-ROMs. This latter fact also suggests why fast (50×plus) CD-ROM drives are also increasingly a "must-have" for gamers and, as DVD technologies are popularized, why most gaming systems are now shipping with DVD drives built in. For online gamers, fast Internet connections are necessary, giving rise to a host of "fat pipe" solutions for the home, including IDSN, ADSL, satellite, cable, and dual-modem configurations.

In other words, the computer gaming industry is much more than software; it requires factory labor, large manufacturing plants, and massive distribution systems as well. In a sense, this part of the computer gaming industry is a multibillion-dollar industry in its own right, one that many governments have sought to regulate over the years with a host of tariffs, taxes, trade union contracts, and import/export rules. By 1984, in fact, the U.S. International Trade Commission had recognized this rapidly growing economic sector and drawn up a comprehensive report titled "A Competitive Assessment of the U.S. Video Game Industry." This report, which is over one hundred pages long, details the results of a comprehensive international survey of fifty-four game manufacturers (Watkins). Its findings, which have now been proven to be mostly accurate, were that the United States and Japan would continue to dominate the computer game industry, that copyright and patent infringement would be the major industry battles in the next twenty years, and that the industry itself seemed destined to soar, especially in the home video game sector.

One consequence of the booming game industry has been the rapid development of several technologies upon which the evolution of computer gaming depends. Video cards, the part of a computer's subsystem that processes the instructions related to graphics, have for more than a decade had their development driven primarily by the computer game industry. In a business where eye candy—detailed, smooth, and realistic computer imagery—is considered more important by the audience than almost anything else, game makers must constantly work to improve the look of their games. Apart from developing new software-based techniques for storing and retrieving image data more rapidly, the most common way developers improve graphics is by working closely with the graphics hardware engineers who design video cards. Such technology can dramatically improve a game's performance and thus is a tempting and relatively small consumer investment that can have impressive returns: animation will be smoother, shadows and smoke will look more realistic, and colors will be more vivid. As one video card standard replaces another, however, game designers, driven by competition with other designers, work to get the most out of the latest technology. Existing video card technologies begin to bog down under the increased demands of more intricate games, spurring new developments in the video card industry. And so it goes: game makers chasing after the latest video capabilities to make their games better looking (and hopefully better playing), thereby attracting more players who in turn must buy the video cards that will make the games look as good and perform as well as they're supposed to.

The same is true of the audio card industry. Gone are the games that warned, rewarded, or mocked players with buzzes, clicks, and electronic tones. Today's games are replete with musical scores and sound effects digitally rendered in Dolby stereo and surround sound. An appropriately equipped gamer can tell if a bone-rattling skeleton is approaching from behind and to the left, or from the right and up on a balcony. As with video cards, this capability has been off-loaded from the CPU to the audio card, and like video cards, the evolution of audio cards is circularly driven by manufacturers/designers/consumers. These shortcuts around the bottleneck of Moore's law—which dictates that the speed of CPUs doubles every eighteen months—have been of enormous importance to the development of the computer gaming industry and are major contributors to its economic force.

But even this is not the whole story of computer gaming's economic force. Since the late 1980s computer gaming has yielded numerous spin-off industries. Action figures of popular computer game characters are now common and can be found in any large toy store: Duke Nukem, Lara Croft, Mario, Pokemon, and the variety of heroes and villains from *Mortal Kombat* and *Final Fantasy* all have shelf space within a few yards of Barbie, Ken, and G.I. Joe.

Web sites are another subindustry for gaming, providing players with a virtual space to get help with difficult game levels or puzzles, compare scores, and chat with other fans. These sites are usually sponsored by advertisers who run animated banners—tiny electronic billboards—that "inform" players of new games and game accessories or alert them to other Web sites where they can find similar information and community. Often the Web sites are sponsored by game manufacturers themselves, who use these independently developed digital venues to monitor player enthusiasm and to extend their technical support network for very little cost to the company. The corporate sites themselves, in fact, almost always provide links to fan Web sites, since such sites provide free hints and strategies for their games—an excellent way to keep player frustration, which can have financially disastrous consequences, under control.

Usenet newsgroups for computer games, usually located under the rubric "alt.games," also serve as a very loose community. Such newsgroups, of which there are dozens for computer games alone, allow players to post e-mail requests for help, provide impromptu game reviews, and disclose undocumented features that they've discovered. Newsgroups are also known to be popular feedback venues for manufacturers, and it's not uncommon to see messages posted that directly address corporate executives and game designers. Insiders know that newsgroups are one of the first places to check for industry rumors of game sequels, movie adaptations, and bankruptcies.

In the print medium there are two other subindustries: glossy strategy books that provide step-by-step walk-throughs for particular games, and novelizations. Large computer stores typically have several dozen strategy books, each for a different game. These guides generally do not provide any information that cannot be obtained for free off the Internet, but the information is usually organized more efficiently and also provides an assortment of game-related material, such as a "The Making of . . . " chapter, interviews with the game's designers and programmers, and a more complete list of credits than is found in the game. Game novels, while not terribly popular, are available for hard-core fans; they tend to be available only for the top-selling games in the role-playing and strategy genres. The games *Wing Commander, Final Fantasy, Gabriel Knight,* and *Quest for Glory,* for example, all have had novels written about their environments and characters and are often formulaic in the ways that *Star Trek, Star Wars,* and *Dungeons and Dragons* spin-off novels are.[10] All of this print-based spin-off paraphernalia contributes to the development of economic force, not through generating huge profits but rather through cementing consumer loyalty to franchisable brands.

Another component of the economic force of computer games—albeit a small one—is the fanzine and other related fan paraphernalia, all of which exist in relatively small quantities and most of which is distributed electronically and at fan conventions. Fanzines—underground fan publications that explore every detail of a computer game and its development—usually exist only for the best-selling games. Desktop themes (specially designed collections of background computer screen images, animated cursors, music, and sound effects that replace the operating system's default collection) are also popular, as are screensavers that provide a slide show of images taken from one's favorite game. These, too, are part of the computer gaming industry, providing die-hard gamers with a tie-over fix between game-play sessions and providing an immersive experience for players newly enthralled by a game.[11] All of these forms of fan paraphernalia work to generate and maintain players' appreciation of particular games, a crucial factor in the economic force of the computer gaming industry, because appreciation can be turned quickly into profit.

Software supplements, too, figure into the economic force of computer games. Dozens of new algorithms—mathematical formulas that describe, for instance, a general set of instructions for quickly compressing, decompressing, storing, and retrieving large amounts of video data—have been developed by software engineers who specialize in computer gaming. Some of these algorithms end up patented, then licensed for other applications, such as computer-assisted drawing and virtual reality walk-through programs. Similarly, interface design has had a significant impact on nongame software engineering trends. Because most computer games need to be designed so that playing them is intuitive—gamers are notorious for not reading instruction manuals until after they've played for an hour or more—their look and feel must be instantly discernible. Game designer Chris Crawford observes that users tend to evaluate interfaces not in absolute terms but relative to other similar applications or ways of doing the same task. Balancing a checkbook, for example, is a task that has spawned many computer programs, but because the interfaces on many of these applications are even more complicated than simply using a pencil in the check register at the back of a checkbook, many computer users try and then abandon the electronic method. Crawford notes that this phenomenon is especially relevant for game developers to understand because players often have no other model to which they can compare a game's interface. Thus, says Crawford, "a game's user interface must . . . be not merely functional, nor even easy to use—it must also be fun" (103). This idea of making the interface fun is one that has now thoroughly suffused the home software market.[12] A wide range of nongame software applications now sport "fun" interfaces, from the "Snappy Video Snapshot" device's software to the interface on Norton's SystemWorks. Both of these programs use colorful interfaces with interactive buttons that glow, depress, and click or beep when the user selects them. Increasingly, Web pages also draw on the usability principles established and practiced by the computer gaming industry, and some sites extend their gamelike interface design into computer gaming itself, as can be seen at several U.S. Armed Forces Web sites.[13]

This influence of gaming on the software design industry in general constitutes an economic force for computer gaming itself, because the effect of computer gaming's careful attention to usability and player appeal has been to popularize all aspects of home computing. As many commentators have observed (Norman 73; Watkins), computer games themselves spurred the home computer market, beginning in the early 1980s and continuing today, a fact largely due to the constantly evolving interfaces developed by game designers. The contribution that computer game software engineering has made to the computer industry—and mass culture—therefore, has been enormous, generating, or helping to generate, hundreds of billions of dollars in revenue, even in companies that have nothing whatever to do with computer games. There is ample evidence, then, that the economic force of the computer gaming industry is steadily rising and that this force, when applied to those antagonisms related to computer gaming, is an increasingly influential factor in how those antagonisms are represented, shifted, and stabilized. The scholar who is attentive to how economic force shapes both industry and consumer perceptions about computer games and gaming will be quick to recognize when it is being used to mask other exercises of power, to promote particular interests, and to mollify or even repress contending voices also engaged in the struggle to control how games mean.

Computer Games as Instructional Force

The fifth and last force that plays an important role in how the struggles surrounding computer games are shaped and shifted is one that consistently occupies a marginal place within the industry and a polarized position among consumers: instructional force. This particular force involves the ways that computer games teach people things. When I say that this force has a marginal place in the industry, I mean that, excluding "edutainment" titles like *Where in the World Is Carmen Sandiego,* game developers do not typically consider how their games educate players. This is not to say that developers do not consider such issues at all—they do. But these considerations take place primarily in the context of *playability,* not education per se. Game elements like intuitive interface designs and in-game tutorials are specifically designed to teach players how to work effectively in the game environment. The documentation that comes with games serves a similar function. There is little discussion, however, of what a particular genre, theme, or stereotype may teach players, and it is this lack of consideration of the instructional components of computer games that feeds the polarized positions common among consumers. Game reviewers (professionals, amateurs, and parents and guardians of players) generally fall into two groups: those who think developers shouldn't have to worry about what their games teach—a free-expression kind of argument—and those who think that developers should consider the instructional force of their work because to do otherwise is professionally irresponsible. At the heart of this particular debate is the struggle over what game developers "are": artists, businesspeople, or both. I address this struggle in detail in chapter 3.

There are two other ways that instructional force is being developed and used to shape this and other computer game–related struggles, however: educational curricula focused on computer game development and the innovative use of popular computer games to teach skills that are only marginally related to a game's content. As of late 2003 the only university departments that regularly develop curricula focused on computer game development are software engineering and education. There is also now a handful of programs in university media labs and for-profit educational institutions that specialize in teaching game development, a phenomenon that has more than a few industry insiders concerned that computer games will be homogenized as a result. This debate, too, is related to the art versus business antagonism noted earlier.

Less frequently—much less frequently—programs in rhetoric, cultural studies, media arts, and communication sponsor courses that examine computer games in particular social and theoretical contexts like gender and race politics, literary and film studies, and postmodernism. A similar development is the use of computer games as pedagogical tools, especially among teachers who see educational advantages to the virtual realities that computer games—and the tools used to build them—present.[14] But regardless of the intentions of developers and teachers, the instructive force in games is always at work, transforming some kind of ignorance into some kind of knowledge. The scholar who is able to discern how this instructive force is being brought to bear—intentionally or not—on the antagonisms that surround computer games will be afforded an excellent opportunity to understand, critique, and when necessary, work to change how this particularly influential force is and is not applied.

So, Why Study Computer Games?

This overview of the influences that both impinge upon and are enacted by the computer game complex should make it clear that while gaming's effects are well recognized, the interpretations of those effects are contradictory and complex. This tangle of opposing views tells us that computer games are a site of struggle, a point in the dialectic where rhetorical forces are exerted in an effort to gain dominance over competitors, technologies, players, concerned citizens, and the media. The people who enact these manipulative forces and the networks within which they work differ in their sociopolitical agendas, their ideas about what constitutes fun and games, their understandings of the importance of history, and their sense of their complicity in exclusive or inclusive cultural systems. But although recognizing this complexity makes it impossible to responsibly ascribe intentionality to one developer or even to the computer game industry as a whole, it also makes it impossible not to recognize that the influence of all of these forces through computer games does real work in the world. The creation and playing of games entail different kinds of work, of course, but they all manufacture values ranging from the economic to the moral. And like any piece of artwork, a "gamework" is itself a medium through which these values are articulated and reproduced. The purpose of this book is to reveal and explore some of that work and to offer a *rhetorical method* to others who wish to explore on their own the problems and possibilities of gameworks as influential cultural artifacts. This method, which I will put to use in the second half of the book, is the subject of the next chapter.

2
A Grammar of Gamework

At precisely 6:00 P.M. Mountain Time, Sara dials into her Internet service provider, hisses "y-e-s-s-s" when she snags a clean data line, and double-clicks on a screen icon labeled HEAVY GEAR. As soon as the battered plate armor interface appears, she rapidly navigates her way through the selections: Main Menu, Multiplayer, Campaign. A tactical information screen replaces the game's setup interface: dirty blue neon piping outlines various panels that provide details about her other teammates and her Gear's weaponry, armor, and maneuverability statistics. Two other panels, outlined in black, give a summary of her team's mission and display a reconnaissance video that is meant to help clarify her objectives. After reviewing the information, Sara punches the LAUNCH button and in thirty seconds finds herself looking out of the cockpit of a four-story-tall battle robot and across a vast desert of shifting red sand.

Sara has come to find the deep rumble of the Gear's enormous engine both soothing and exhilarating, and she scans her heads-up display with satisfaction: weapons, stealth, armor status, radar, speedometer, and navigational instruments. She taps into the tactical computer to see if the other members of Red Tide Squad, an all-female team of Gear Commanders, are assembled.

"Red Monkey to all Red Tide pilots, identify," Sara—aka Red Monkey—types into the communications console. One by one, four other players send their identification signatures, and each of their exact positions appears on a satellite view of their headquarters that Sara has called up on her screen.

"Red Rose, A-O-K."

"Red Menace, all systems go."

"Red Baroness, check. Good to see you, Red Monkey!"

"Red Eye, ready, Squad Leader."

Sara grins a tight-lipped smile, furrowing her brow as she quickly types, "I'm transmitting your nav coordinates now. Stay in a loose right echelon until we hit Nav 1, then peel from the back to your respective stations. Radio silence and passive radar 'til first contact. Keep your eyes and ears open, girls, and let's bring the Curse of the Red Tide down on their HQ. Move out!"

~

One of the challenges of describing how meaning is made in a particular situation is discerning an explanation that doesn't compromise that situation's culturally transitory nature. This is especially difficult with phenomena that reside in the public sphere. Contemporary rhetoricians like Barry Brummett, William Covino, and Cynthia Selfe, for example, know well the difficulties of describing the techniques by which horror movies, Bruce Springsteen songs, or university Web pages manipulate an audience's consciousness. Such popular experiences play on people's imaginations in so many ways and depend on so many factors that the idea of developing a unified explanation for them is a daunting prospect, to say the least.

The complexity—or even impossibility—of such a project should not, however, deter scholars from trying to understand these meaning-making processes. Such attempts can discover both the details and the broader contexts of particular manifestations of cultural influence such that even though they are incomplete, they are still extraordinarily revealing. Two consequences of the critical revelations that emerge from these attempts are that they create opportunities for transformative action and that they highlight the fact that critique is a never-ending, never-perfectible process. This chapter proposes one approach to revealing these processes' work within the context of computer games and the people and industries linked to them. While this approach is strongly influenced by rhetorical theory and critical cultural studies, readers not well versed in these disciplines needn't fear. Computer game studies is new to most people, no matter what their background, and for that reason the first part of this chapter serves as a brief orientation, particularly to concepts like "rhetoric," "dialectic," and "ideology." Also, because there is some debate over what exactly constitutes a "computer game" (not to mention why I prefer that term over "video game"), I will propose a definition of that too. By situating these terms and concepts at the center of a flexible critical method, analyses of the *computer game complex*—the combination of computer games, gamers, and the industries that support them—can be developed. At the end of the chapter I will suggest how the method I have proposed can help scholars to understand better not just the work of computer games but also the contexts in which they flourish, even when they do not seem immediately connected to them.

Rhetoric and Dialectic

For centuries, scholars have debated over the nature and purview of rhetoric and dialectic, and they have argued for almost as long about the relationship between the two. In the context of computer game studies there is little reason to rehearse these debates, and for our purposes it will suffice to note that *dialectics* is a way to search for truths, while *rhetoric* is a way to convey truths. The use of "truths" here is not meant to be absolutist; rather, by linking rhetoric and dialectic to truth I mean only to signify their ideal relationship to praxis, that is, to endless processes of studying the world (dialectical inquiry) and using the fruits of that study to change it (rhetoric). The truths after which dialecticians strive are dynamic, nonlinear, and multivalent, and their assemblage into logical stories that make sense in some way—rationally, emotionally, spiritually, and so on—is achieved through rhetorical means. The interplay between dialectical inquiry and rhetoric, then, is what enables the construction of histories, scientific facts, political exigencies, and a host of other discursive formations.[1] Understanding the dynamics of this relationship is essential for scholars who are working to understand a sociocultural dynamic in which artifacts like computer games are always already embedded.

It is also important to clarify the relationship between rhetoric and dialectical inquiry because doing so necessitates a coming to terms with truth itself, that is, the dialectic. The dialectic is an existential condition in which struggle and change are the only constants and to which all materiality is subject. These dialectical struggles, or *contradictions* as we may call them, have both unique and shared qualities. Some writers—Mao Ze Dong, for instance—have observed that contradictions may be antagonistic or nonantagonistic. *Antagonistic contradictions* are struggles that are closed off from the changes that dialectic makes possible; consequently, they can be resolved only by coercion (i.e., force). Conversely, *nonantagonistic contradictions* are struggles that are open to the changes of the dialectic; consequently, they can be resolved by rhetoric.

It is important for computer game scholars to recognize these relational dynamics between the dialectic, dialectical inquiry, and rhetoric, as well as the distinction between antagonistic and nonantagonistic contradiction, because the computer game complex depends on these dynamics—arranged in particular configurations—to thrive. The ability to influence which parts of that complex thrive and which ones don't, therefore, requires an understanding of the current dialectical and rhetorical configurations and a tactical sense of how to realign them. This brings us to *ideology.*

In effect, the dialectic is host to a vast number of webs of *eluctable and ineluctable rhetorical events.*[2] Each web is a contradiction, each rhetorical event one of its strands. While dialectical inquiry helps identify and explain struggle and change within the dialectic, this can be accomplished only by studying the rhetorical events that together articulate particular contradictions. Thus, *rhetorical analysis* is a component of *dialectical analysis,* though rhetorical analysis can also stand on its own. When rhetorical analysis is used to facilitate an understanding of the dialectic, it is called *rhetorico-dialectical analysis,* or in shorthand, "dialectics." Otherwise, it's simply called "rhetorical analysis."[3]

At first glance it may seem as if ineluctable rhetorical events are undesirable, but this is far from the case. Such points of stability are crucial for identity formation, constituting as they do the stepping-stones of philosophy, theology, morality, ethics, and politics. In this capacity, ineluctable rhetorical events are the basis of ideology, which is made manifest on three levels: inclusive, homologous, and idiosyncratic. *Idiosyncratic ideology* is the unique set of assumptions, rules, and constraints that determine how an individual makes meaning out of his or her experiences. We can also call this, following Brummett, et al., one's "mosaic." This idiosyncratic ideology is not, of course, *completely* idiosyncratic; many—perhaps even most—of the assumptions, rules, and constraints that determine meaning-making are learned from others in the community and then naturalized to the point of becoming "common sense." Drawing on the mosaic metaphor, each assumption, rule, and constraint—idiosyncratic or not—is relatively innocuous on its own but when combined with other assumptions, rules, and constraints begins to form a picture, to "make sense." Idiosyncratic ideology is that which transforms what might otherwise be a jumble of assumptions, rules, and constraints into something with a recognizable logic.

Ideology at the communal level is homologous and, again following Brummett, we may refer to such ideologies as *homologies.* Just as idiosyncratic ideologies are influenced by communal homologies, homologies are influenced by societal or *inclusive ideologies.* These ideologies are comprised of the set of assumptions, rules, and constraints on meaning-making that operates across homological boundaries. Again, drawing on the metaphor of the mosaic, homologies are mosaics that make sense not only to an individual but to an entire community as well.

Ineluctable rhetorical events articulate the points in the dialectic in which the conversation is closed and the ideology—at whatever level—has been established. This is not to say that ideology or ineluctable rhetorical events are outside the dialectic. They are integral components of it, forming as they do, definite points of resistance to other competing ideologies and ineluctable rhetorical events. And eluctable rhetorical events, too, are determined by ideologies. Since it is ideology that determines how one makes meaning, then any semiotic event producing or meant to produce a *metanoetic experience*—a change of mind—is always already determined by a set of assumptions, rules, and constraints that dictates the importance of such change. Additionally, *metanoia* itself always results in the transforming person being able temporarily to create ineluctable rhetorical events only in matters concerning the subject of the dialectical analysis. In other words, ideology governs the direction of all the rhetorical events that constitute it. In turn, rhetorical events articulate the variety and type of struggles that constitute the dialectic and push or discourage it from change. An analysis of the dialectic at the point of a particular struggle, therefore, must necessarily involve a rhetorical analysis, which must necessarily be both ideologically determined and involve an ideological analysis. Dialectical inquiry is always ideological. Rhetorical analysis is always ideological. Metanoias are always ideological. Only the dialectic is unhindered by ideology, because its very motion is that of ideologies in constant conflict. The computer game complex, as we shall see, is a striking example of how ideology, rhetoric, and the dialectic play with each other in ways that despite the plethora of contradictions—antagonistic and not—allow it to expand at an explosive rate.

Propositions of the Gamework

To recapitulate: rhetoric acts within the dialectic to alter particular antagonisms according to ideologically informed logics. But how does this understanding facilitate the critique of computer games, gaming, and the industries that support them? Primarily they do so by bringing into focus five general propositions according to which computer game scholars may begin their analyses:

1. Computer games are comprised of rhetorical events that work to make meanings in players;
2. These rhetorical events are constructed primarily out of: (a) develop-

ers' and marketers' idiosyncratic, homological, and inclusive ideologies, and (b) players' (or more generally, "experiencers'") interactions with the systems put in place by the developers, which are also influenced by their own idiosyncratic, homological, and inclusive ideologies;

3. The set of ideologically determined meaning-making rhetorical events that comprise a computer game is designed to transform players in some way;
4. Since all rhetorical events take place within the context of the dialectic, where various kinds of struggle are always being engaged, the rhetorical events of any given computer game are also always complicit in those dialectical struggles;
5. Since dialectical struggles are never wholly discreet, any given computer game–related rhetorical event is always connected to other rhetorical events and struggles that are not game-related.

These five propositions raise numerous questions about the computer game complex, from the local (e.g., What are the rhetorical events in *Unreal Tournament*?) to the general (What society-level antagonisms does the electronic entertainment industry engage, and why?). These propositions also suggest that the computer game complex always involves producers, artifacts, and consumers. As a consequence, computer game scholars need a critical approach that can be focused enough to reveal the subtleties of how rhetoric works on and through producers, artifacts, and consumers individually and also be flexible enough to accommodate these subtleties within a broader framework that links producers (game developers and marketers), artifacts (computer games), and consumers (players) to each other and to the dialectic in which they all participate.[4]

In general, analyses of cultural artifacts like computer games are doomed to remain little more than interesting hermeneutic exercises if they are not somehow connected to an understanding of the dialectic. By describing how an artifact (for example, an arcade game emulator) affects discursive systems that exist seemingly beyond the artifact's own discursive system (for example, U.S.–China trade relations), the computer game scholar addresses the "so what" question that might otherwise render irrelevant an astute analysis. A first step in making this connection is to identify how a specific rhetorical analysis points to particularly contentious issues, issues that may be at the heart of larger social struggles and transformations. Locating such sites of struggle and change—the initial work of a rhetorico-dialectical inquiry—often only requires one to pay attention to how the specific subject under analysis is variously represented. Do different communities value this subject in different ways? Are there contending views of the purpose of the subject? When the subject is made manifest, either in several different media or within the same medium, are the manifestations notably different? Do descriptions or explanations of the subject differ dramatically from author to author? All of these questions can help to identify a point of struggle within the dialectic and so also indicate connections between, say, a particular computer game's rhetoric and the broader social antagonisms that rhetoric feeds and is fed by.

Another way to establish a connection between a rhetorical analysis and the dialectic is to explain how in-game struggles (miners versus company thugs, for example, in *Red Faction*) are representations of real-world struggles. An analysis of this sort will point the scholar toward at least two important sites of inquiry. First, what are the components of a given struggle? For example, who is involved in the struggle, and what interests are they serving? What ideologies are in contention? What factors, historically—including fictional in-game histories—have contributed to the current state of the struggle? What do participants in the struggle say are their objectives? Does the struggle seem to be more antagonistic or nonantagonistic?

The second site of inquiry involves the implications of representing a given struggle in a particular way. For example, given the fact that all computer games teach something to players, what does a game like *Red Faction* teach people about organized worker resistance to company practices? What metonymies have been implemented in order to make engaging this particular struggle "fun"—and at what cost? In what ways might these implications of how a struggle has been interactively represented in a computer game serve certain real-world interests and support or compromise real-world ideologies? Doing this kind of analytical work generally involves researching real-world struggles and discovering the relationships, viewpoints, and disagreements that exist among its participants. Answers to questions like these will provide a deeper context for analyses of the computer game complex and clarify its scope and embeddedness in the affected sites of struggle.

Finally, the connections between an artifactual analysis of a computer game and the dialectic can be discovered by examining the mechanisms of the struggles that the scholar has identified: By what means are they perpetuated? What techniques do participants use to gain or assert their power in the struggle? What techniques do they use to diminish their oppositions' power? What are the indications that the struggle is or is not an antagonistic one? By answering questions such as these, explanations for how particular struggles affect dialectical transformations and what the effects of such transformations might be on related struggles outside the computer game complex will be readily forthcoming.[5]

There are, of course, an infinite number of ways to make such explanations. Particular sites of struggle will suggest certain kinds of analysis. Topoi, various kinds of evidence, literary tropes and figures, physical gestures, aesthetics, grammars, lexicons, and protocols—all of these may become ideologically weighted instruments of analysis. Other scholars may use principles drawn from anthropology, psychology, cognitive science, economics, philosophy, linguistics, semiotics, or some combination of these. None of these is necessarily more correct or accurate than others. Rather, they each offer different ways of interpreting "artifacts." In the context of analyzing computer games, each of these methods is simultaneously rich with possibility and limited and problematical. What makes them suitable and rich is that they are all flexible systems that have been contextualized within the struggles they are meant to address. What makes them problematical is that none of them was specifically designed to address the unique blend of features, constraints, and rhetorical mechanisms of even the most poorly designed or archaic computer game. While it is possible to thoughtfully adapt nearly any existing analytical framework to the computer game complex, my aim in this book is specifically to develop an analytical framework that has been constructed from the beginning as a way of examining the unique and powerfully influential medium of computer games. In the remainder of this chapter I continue to build on the relationship between rhetoric, dialectic, and ideology I've outlined above in order to describe this new framework. My chief end is to detail a method for analyzing computer games, gaming, and the computer game industry that is both instructive about the meaning-making work they do in particular sites, struggles, and discourses and that also reveals how those rhetorics affect the motion of the dialectic in general.

The Problematic of Play

Game, along with the related words "gaming," "play," and "simulation," is among that class of terms that people regularly use but are rarely required to define. Yet in a project like this one, games—how they're made and played, and why they have the effects they do in the dialectic—are precisely what are under investigation. The importance of arriving at a working definition of these terms, therefore, is critical. Playing games of one sort or another is an important, even necessary, part of life. Indeed, human behavior specialists—from ancient teachers like Quintilian to twentieth-century historians like

Johan Huizinga to contemporary psychologists like David Cohen—have long recognized the importance of play for healthy human development. The ancient ball courts of Mezo America, the Chinese board games of millennia ago, and the thriving computer game industry today all attest to the importance that humans place on playing games.

The extent to which the language of gaming and play saturates our discourse also testifies to their social importance. In addition to such common understandings of *play* as "a story in which actors take on the role of its characters before an audience" and "to engage in activities considered frivolous and fun," the term also sometimes suggests a more covert kind of acting, as when we agree to "play along," "play ball," "play the game," and "play dumb." Play can also be forced upon us—for instance, when we realize we are "playing the fool," "playing into the hands of someone," or being "played down to." Play can be strategic, as when we have to "play up our strengths," "play both ends against the middle," "play our cards right," or "play head games." Sometimes people "play hardball" or "make a play" for what they want. "Playboys," "playgirls," and "players" in general typically "play things by ear," are always "playing the field" and "playing off one sucker against another." Play can also be an avoidance tactic, as when someone "plays possum," when we wait for others to "play through," or when we "play for time." Play can be descriptive, as when we get a "play-by-play" or when an action is judged to be "out-of-play." And sometimes (perhaps as in this paragraph, which is just a long "play on words") an idea gets "played out."[6]

Professional computer game designer Chris Crawford has also thought about the ubiquity of game- and play-related phrases in language, and he notes that this popularity creates at least two barriers to understanding the nature of games: "First, liberal use of gaming terms promotes an exaggerated idea of our own understanding of games. We fail to give the subject the careful and critical analysis that we reserve for more academic topics, and we blithely ignore the complexities of game design. . . . The second obstacle is ambiguity. We have applied the principles and concepts of gaming so widely that we have diluted their original meanings" (1–2). Leaving aside the improbability that we could ever grasp the "original meanings" of any game—old or new—Crawford does raise a good point: games have much more complicated origins and effects than most people imagine. The research summarized in the previous chapter catalogs just some of these effects, mainly the psychophysiological ones but also some of the pedagogical, economic, and sociological ones.

In his book *The Art of Computer Game Design,* Crawford's objective is not to document the effects of games, however, but rather to identify the most common features of games. His goal is to develop a common lexicon of computer games so that he and other computer game designers are able to describe their work and ideas clearly to one another. By his own admission, Crawford works by "bulldozer and scalpel" (2). He first identifies four major categories of games (board, card, athletic, and computer), then distinguishes among several related concepts: a puzzle isn't a game, nor are most racing events. Every game (computer-based or not) has four components, says Crawford: representation, interaction, conflict, and safety. A game is representative because it is "a closed, formal system that subjectively represents a subset of reality" (4). Its structure is self-contained, its rules are complete and explicit, its various components and participants interact with each other directly and often in complex ways, and the game's environment is the peculiarly integrated product of the game designer's and the player's fantasy. In this game fantasy, only pieces of reality apply, not entire models of nature or behavior (4–6).

Interactivity, argues Crawford, is an equally important game element. Games allow players to explore a virtual space and context nonsequentially, generating causes, observing their effects, and reacting to the causes and effects generated by other players or by random events: the miraculous half-court shot at the buzzer, the rained-out game in the eighth inning, or the "match" at the end of a pinball game that results in an extra ball or free credit (7). Because of this interactivity, Crawford says, games are "alive," evolving constantly as a result of all the interpersonal material generated and thrust into the game environment (8–10). Games are active challenges, changing according to the players' behaviors, attitudes, styles, and decisions. But Crawford also notes that interactivity is necessarily limited in a game because of its rules and structure. Unlike a doll or model airplane, which allow a player complete freedom to imagine different rules and scenarios each time he or she picks them up, a game is relatively stable.[7] Part of this stability arises out of the consistency of the play sphere: the chessboard, the baseball diamond, and the universe of *StarCraft* are all fixed. Game stability primarily arises, however, out of rule systems. Huizinga writes: "All play has its rules. They determine what 'holds' in the temporary world circumscribed by play. The rules of a game are absolutely binding and allow no doubt. . . . Indeed, as soon as the rules are transgressed the whole play-world collapses. The game is over" (11). The relationship between interactivity and rule systems is particularly important for computer game scholars to consider because rules constrain interactivity. The decisions made concerning the limitations of interactivity directly impinge upon a game's "appeal" and "gameness" and carry signs of how game developers have conceived of their audience.

Conflict, the third universal feature of games, can be passive or active. If it is passive or static—an obstacle to be overcome—it's only a puzzle, not a game. But if the conflict is active, if it responds to the player's motion and tactics with reciprocal motion and tactics, argues Crawford, then it may reasonably be considered a game (11–12). Crawford is emphatic about the importance of integrating conflict (which is not to say violence) into games, and he even goes so far as to suggest that designers who have sought to create games based on models of cooperation instead of conflict have met with failure because their fundamental premise is flawed (11).[8] This claim is one of Crawford's most powerful—if brief—attacks on the alternative gaming crowd, a collection of game designers committed to moving away from the development of games featuring greed, imperialism, self-promotion, and violence. For Crawford, life itself is dialectical—that is, inherently conflictual—and so games that reproduce these conflicts, even in exaggerated ways, are inherently compelling. There are, of course, gender-related implications for such a position, not the least of which is that since many girls are raised to circumvent conflict, they also learn to avoid games that revel in conflict, even at the possible expense of forgoing the kinds of skill acquisition that some of these games promote: pattern recognition, long-range tactical planning, and facility with computers, to name just a few. But this observation that the best games entail conflict is a crucial one as we attempt to understand the relationships among computer games and gaming, the discourses that address them, and the fundamentally conflictual dialectic within which they work.

Finally, Crawford observes that games allow all of this exploration and conflict in a safe environment: "a game is a safe way to experience reality" (12). Here, Crawford takes some liberty with the concept of "reality," but his observation that "[i]n a world of relentless cause and effect, of tragic connections and inevitable consequences, the dissociation of actions from consequences is a compelling feature of games" is both accurate and disturbing (12). The safety factor of which Crawford speaks is broader than he imagines: not only does it allow players to experience dangerous situations without experiencing the real consequences that such situations would have on their bodies or minds were they to enter them in real life; it also provides them an opportunity to escape the "relentless world of cause and effect" that they have come to believe is usually beyond their control. The computer game worlds that players enter are worlds where causes and effects are made to seem almost entirely subject to player control.

Divided up into these four components, "game" as a concept hardly seems like something fun. Indeed, it sounds more like work. And if games are not always fun, one might well ask why people play them. Crawford's answer is surprising but brings the relationship between computer games and rhetoric right to the surface: "the fundamental motivation for all game-playing is to learn" (13). The problematic of play turns on the fact that play, and games in particular, does work outside the perimeter of the play space and does so invisibly. Evoking the antics of lion cubs that playfully scratch, growl, and bite each other, Crawford observes that such games are, in fact, "a deadly business," the good-natured and unintentional practice of vital survival skills (13). Interestingly, Crawford doesn't detail what humans learn in their games, not even in the computer games that he so expertly designs. Instead, he simply notes that playing games is a fun way to learn and that sometimes players don't even realize that they're learning.

Crawford's abandonment here of this line of inquiry is indicative of a boundary most computer game developers are reluctant to cross. To meditate on what their games might incidentally teach would surely cause developers to pause too long to ever bring their games out of development. Crawford skirts the problematic of play simply by observing that even though designers know what motivates people to play, they can never take into account "taste," which in Crawford's view seems to be a dynamic ratio that includes all of the motivational forces that can come to bear in and on a player. Instead of cogitating endlessly on the work games do, Crawford—understandably—advocates a more practical approach: track the "evolving taste of the public" to see what general preferences and tolerances exist, then aim toward this target, taking care to lead the shot. In other words, give the players what they want, or more precisely, what they *will* want. Left in the wake of this practical turn is the matter that games always teach, and so Crawford shifts his initial philosophical view of gaming into a commercial one: the computer gaming industry itself is its own kind of game, one that involves reading the signs of consumer trends and designing and integrating numerous complex systems so compellingly that players find it difficult to disengage from them.

It is precisely where Crawford leaves off his philosophical inquiry, however, that computer game scholars can join in: games do work, especially teaching work. This gamework changes lives and cultures, and it is the work of scholars to explain how. Do computer games catalyze the same kinds of work—socialization, obedience, problem solving, competitiveness—as when people play chess, softball, or tag? What are some of the incidental learnings people glean from the computer games they play? And to what extent do computer games act upon people in ways that are masked by their entertaining features? To answer these questions and to discover their rhetorical and dialectical implications, we must make one final definitional foray to become familiar with what is meant by the terms "computer game" and "computer gaming."

Computer Games and Gaming

As noted in the preface, I prefer "computer game" over "video game" as the generic term for the subject of this book, because it is the presence of computers—not video, which is only one of several components in an electronic game—that defines both the technological platform and the aesthetic of this medium. Whereas Chris Crawford defines a computer game as a computer-based, semi-realistic scenario in which a player safely interacts with conflicts of the designer's making and learns things in the process, Brian Reynolds, another prominent computer game designer, operates from a simpler definition. "A game," he says, "is a series of interesting choices" (Saltzman 42).[9] By this Reynolds means that a computer game—a good one, at least—allows players "to interact with a story rather than simply sit passively and receive it" (42). Similarly, journalist Steven Poole argues that computer game designers should be guided by an "aesthetic of wonder" and observes that "Modern videogames—dynamic and interactive fusions of colorful graphic representation, sound effects, music, speed and movement—are unquestionably a fabulously sensual form" (12). Poole emphasizes that what makes this new artwork so compelling is that "You *play* it" (13, emphasis in original).

Unfortunately, say some critics, computer game development is primarily driven by an aesthetic of domination rather than an aesthetic of wonder. Cornelia Brunner, Dorothy Bennett, and Margaret Honey, for example, justly criticize computer games for being "one-dimensional" and strictly designed to "appeal to boys" (81). From this gender-critical perspective, Brunner, Bennett, and Honey observe that:

> Games have traditionally privileged:
> • Victory over justice.
> • Competition over collaboration.
> • Speed over flexibility.
> • Transcendence over empathy.
> • Control over communication.
> • Force over facilitation. (81–82)[10]

Extending Chris Crawford's philosophical view into cultural critique instead of practical business acumen, Brunner, Bennett, and Honey argue that computer games' interactive features and aesthetic virtues often distract critics from trying to understand what games teach on social and ideological levels.

In the context of the gamework, then, we can say that "computer game" has an operative element, a teaching component that transcends the obvious and in some cases may be decidedly covert.

Game designers Andrew Rollings and David Morris demonstrate Brunner, Bennett, and Honey's observations even as they argue that computer games are a kind of "entertainment software" that—apparently unproblematically to them—requires users to develop "strategies to play them effectively" (22). Games, say Rollings and Morris, always have one or more of the following goals:

- Collect something (point-scoring games, and so on)
- Gain territory (the classic war game from *Go* onward)
- Get somewhere first (a race, either literally or figuratively—for example, an arms race)
- Discovery (exploration or deduction—very rarely an end in itself)
- Eliminate other players (23)

Rollings and Morris's list, which was published two years after Brunner, Bennett, and Honey's feminist critique of the industry, indicates how entrenched the aesthetic of domination is. Victory, competition, speed, transcendence, control, and force remain the accepted "first principles" of computer games and exemplify the problematic of their constitution.

One problem with both of these aesthetics, at least for scholars, is that they focus on the developers' objectives rather than on the medium's effects and the work required to create them. The aesthetic of wonder, for example, asks how a game can be made more cooperative, while what a scholar wants to know is why a "cooperative" game is perceived as such. The aesthetic of domination asks how a game can be designed so that players are thrilled by ramming cars off the road, whereas a scholar wants to know how developers are able to actually answer such questions accurately. What is needed, then, is a definition of "computer game" that fits a critical, rather than a developmental, project. Such a definition would take into account the most common ideas about the constituents of computer games, but would do so within their context as a socioculturally situated medium between developers and players.

Computer games, let us say then, are a form of entertainment that depends on the interactions between players and game designers. These interactions are mediated by computer technology, including a variety of peripheral hardware and software interfaces (joysticks, keyboards, buttons, menus, graphics, music, sound effects, force feedback). Consequently, computer games are sensational and generate psychophysiological player responses to game designers' largely predetermined stimuli. These stimuli include the central challenges of the game (e.g., scoring baskets, shooting "enemies," finding treasure, negotiating exchanges of goods, exploring a place), as well as the mood of the video, audio, tactile, and olfactory components of the game. Since responding to stimuli in a strategic manner in order to achieve particular goals constitutes learning, computer games also teach players through game rules, protocols, constraints, and representations; this learning always has unintended consequences. Computer games are thus influential and transformative. With these working understandings of rhetoric, dialectic, and computer games at hand, we now turn toward the project of integrating the dynamics among rhetoric, dialectic, ideology, computer games, and the problematic of play into a method by which the unique phenomena that comprise the computer game complex may be studied.

The Grammar of Gameworks: Analyzing the Computer Game Complex

Douglas Kellner has argued convincingly that critical cultural studies has reached a point where isolated analyses of means of production, texts and artifacts, and audience reception of the products of the culture industry are no longer sufficient. This is so, he says, because the combination of globalization and telecommunications has articulated production, artifact, and consumption so tightly that to study just one is to exclude two-thirds of the system that gives each component of the network its power. Therefore, says Kellner, cultural studies needs to embrace a "multiperspectival approach" to the critical projects it undertakes.

In many ways Kellner's idea is not new. Marx and Engels certainly adopted a multiperspectival approach when they linked politics, economics, and social theory to analyze the evolution of capitalism, the construction of the bourgeoisie, and the conditions of the working class. Members of the Frankfurt School, too, advanced multiperspectival projects, critiquing the interplay among capitalist mass media, technology, and the arts such that they homogenize culture and turn it into a massified industry promoting capitalist values. Finally, the Birmingham School has promoted some multiperspectival approaches to cultural studies, primarily through work that attends to the production, distribution, and consumption of working-class cultures and cultural artifacts. What Kellner uniquely contributes, however, is a clarified and revivified call for contemporary scholars to engage in multiperspectival cultural studies that shun the divisions between academic disciplines and that actively investigate the relationships of cultural artifacts "within the three dimensions of: (1) the production and political economy of culture; (2) textual analysis and critique of its artifacts; and (3) study of audience reception and the uses of media/cultural products" (25). Rather than studying only the processes of an artifact's production, or only that artifact's reception by consumers, a multiperspectival approach would examine all three dimensions together as an integrated system, or as Clifford Geertz might call it, a "web of significance."[11]

Given the varieties of influence that impinge upon and are advanced by the computer game complex through rhetorical and dialectical processes, and given the attention that developers like Chris Crawford (among others) have paid to the relationships among developers, technologies, and players, and given the problematic of play—which raises the question "What do computer games teach?"—it seems clear that a method designed to critically investigate computer games must be multiperspectival. It must not only suggest a way to conduct a political economy of a particular game, but it must also suggest how that political economy is integrally related to the people who play that game and to how that game is situated, for instance, in the history of game development. A multiperspectival approach to the study of computer games must take into account the variety of agents who exert meaning-making power on them, including developers, marketers, pundits, players, and politicians, and must accommodate the different ways that ideologies intervene in all of these relationships. In short, a method for critiquing computer games must take very seriously the wide variety of work that they do and enable. In the remainder of this chapter, I propose such a multiperspectival method.

Introduction to the Grammar of Gameworks

We saw in the first chapter that the discourse used to describe, defend, attack, and exploit the characteristics of computer games is highly conflictual. Such radical disagreement indicates that a plethora of dialectical struggles, ranging from the economic to the tactile, underlies the many discourses of the computer game complex and that these struggles are invigorated by the rhetoric of its participants. But how does one describe these struggles within the unique context (interactive play in virtual worlds enabled by complex technologies) that computer games present? What is it that is fundamental to all the major and minor skirmishes concerning the value and import of computer games and the industry that drives them? To answer such questions requires the computer game scholar to work deductively, from specific cases in which rhetorical events signal local attempts to change people's minds on particular issues, to general understandings of why such suasory events may have been considered necessary (or unavoidable) in the first place. As I suggested earlier, the benefit of clearly identifying the dialectical struggles both in and surrounding computer games—even if this identification is only tentative—is that it refreshes one's ability to see what is at stake for anyone enmeshed in them. In this way the analysis of computer games facilitates scholars' efforts to influence the dialectical struggles about which they are concerned. It is, to put it another way, a means by which critique can shape a community's progress.[12]

Since computer games, gaming, and the industries that support them together comprise a unique sociocultural context—a "complex," as I have been calling it—any framework set up to organize an analysis of this context would have to address both the features common to external cultural artifacts and those features that indeed make the complex of computer games "unique." The method I propose here does this by drawing on terms from several disciplines: the history and theory of rhetoric and dialectic; artifactual studies; the academic literature on computer games and gaming; industry literature on professional computer game design; both academic and industry literature on marketing (especially the marketing of computer technologies); and personal experience in computer game playing and (to a much lesser extent) design. As a consequence, this method provides a description of how meaning may be made and managed specifically by those who design, market, and play computer games, and it simultaneously offers a way for computer game scholars to talk about the processes and techniques involved in this meaning-making process. As such, the method provides a way for critics to interpret the clues left behind by everyone involved in the struggles that comprise all aspects of computer games.

This method also takes into account the variety of influences—described earlier as mass culture, mass media, psychophysiological force, economic force, and instructional force—that commingle in the making, marketing, and playing of computer games. In addition to recognizing the role of people (or "agents") and influences in the computer game complex, the method also takes into consideration how rhetoric specifically is used to negotiate meaning, how the computer game complex makes these meanings manifest in particular industry-specific tropes, and the kinds of locales (personal, communal, societal) in which this rhetoric has transformative effects. All of these elements—agents, functions, influences, manifestations, and transformative locales—comprise a "grammar of gameworks," a set of interrelated terms that constitute a method specifically designed for investigating the computer game complex.

Organizationally, this grammar is pliant and systematic; each element is related to all the others, and together they give substance to the underlying and sometimes ephemeral dialectical struggles they describe.[13] An analysis of a particular computer game, game genre, or industry practice that uses the grammar of gameworks might well trace a nearly unique path among these elements but will always have as its aim the explanation of how the ideologically determined rhetorical events of a computer game,[14] a response to a computer game, or particular company's development cycle makes meanings that have the consequence (or are intended to have the consequence) of creating or prohibiting transformative experiences—experiences that ultimately shape struggles under way in the real world and that may have no overt connection to the computer game complex itself.

The grammar of gameworks offers scholars a way to systematically reveal the overt and covert contradictions, antagonisms, and imperfections that surround and inhabit computer gaming and helps to explain these contradictions in such a way that their critique provokes radical action.[15] If, for example, an analysis suggested that *Redneck Rampage* was a parody of the "first-person shooter" game genre and of a particular stereotype of rural working-class Southerners—each of which could constitute powerful economic and social antagonisms—then the scholar would be in a better position to act on this analysis, perhaps choosing to include the game in a curriculum, to advocate for the production of similar games, or perhaps simply to challenge other scholars who too quickly condemn violent video games. On the other hand, if *Redneck Rampage* was determined to be bigoted and pointlessly brutal, exemplifying two common traits of many successful games in this genre, then the scholar could effectively narrate these critiques—again by linking them to underlying antagonisms such as those that determine the role of mass media under capitalism—and act to discourage people from "playing" in this way. In ways like this, analyses of computer gaming are metanoetic: they work to change people's minds, not only about the ethics of computer games, and not only about the ethics of representation and play. They also reveal the contradictions at the heart of contentious discourse by studying how the people involved in computer gaming—producers, marketers, players, and other incidental participants in the industry—try to transform each other and are themselves transformed. Ultimately, the "grammar of gameworks" provides scholars with guidelines for articulating how computer gaming is and is not transformative. Let us look then at the details of this grammar, beginning with agents in the computer game complex, then proceeding through functions, influences, manifestations, and transformative locales.

Agents

Every computer game begins with an *agent:* someone—or some collective—is always behind the management of meaning.[16] Kenneth Burke writes that "[t]he agent is an author of his acts, which are descended from him, being good progeny if he is good, or bad progeny if he is bad, wise progeny if he is wise, silly progeny if he is silly" (*Grammar* 16). While this oversimple definition is problematical, it does serve to remind us of the human beings who comprise the computer game complex.[17] It also helps us contextualize agents' actions, which take place in specific scenes. Interpretations of the scene, of course, will vary depending on the observer, and Burke is careful not to restrict the definition of "agent" to corporeality: "[T]he term *agent* embraces not only all words general or specific for person, actor, character, individual, hero, villain, father, doctor, engineer, but also any words, moral or functional, for *patient,* and words for the motivational properties of agents, such as 'drives,' 'instincts,' 'states of mind.' We may also have collective words for agent, such as nation, group, the Freudian 'super-ego,' Rousseau's '*volenté générale,*' the Fichtean 'generalized I' " (20). This allowance for nonindividual, noncorporeal agents is of special importance to computer game analysis because of the displaced agents that game players control. *Avatars* as displaced agents warrant their own section in the next chapter, where I describe the rhetorical effects of multiple real agents (game designers) constructing a single *virtual agent* (e.g., Duke Nukem or Lara Croft) in a computer game that a player may comfortably inhabit. Such interactions among a multiplicity of real and virtual agents create complex webs of meaning.

There are four primary agent categories in the computer gaming industry, each of which has many subtypes. The first includes those people who are responsible for the construction of games. These agents, typically called *developers,* include writers and level designers, hardware and software engineers, visual artists and musicians, and producers and their staff who typically work to fund a game's development process.

The second agent category includes those people who are responsible for getting games to consumers. Although I will use the term *marketers* (or in certain cases "reviewers") for these agents, this category contains a more diverse professional range than that term suggests. In addition to advertisers, who write copy and design packaging, and store owners, who sell the product on their store shelves, there are also those involved in the distribution process. This group includes logistics experts, who figure out the best way to get the product from the factory to the store or the customer, all the people responsible for carrying out the logistics experts' plans—including office staff, truck drivers, and system administrators—and corporate identity consultants, who help keep new product developments in line with a (sometimes) well-crafted public image.

The third agent category includes game *players* themselves. The range of these agents is broad, from players who exclusively use one gaming medium (arcade, console, desktop computer, handheld) or who play only one type of game (shooters, role-playing games [RPGs], strategy, sports), to those who enjoy a variety of genres and will play games anywhere.

Finally, there are *virtual agents,* a category that includes those entities that game players inhabit while they are immersed in a game. These agents—or avatars, as they are usually called—technically exercise no independent control themselves, since they are always responding to some combination of the players' directions and the programmers' instructions. In early games, virtual agents were completely scripted and allowed the player no latitude for blending her or his own agency with the avatar's. The player, in the guise of the virtual agent, could do only what the programmer had made allowances for in the code. Virtual agents in early first-person shooters, for instance, could not fire upon friendly game characters. In more recent games, however, such hostilities are not prohibited. In fact, firing upon allies will cause them to identify such behavior as hostile and develop countertactics (e.g., retaliate or run away) specific to the particular virtual space the player is currently occupying. Such open-ended game character behaviors are made possible through artificial intelligence (AI) programming, which game designer Toby Simpson says instills personality into game characters without requiring the programmer "to fully understand how a system works" (Saltzman 205). Virtual agents, then, exercise shared agency, a fact that figures importantly in understanding the rhetorical events that make computer gaming so compelling.

For scholars of the computer game complex, a comprehensive awareness of how the different agents are involved in making and managing meaning is crucial. Developers contribute to this work throughout the construction of games. They influence—by various negotiations and impositions of power—the production process and determine how a game looks and feels. Similarly, marketers largely effect their influence by interpreting and responding to the business side of the computer game complex. Advertising and consumer trends, supply networks, and distribution outlets, for example, are the domains where marketers work. The agents who are players also manage meanings in ways that are important for scholars to account for; players not only have considerable power over how successful a game is through their power as consumer-judges, but they also influence the future of game development through their feedback on existing titles. Finally, avatars are agents of influence who serve as mediums (in the spiritualist sense) between the real-world will of the player and the game world's response to that will. Computer game scholars can develop rich accounts of their subjects by understanding the unique ways that all of these agents work to make and manage meanings both inside and beyond the computer game complex.

Functions

Regardless of whether agents in the computer game complex are real or virtual, or are production-, marketing-, or consumption-oriented, they would have little influence on anything if they did not embody and enact particular approaches to managing meaning. Agents depend on (both consciously and unconsciously) the various ways that rhetoric works in different circumstances to effect change. Barry Brummett offers a useful taxonomy of these ways—or more accurately "functions"—that is particularly helpful for understanding how agents use (and are subject to) meaning-management processes. In *The Rhetoric of Popular Culture,* Brummett explains how it is that artifacts of popular culture, such as films, manage meaning and in turn are managed by the meanings that prior artifacts have encouraged.

Meanings are made and managed through rhetorical events in roughly three ways, says Brummett, each of which is identifiable when it is made manifest in discourse. The word "roughly" is important to note here, because Brummett astutely points out that, in fact, rhetoric operates along a continuum; the three functions he names are simply three key points on that continuum that allow scholars to speak of rhetoric as *tending* to function in one way more than another. Brummett writes, "At one end of the continuum, rhetoric serves an exigent function: it addresses exigencies of the moment, pressing problems, perceived quandaries, and frank questions. . . . Any time a pressing need arises that implicates the management of meaning, rhetoric then functions at the exigent level" (39). Brummett observes that the *exigent function* of rhetoric is characterized by discursive interventions by and on agents, which have "at least three characteristics: (1) People are consciously aware that a rhetorical function is being performed because it is manifest in signs that suggest explicitly suasory intent. . . . Members of the public know that someone is trying to influence them; those who are attempting the influence know that they are doing so. (2) Because rhetors know that they are specifically attempting to influence meanings, they take (or are in a position to be expected to take) responsibility for doing so. . . . (3) [I]nterventionist messages take the form of discrete texts defined by their sources" (40).

In the center of the rhetorical continuum, Brummett situates the *quo-*

tidian function: "[H]ere are managed the public and personal meanings that affect everyday, even minute-to-minute decisions. This level of rhetoric is where decisions are guided that do not take the form of peak crises (as in the exigent function) but do involve long-term concerns as well as the momentary choices that people must make to get through the day" (41). Like the exigent function, the quotidian function of rhetoric is made manifest by three characteristics. Unlike the exigent function, however, the characteristics of the quotidian function are *appropriational:*

> To perform the quotidian function, people *appropriate* phrases, slogans, actions, nonverbal signs, etc. that are already available in the society or organization within which one is acting. . . . In contrast to interventionist manifestations, people are (1) *relatively* (recall that we are dealing with a continuum) less consciously aware that the management of shared meanings is under way. . . . Because people are less consciously aware that meaning is being managed, they are (2) *less likely* to take or assign responsibility for a rhetorical effort. . . . Because the construction of texts is relatively less consciously and clearly defined by a responsible source, the appropriational manifestation of rhetoric involves (3) *diffuse* rather than discrete texts. (42–43)

At the other end of the meaning-management continuum is the *implicative function,* which "includes the management of meanings that are unproblematic and taken for granted" (46). "The farther to the right on the continuum we go," writes Brummett, "the more sedimented and unquestioned are the meanings. The far end contains the *conditions* for common sense, the ways a society constructs its categories of thought and language, such as gender and race, its fundamental values, its most unquestioned priorities" (46). The implicative functions of rhetoric are executed by what Brummett calls *conditional* manifestations, which work to manage meaning in transparent ways. These conditional manifestations will usually be

> (1) far from our conscious awareness. . . . People are usually not aware of the suasory function of actions and objects when that function is directed at the *maintenance* of the most foundational conditions of thought and language. . . . (2) Because people are usually not aware of the rhetorical function served by the conditional categories of thought and language, nobody explicitly takes, or expects another to take, responsibility for producing the categories *as rhetorical.* Indeed, as we go from the left to the right of the continuum, the more rhetoric becomes

> a communal "product" of socially held systems of meaning and less the result of individually planned interventions. . . . Thus, (3) people have no sense of a text at all in the conditional manifestation of rhetoric. (46)

Further, Brummett suggests that conditional rhetoric embodies

> the basic values, grammatical categories, fundamental assumptions, and rules of thought and language that are conditions for, and are implied by, rhetoric's other manifestations. . . . The conditional manifestation of rhetoric is rarely thought of at all, and when it is, it seems like a ghost haunting the houses of "real" texts, faintly seen assumptions and conditions hovering just beyond the clear and concrete signs and utterances of speeches and everyday life. Conditional rhetoric is always what props up or grounds the meanings of interventionist and appropriational manifestations. The texts of conditional rhetoric are therefore *shadow texts* rather than discrete or diffuse. They "follow" other texts, ever present, rarely if ever consciously noted, dependent on other texts for their existence, yet providing reassurance of the fundamental "reality" of the meanings embodied in other texts. (46)

The purpose of critical exercises such as those that examine horror films—or computer games—is, in Brummett's view, not necessarily to explain how agents *did* work to manage meanings, but rather serves "to illustrate how [agents] *might* [have done such work], so as to expand the rhetorical repertoires of those who read or hear the critical analysis" (125).

While I agree that an important role of professional criticism is to "expand the rhetorical repertoires" of other critics, Theodor Adorno's concern that too often cultural criticism merely feeds the culture industry it purports to be critiquing rings in my ears.[18] For that reason, I want to emphasize that analyses of the computer game complex should not only influence other critics and scholars but should also be used by them to take an active role in influencing the computer game complex itself. A concerted effort to reflect on the contradictions made apparent within the computer game complex and the dialectic of which it is a part—an effort that the grammar of gameworks is meant to facilitate—will help scholars and critics become activists working to generate transformations of both the complex and the dialectic.

Finally, it is important to note that frequently the apparent absence of a relationship between an agent and the mode in which rhetoric is functioning in a particular case can tell scholars a good deal about how meaning is being managed and used to shape the perceptions and even the logics of a particular struggle. For instance, computer game scholars might initially be inclined to dismiss the possibility that there exists a relationship between an agent/player and a rhetoric that is functioning exigently. How, one might wonder, could computer games—or some other aspect of the computer game complex—address "exigencies of the moment, pressing problems, perceived quandaries, and frank questions"? Such relationships, however, do turn up, particularly when psychophysiological influences intercede. Several studies have shown that many people—youth and adults—play computer games to escape the stress of their lives, clearly an example of how agent/players invoke the exigent function of rhetoric. So while it is possible and sometimes necessary for the rhetorically minded computer game scholar to ignore certain agent-to-function relationships, it is extremely rare for these relationships not to exist in some form, or for them to be inconsequential to the emerging understanding of the dialectic to which the entire computer game complex is linked.

Influences

The struggles that comprise the dialectic are constantly shifting as a host of rhetorical (i.e., meaning-making/managing) events—influences that both change and stabilize power—are implemented toward particular ends. As I described in chapter 1, these struggles always reside at a nexus of forces that directs how the struggles evolve. The forces—or *influences*—that are operative within the computer game complex were explained earlier in some detail, but their importance there was to illustrate how computer games wield those forces to shape other external cultural artifacts and phenomena, including everything from mass culture to mental health, and from mass media to the International Monetary Fund. As I discuss it here within the specific context of the grammar of gameworks, however, I want to clarify the fact that influences also shape the computer game complex itself.

The five major influences on the computer game complex are the same as those that the complex itself imposes on culture: mass culture forces, mass media forces, psychophysiological forces, economic forces, and instructional forces. *Mass culture influences* include voluntary experiences generated by a few specialists for consumption by thousands (or more) and at a profit. Computer games at the turn of the millennium are influenced by mass culture and in turn influence mass culture. The scenario that opens this chapter—the women logging on to a gaming network to play a combat simulation—is a good example. On the one hand, the virtual environment in which "Sara" and her friends are playing is a stock landscape from a mid-to-late-twentieth-century sci-fi genre depicting postapocalyptic struggles among survivors. By drawing heavily on the tropes and clichés of genre fiction, the developers have produced a game heavily influenced by mass culture. On the other hand, the players are all sharing in an experience with thousands of other players, an experience that to a considerable degree has been preprogrammed and for which they must all pay a "play fee." Such "massive multiplayer games" (MMPGs) have spawned dozens of imitations so that now even people who don't play computer games know that MMPGs exist. In this way, mass culture is influenced by the games.

Mass media—radio, TV, newspapers, popular magazines, and film, for example—also influence the computer game complex. Mass media are those communication channels that tend to be one-way, originate with a very small number of people and are distributed to many (often millions), offer minimal opportunities for feedback, are easy to disengage compared to a live interlocutor,[19] reach audiences quickly, and can have knowledge-making or knowledge-changing effects in audiences (Rogers 193). Until recently, newspapers, popular magazines, books, TV, movies, and radio were the major mass media, but today the Internet and World Wide Web have also entered the mass media arena. Computer games are currently at the fringe of mass media, not reaching quite as many people as TV or movies. That gap is closing rapidly, however, as genres blur and software titles hit the market billed as "interactive movies" and capitalize on popular concepts from other media like computer games based on TV shows (e.g., *Survivor* and *Who Wants to Be a Millionaire*). Despite their status as fringe mass media, however, computer games nonetheless have all the characteristics of other mass media: they tend to convey their content unidirectionally, are designed by relatively small teams but are consumed by thousands or millions, offer little opportunity for players to give feedback to designers, are easily selectable, are quickly distributable through retail outlets and online sales, and, as many researchers have shown, do often have the effect of changing what players know and do.[20] Additionally, as many game developers and psychologists have observed, computer games' interactive elements make it a mass medium with powerful new techniques by which players may be mentally, physically, and emotionally engaged.[21]

But the computer game is not an entirely new mass medium, nor are computer gamers a radically new kind of player, nor is the electronic entertainment industry that supports computer games wholly unique. Rather, computer games draw heavily on preexisting media concepts and models, partially because mass media such as TV and newspapers have become naturalized to developers (and so they design their games within the confines of these more familiar media), but also because they know that many people will feel more comfortable working with a game—building, marketing, and playing in it—if it is like other media with which they are already familiar. In this way, computer games act not only as media that reproduce the content of more traditional mass media (e.g., the stereotyped depiction of leftist Balkan guerrillas in Tom Clancy's interactive novel/game *Rogue Spear*), but they also validate those traditional forms of mass media by imitating them within the games themselves (e.g., the use of in-game mock-TV reports to communicate information to players about their current status). I will discuss the implications of these reproductions in part 2, but at this point it simply needs to be understood that in analyses of the computer game complex guided by the grammar of gameworks it is sometimes crucial to examine how it is that mass media are being used specifically to change (or at least try to change) how people think about the conflicts represented within it.

Another influential force that occupies a position in the grammar of gameworks is the one that effects psychophysiological changes, that is, those influences that directly affect the body and mind. While mass culture and mass media also have accidental psychological, and to a lesser extent physiological, effects on participants in the computer game complex, they are usually minor when compared to the effects generated by intentional and/or consequential *psychophysiological influences.* Game developers and marketers purposely devise tactics to engage players' emotions, challenge their intellects, and test their bodies. Research has shown that some computer games can cause players to sweat, to go without food or using the toilet, to get violently angry or frustrated, to enable the release of stress, and to learn complex rule systems very rapidly.[22] The variety of psychophysiological responses that computer games induce, in fact, is quite astounding, ranging from simple changes in concentration or heart rate to dangerous levels of addiction and nerve and tendon damage. These influences are moderately well understood and are often used by game developers, are sometimes exploited or masked by marketers, and in varying degrees, are anticipated by players. By recognizing how these influences shape particular struggles within the dialectic and how they are related to the computer game complex, the computer game scholar will be able to ask and answer specific questions that reveal the ideologies informing them. In this context, the grammar of gameworks exposes the kinds of experiences that agents in the computer game complex privilege and at what cost. The grammar of gameworks takes seriously the fact that when certain desired responses are compelled, the effects of such compulsion are felt in all the computer game complex agents, both personally and communally. Thus, the grammar of gameworks makes it possible for scholars to investigate the effects on game developers and the game industry that the elicitation of such responses has and to critique the interests served in gaining these responses. Analyses such as these provide compelling evidence for how the struggles within the computer game complex are also being played out in the larger dialectic.

Economic force, another of the influences that acts on and through the computer game complex, is most apparent in the monetary resources extant in a situation: Is the developer a small independent company with limited capital? Or is it Microsoft? Is the marketing budget large enough for TV commercials or only for ad banners on computer game Web sites? Will the game cost players fifty dollars at a national computer store chain, or is it available only as downloadable shareware from the Internet? Even from this limited perspective, a host of questions arise, including how much games cost, who can afford them, and what effect these costs have on individuals, communities, cultures, and societies.

But there are broader economic forces at work in the context of computer games, gaming, and the computer game industry. As I discussed briefly in the previous chapter, and as I will discuss at length in chapter 5, the economic force of the computer game complex extends far beyond the cost of games themselves. Thousands of attendant expenditures support any given computer game: hardware that stores, runs, and displays it; software that controls the interface between the game and the hardware; peripherals that allow players to improve their experiences of the game; network servers that connect players to each other and provide game hints and strategies; feature-length films based on the game; and a growing market for game-related collectables such as action figures, comic books, novelizations, fan and strategy magazines, posters, mouse pads, jewelry, screensavers, soundtracks, and even clothing, housewares, and food. These game-related products, some more necessary for game play than others, provide enormous incentive to game developers and marketers who have dreams of success and wealth and offer players a variety of ways to dispose of their income. As an industry, computer games and gaming provide thousands of jobs, though many of them are low-wage positions that are farmed out to exploited workforces both in and outside the United States. From the perspective of labor alone, the economic force of the computer game complex is enormous due to its integral and expanding role in global markets. As such, it is tied into a network of even larger economic forces—capitalism, socialism, communism, globalization, national and international tariff, tax, and import/export laws—all of which influence how this exploding entertainment industry represents itself and is represented by others.

These representations are eventually concretized in more or less subtle ways in the artifacts generated by the computer game complex. Many such concretizations are apparent in the ways developers try to "localize" their games, for example. Game designer and producer Bob Bates, for instance, is particularly adamant about the importance of localization—customizing products for different markets—in *Game Design: The Art and Business of Creating Games:* "These days, more than half of a game's revenue is likely to come from outside the United States. [Computer game] publishing has become a worldwide business and making multiple-language versions of games is standard practice" (196). Both Bates and Rollins and Morris also emphasize the fact that localization efforts must address more than just language issues. Colors, status bars, interface orientations, visual metaphors, and audio tracks all should be considered in the localization process, they say. Brazil, for instance, has very strict restrictions on the representation of violence in computer games, Germany prohibits the publication of the swastika, and in India and China the color white—not black—symbolizes death.[23] As developers work through issues such as these, they make available to the scholar signs of the relationship between in-game struggles and the dialectical struggles of the real world.

Finally, we can observe the effects of *instructional force* as an influential element in the grammar of gameworks. Although computer games—including "edutainment" titles like the Maxis "Sim" series (e.g., *Sim Earth, Sim City, Sim Farm,* and *The Sims*) and Brøderbund's *Where in the World is Carmen Sandiego*—have only recently been associated with organized educational pursuits, the evolution of computer game technology suggests that as virtual reality (VR) systems become commonly available, immersive and interactive teaching games will rapidly emerge. Several educational organizations have already begun to try to take advantage of the experiential quality of VR, the most successful among them being companies like Immersion Studios and not-for-profit institutions like Alternative Educational Environments. Apart from their use of specifically educational titles, however, few educators are taking advantage of computer games' instructional potential. Such a dearth of attention does not mean that the instructional force of computer games and gaming is unimportant or noninfluential, but merely that it is underexamined. A scholar drawing on the grammar of gameworks might, for example, recognize how rhetorical events are used to teach players certain precepts, values, or skills, then inquire into the nongaming implications of such instruction. Such a scholar might also investigate how developers have situated instruction within the game environment, how the game is marketed as instructional (or not[24]), or how players describe what a game teaches them.

If Chris Crawford is right that "the fundamental motivation for all game-playing is to learn," then the instructional force of all elements of the computer game complex, regardless of how much attention it receives from scholars and professional teachers, will likely be increasingly influential as the industry expands. Certainly those who strongly question the value of computer games—people such as Dave Grossman (*On Killing*) and Craig Wessel (*A Parents' Guide to Computer Games*)—are concerned about what games teach people about sex and violence, but these topics function rhetorically at the exigent level. That is, they are so immediately troubling that responding to them is relatively uncomplicated. More troubling is how computer games may be exerting instructional force at the quotidian and implicative levels, how they may be offering instruction in making everyday decisions and defining the logic by which players interpret the real world. Influence of this sort has been studied extensively in other forms of mass media but is relatively undeveloped in studies of the computer game complex. Understanding instructional force as one influence among others and as a component of meaning-making events that are situated within larger dialectical struggles can again help the scholar understand what interests are at stake in those struggles, since instruction necessarily reveals the values of both teacher and student. The scarcity of work on the instructional force of computer game development, marketing, and play, therefore, should be seen as unexplored, rather than uninteresting or unnecessary, territory.

Manifestations

In my earlier discussion of the term "computer game," I cited Chris Crawford's observation that all computer games have four components: representation, interaction, conflict, and safety. To Crawford, these components are necessary elements in a computer game, and he offers them as a framework for novice game designers. To make a computer game, implies Crawford, the developer must incorporate these four components. Looking at computer games from an analytical perspective, however, representation, interaction, conflict, and safety may be understood as that manifested set of meaning-making events that uniquely mark computer games as cultural artifacts. On the one hand, developers may choose to address the *representational manifestations* by developing a complex set of rules that determines what a game's players may and may not do in the virtual environment: they cannot walk through walls, they can fly if they've found the magic wings, they cannot see in the dark unless they've purchased night vision goggles. On the other hand, a player may address the representational component by learning and accepting these rules, or perhaps by cheating them by finding out and using the secret codes that game programmers routinely insert in games so that they can more easily debug them. In the latter case, the player who types the phrase "iamgod," for instance, will suddenly find his or her avatars able to walk through walls, fly through ceilings and floors without wings, see in the dark without technological assistance, and be indestructible.

The computer game scholar, however, can understand the representational rules as a *manifestation* of the developers' rhetoric, each rule corresponding to a meaning-making or meaning-managing event. This rhetoric is signaled by the computer-coded description of what "makes sense" to the programmer(s), that is, by the game's logic. By prohibiting players from walking through virtual walls, developers signal to scholars that this particular artifact was built using a fairly conservative representation of materiality: you can't walk through walls in the game, because you can't walk through walls in real life. What's important to recognize here is that unlike real life, where relatively fixed physical properties determine how substances such as flesh and brick interact, the interactions among virtual substances are all determined by game developers. There is nothing stopping a virtual body from passing through a virtual wall except a line of programming code. By recognizing these programmed "laws" that define a game's represented reality, a scholar may begin to see how a computer game's developers make their rhetoric—their attempts to manage meanings for players—manifest.

The other game components that Crawford identifies have similar importance as manifestations of rhetorical events. *Interaction,* for example, gives a game "life" because it adds a dynamic evolutionary quality to the play. As a player responds to certain situations in the game, those responses figure into other situations that may arise seconds or hours later in the game. This sense that the player is having a direct effect on the flow of the game is very compelling and is crucial to keeping players engaged. Game marketers are quick to advertise this capability with phrases such as "no two games the same" and the more technical "adaptive campaign design." Such phrases are common indicators that a game's software/player interactivity is high. As a component in the grammar of gameworks, interaction reveals the specific ways that game developers attempt to captivate players. Such manifestations can tell the scholar a good deal about how particular developers and marketers seem to have understood the people who play their games and how such understandings lead developers to implement those types of rhetorical events that they believe will compel gamers to spend money and time on their product.

One way to approach the *interactive manifestations* of a game is to look at all the ways that interactivity has been designed into and out of it.[25] Such an analysis would bring to light those qualities that particular developers assumed would be compelling to players and useful to the game's marketers. Looking at player responses to the interactive features of a game also reveals how people do or do not adapt themselves to the assumptions and proclivities of the developers and marketers. Both of these types of analysis reveal instances of how meaning-making events are used to parlay transformations within the dialectic, and both types of analysis are called for in multiperspectival examinations of cultural artifacts like computer games.

Conflict is another—and perhaps the most discussed—manifestation of rhetorical events within the context of the computer game complex and provides an especially good opportunity for understanding how broader dialectical struggles are uniquely dramatized in the computer game complex. Conflict depends on opposition, and the ways that such oppositions are constructed, marketed, and engaged suggest how different agents use rhetorical events to gain control of an underlying dialectical struggle. What transformative mental processes are set in motion by creating an interactive conflict between Michael Jordan and Larry Byrd, as in the classic computer game *Jordan vs. Byrd: One-on-One*? Or by the mysterious conflict among a father and his two sons in *Myst*? Or by the interactive story about a newlywed couple occupying a mansion haunted by a crazed stage magician who brutally murdered several of his wives (*Phantasmagoria*)?

It is easy to see how each of these conflicts might evolve into compelling stories and computer games in the hands of capable game developers. It is also easy to imagine how different players would respond to these types of virtual conflicts. The question for the analyst of the computer game complex, however, is "What can the construction of these virtual and narratologically specific conflicts tell us about the dialectical struggle, particularly as it concerns the oppositional discourses of the computer game complex itself?" Conflicts of the virtual sort, like the representational rules that define the parameters of a game, are stylized, even aestheticized. The decisions that developers make, not only in representing a conflict but also in identifying some set of relationships as conflictual and as having mass appeal, reveal a host of rhetorical events at work, not only *by* the developers but also *upon* the developers. An analysis that draws on the grammar of gameworks examines these rhetorical events that center on the identification, representation, and stylization of particular conflicts, and contextualizes them within the framework of an ongoing analysis of dialectical struggle.

Crawford's fourth and final element common to all computer games observes that they allow players to safely engage in risky and challenging activities. This is an interesting rhetorical event in and of itself, because—at least as most developers frame it—the concept of *safety* takes into consideration only corporal safety, not cognitive or emotional safety. It also does not consider the unsafe physical practices that many—perhaps most—gamers engage in, particularly those behaviors that lead to tendon decay and nerve damage. If computer games are "a safe way to experience reality," as Crawford argues, what conclusions might an analyst of the computer game complex draw from the safely simulated conflicts of revenge fantasies that constitute the lion's share of plots in most martial arts games (e.g., *Street Fighter*)? An outspoken critic of violent computer games, Dave Grossman argues that games like *Doom* and *Duke Nukem* are so rhetorically powerful that they are able to convince some people to suppress their natural repulsion to killing. In essence, Grossman is arguing that computer games are inherently *unsafe* because they actively work to shape and transform the mind while giving the overall impression that playing the game is harmless because the body is not in immediate physical danger. "Safety," then, is usually a clear manifestation of developers' meaning-making events (because they engineer it), of marketers' meaning-making events (because they often exaggerate the "danger" of a game to heighten its salability while confining their thinking to corporal safety), and of players' meaning-making events (because they don't usually seriously consider what variety of real dangers might accompany the "safe" gaming environments into which they so readily enter).

It is important to note that of all the elements in the grammar of gameworks, "manifestations" is the one most closely related to those features of the computer game complex that make it a unique site of artifactual inquiry. Arguably, representation, interaction, conflict, and safety all come into play in other media like film or TV, but I contend that their blend in those other media is fundamentally different than in computer games and that the motivations and techniques behind computer game development are likewise fundamentally different. This is not to say that computer games are better or more engaging or even more influential than films, TV, or popular magazines but rather that they are essentially different artifacts. The manifestations of rhetoric in the computer game complex, therefore, manage meanings differently than, say, movies or even "choose-your-own-path" novels popular among younger readers. Through their rhetoric, computer games require players to practice being the subjects that developers have invented. Less interactive media like film and TV insist on viewers' subjectivity, to be sure, but they don't require viewers to work at optimizing their performance of that subjectivity. Computer games do. Other media are to be understood or appreciated by their audiences, whereas computer games are to be won. Huizinga touches on the importance of this distinction:

> Winning means showing oneself to be superior in the outcome of a game. Nevertheless, the evidence of this superiority tends to confer upon the winner a semblance of superiority in general. In this respect he wins something more than the game as such. He has won esteem, obtained honour; and this honour and esteem at once accrue to the benefit of the group to which the victor belongs. . . . But the following feature is still more important: the competitive "instinct" is not in the first place a desire for power or a will to dominate. The primary thing is the desire to excel others, to be the first and to be honoured for that. The question whether, in the result, the power of the individual or the group will be increased, takes only a second place. The main thing is to have won. (50)

To win a computer game requires the player to perfect his or her role in the game: adventurer, sniper, quarterback, starship captain, railroad tycoon. Failure to accept and actualize this rhetoric is not merely to lack understanding, as it would be among filmgoers. Rather, it is to lose, to be inferior, to be a detriment to one's group. Matters such as these involve the final element of the grammar of gameworks, transformative locales, and make these differences clearer still by suggesting how computer games and the industry that supports them work to shape the ideologies of all those who interact with them.

Transformative Locales

The shaping of meaning is necessarily dependent on the locale in which meaning-making events are invoked. The transformations that these events inspire are not always radical, though they can be. Rather, they tend to be slight changes of the mind or heart—what ancient Greek philosophers and medieval theologians called, as I noted earlier, *metanoias*. These small changes occur when rhetorical events cause a person to see the world in a subtly different way, a difference so slight it may not even be recognized. The three categories of ideology that I described earlier—idiosyncratic (i.e., personal), homologous (i.e., communal), and inclusive (i.e., societal)—are the locales within which transformative experiences take place. Some meaning-making and managing events are aimed at a particular locale: a personal letter from one friend to another will work on a person's idiosyncratic ideology; a published letter to the editor of a local newspaper will work on the homological ideology of the community; a state-of-the-nation address will work on the inclusive ideology of the society. Some suasory events, however, cross locale boundaries, as when computer scientist Joseph Weizenbaum jokingly developed the ELIZA computer psychiatrist program for a friend and accidentally fueled the race to develop artificial intelligence (not to mention contributing significantly to the popularization of the concept). Technological innovation, in fact, is one of the most common sources of locale boundary crossing, as we see from studying the history of the acceptance of such devices as the lightbulb, sewing machine, phonograph, telephone, radio, automobile, movie camera, television, rockets, and the harnessing of atomic power in reactors and bombs.

Transformative locales in the context of the grammar of gameworks mark the sites where personal, communal, and societal transformations occur in relation to the dialectic. They are points at which the assumptions, rules, and constraints of ideology are altered. This is a particularly important point in the grammar of gameworks because it distinguishes between a "metanoia" and a more rudimentary kind of mind change. Computer game scholars will want to differentiate between, for example, a player who realizes that a particular battle in a war simulation can be won only by means of an air strike and the player who realizes that the entire simulation is constructed on the idea that air dominance is the key to victory in all modern warfare. The former case causes the player to change his or her strategy only vis-à-vis a particular scenario in the game, whereas the latter causes the player to reconsider both local game strategy and the history of real wars.

The complexity of articulating such transformations is great: the war simulation player above has experienced a metanoia and is certainly transformed at the level of idiosyncratic ideology; but the transformative experience was catalyzed by a reflection upon what is a truism among military strategists, that is, it was catalyzed by a homology. How does one describe the transformation, then? The scholar can begin by detailing the most apparent transformative locale—is it mostly idiosyncratic, homologous, or inclusive—then move to an analysis of the other possible locales in order to determine if the transformation has occurred in those dimensions as well.

Consider the relatively recent trend among computer game marketers to put the lead game developer's photograph and a brief biography on the back of the game package. This marketing strategy is comparable to the standard practice among book publishers and magazine editors of putting an author's photo and bio on the back cover or near the byline. Here is a transformation that is homologous—it now happens throughout the industry—and signals a change in how marketers understand computer game consumers.[26] This transformation may suggest that rhetoric has worked to alter the dialectic, a possibility that would require meaning-making events to have been successful in constructing new meanings for the community of game marketers. Knowing, or at least suspecting this, the gamework scholar might then begin investigating agent/marketers, the rhetorical functions they may have been using and responding to, the influences that seemed to be most powerfully at work on the struggle over whether or not to make such a change, and the ways that this particular metanoia might change how rhetorical events are made manifest in the games themselves. Finally, the scholar might investigate how this homological transformation is or is not playing out at the idiosyncratic and inclusive ideological levels: Did the lead developer's portrait on the back of the game box signify a particularly notable professional achievement, or did it cause some people to buy the game because they identified with the image? Or perhaps the developer's photo was a marketing ploy designed to silence critics of an egregiously misogynistic or racist game that was designed by a woman or a Korean American. Whatever the case, considerations of the transformative locales where rhetoric shapes ideology and consequently alters dialectical struggles—both inside and outside the computer game complex—are important for scholars to undertake, especially if they are working to fashion a thorough artifactual analysis. Such an analysis, without an accounting of how ideologies are brought into contention with (and eventually dominate) one another, cannot clearly describe the relationships among the artifact, the modes of production that brought it into being, and the sociocultural contexts that empower and resist those modes.

The Grammar of Gameworks as Multiperspectival Approach to Artifactual Study

With its five interconnected categories (agents, functions, influences, manifestations, and transformative locales), the grammar of gameworks is inherently multiperspectival. Each grammatical category is broad enough to encompass virtually any part of an artifact's production, distribution, and consumption, and together the categories are sufficiently comprehensive to allow virtually any aspect of the computer game complex to be analyzed: games, game genres, game films, game company management practices, and international gaming trends are just a tiny fraction of the topics to which the multiperspectival grammar of gameworks can be usefully applied.

Such flexibility offers computer game scholars many advantages. The broadness of its terms and its inherent focus on how meanings are made and manipulated, for example, make it easy to examine developers (agents of production) and players (agents of consumption) as partners in the construction of meanings about a particular game. The broadness of the terms also makes it easy to describe power imbalances, as when one examines which agents have controlling access to different transformative locales (ideologies), or when one investigates the incorporation of external influences like mass media or economic force into games as a result of particular suasory events that have constructed an exigency. The broadness of the terms in the grammar of gameworks also admits the possibility that everyone in the computer game complex exercises agency but that the power of different agents—made clear through examinations of influences and manifestations, for example—varies. Similarly, the broadness of "transformative locales" acknowledges that ideological power has quantitative and qualitative factors such that relatively weak individual agents can negotiate power inequities more effectively when they cooperate and can be made weaker if they are divided.

It bears noting before moving on to part 2 that multiperspectival approaches to critical cultural study provide scholars with several challenges as a direct result of their flexibility. Chief among these are two that involve matters of audience. The first involves intentionality. How, for instance, does one make legitimate claims about agents' intentions? Unless there is concrete evidence of such intentions, it is usually best to be guided in this matter by Brummett's observation, cited earlier, that a major purpose of artifactual analyses is "to illustrate how [agents] *might* [have done such work], so as to expand the rhetorical repertoires of those who read or hear the critical analysis" (125). Indeed, the processes by which cultural consequences are generated are often so complicated by a raft of intermediating discourses that it would be impossible to posit reasonably anything other than what some of those influences might have been. That said, game development does offer some useful resources to scholars who are examining intentionality in the form of "design documents," which describe—often in exacting detail—the assumptions, goals, and techniques that developers plan to implement in the games they are making. In addition, there are several marketing research firms that specialize in gathering and selling market research data to game developers, data that are frequently used to guide the decision-making processes in game design. Still, it is always a good idea for computer game scholars to reflect critically on their claims while working out multiperspectival analyses so that they avoid being unnecessarily reductive.

The second audience-related challenge that a multiperspectival approach to the computer game complex can present involves identifying the audience for the analysis itself. When scholars study the processes of production, which tend to be fairly technical, it may seem to those who are unfamiliar with these technicalities that the analysis is skewed toward an audience comprised of the producers themselves. This is because the specialized language of production under examination can seem far removed, perhaps even inconsequential, to analyses of the artifact itself. Film-work scholars have struggled with this hermeneutic conundrum for several decades, though today it is typical for film analyses to comment at least briefly on such technical aspects of film production as lighting, camera angle, and shot blocking. Gamework scholars now face similar challenges as they acknowledge and investigate how particular graphics algorithms, physics engines, and hardware configurations fundamentally affect the nature of *gameplay.* At least until some of the more general terms of game production become common in the scholarly community, researchers will need to be mindful of the technical nature of their subject matter and make extra effort to clarify important industry jargon or player cants for their readers. The next chapter, which focuses on the discourse of game development, offers a model of such work.

Finally, it is vitally important to recognize that any of the elements within a grammar of gameworks category may overlap any of the others in that category. For instance, the "influences" of mass media and a developer's explicitly stated intentions to wield psychophysiological force via a computer game's interface may be interconnected, such as in the situation described earlier where the developer attempts to create anxiety in players by showing them an in-game "news broadcast" that points out a player's failings. Games such as *Wing Commander* and *Rainbow Six* use this technique, giving gamers a sense of hopelessness if particular objectives have not been met, or a sense of impending victory if a series of objectives has been accomplished with aplomb.[27] Likewise, the "agents" of the computer game complex may not always be stable; developers who monitor Usenet newsgroups and Web boards to glean surreptitiously feedback from consumers of a particular game in order to make decisions about patch priorities covertly transform agent/players into agent/developers.[28] Such overlap should not be avoided but explored. The grammar of gameworks is a method for analyzing an emergent cultural artifact and the industries that support it. By recognizing how these elements overlap, the critic will do justice to Kenneth Burke's commendation to those who would undertake the difficult task of examining cultural artifacts: "what we want is *not terms that avoid ambiguity,* but *terms that clearly reveal the strategic spots at which ambiguities necessarily arise*" (*Grammar* xviii). Overlapping categorical elements within the grammar of gameworks are just such strategic spots. Critics should attend to these ambiguities, not with an eye toward sorting them out but rather with an eye toward discovering how they mask connections between the computer game complex and the dialectic at large.

The grammar of gameworks is a method that enables rich and insightful understandings of the nature of the particular dialectical struggles located both inside and outside the computer game complex. Its central task is to facilitate investigations of how meanings are made and manipulated in and among computer games, which is to say how the computer game complex negotiates power through rhetoric. The grammar of gameworks takes into account five integral areas of power: agents (who have the power to catalyze transformative effects); functions (the purported and actual purposes of these effects); influences (the external forces that impinge upon agents and functions and that inevitably change the transformative effects of historically situated artifacts); manifestations (the ways that transformative efforts are realized in particular contexts); and transformative locales (the spatiotemporal instances in which ideologies—individual, communal, or societal—have specific transformative effects). As a whole, the grammar of gameworks affords computer game scholars a flexible framework by which they may arrange their examinations of particular dialectical struggles that are playing out in the computer game complex. These struggles become manifest in a variety of ways, including the language of dominant and disempowered discourses, suasory techniques, overt and covert interests being served and ignored, and the points and conditions under which transformations of the struggle are possible. The objective of such analyses is to engage and transform the dialectic of which the computer game complex is a part by acting on particular struggles within it. Naturally such an effort will be ideologically determined at the individual, communal, and societal levels. It will also constitute a series of meaning-making events that may themselves become—together and separately—subject to critique as a component in the computer game complex.

The next three chapters offer distinct analyses of the computer game complex using the grammar of gameworks. As a reminder, appendix A includes a diagram of the grammar of gameworks that shows its major concepts and components and also indicates their relationship to one another. Appendix B includes a diagram of the relationships among dialectic, rhetoric, ideology, and metanoia. Appendix C is a glossary that includes, among other terms in the book, all the key terms discussed in this chapter. One thing that is unavoidably problematical about the diagrams is that they suggest a hierarchy where none exists: agents precede functions, which precede influences, and so on. As I will demonstrate in the sites of inquiry that follow, a scholar may begin with any category or element and work away from that point as he or she sees fit. It is also possible not to address every concept within the method; one might, for example, analyze the discourse of *EverQuest* fans as found within the EQ Web Ring. Such an analysis might consider only agent/players, mass culture influences, and the homological transformative locale. This would arguably be a less-than-thorough analysis, but the complexity of such a project might well call for a carefully abbreviated research design, particularly if it is executed with the intention of revealing new avenues of research. The only requirement of the grammar of gameworks, then, is that it be used to study intentionally how the computer game complex—in part or in total—changes and is changed by the dialectical struggles that are at work around it. The only outcome that is expected of the grammar of gameworks is that it be used to change these struggles through critique-driven action.

PART 2
Introduction to Part 2

In chapter 1 I provided an overview of the influences on and of computer games, demonstrating that although gaming's effects on players are well recognized, the interpretations of those effects are contradictory and complex. I also suggested that those societies in which computer games have become popular are also transforming; virtually every aspect of life is being touched by the influence of computer games, from art to business, and from education to entertainment. Because there exists a tangle of opposing views on what these transformations mean—personally and societally—scholars recognize that computer games stand at a point in the dialectic where a variety of forces may be manipulated such that dominance over competitors, technologies, players, concerned citizens, and/or the media can be a result. As these forces are manipulated, concentrations of power shift, advancing some sociopolitical agendas while others lose ground and altering both personal and collective understandings of what constitutes "play." These shifts, I have proposed, are one way that computer games do real work in the world. Both the creation and the playing of games require different kinds of work, all of which manufacture values ranging from the economic to the moral, and gameworks are the medium through which these values are articulated and reproduced. Computer games, like most cultural artifacts, are materializations of a broad set of integrated sociopolitical interests. Games are designed to appeal to children, youth, and adults of all ages, males and females, who are from many parts of the world. Some games have strong heterosexual elements, while others represent homosocial and homosexual relationships. There are games that appeal to players' desires to hunt, solve, maneuver, and plan; the scenarios in which these desires are met are sometimes lifelike and sometimes fantastic. Despite all of these variations, however, one fundamental concept ties them together: play. Regardless of the genre, all computer games purport to facilitate play. And play, it is important to remember, is also always instructive.

Another important component of the first chapter was its characterization of the computer game complex as being determined by struggles on many fronts: social, scientific, economic, instructional, and so forth. On an almost one-to-one basis, each culturally determined claim about computer games has been met by an equally authoritative contradictory claim. These conflicting discourses point out the variety of logics that inform interpretations of mass culture generally, and computer gaming especially. This rich variety of conflicting discourses suggests that profoundly important interests are at stake and that computer games and gaming are not only sites of struggle themselves but are also representative of broader struggles—struggles being engaged at the cultural and societal levels and within which computer games are only flashy but small-time players.

In chapter 2 I examined the notion of play and its relationship to the computer game complex and from this examination developed a method—a grammar of gameworks—by which scholars might usefully critique the computer game complex within the context of a multiperspectival dialectical analysis. I also suggested in that chapter how an understanding of the dialectic might emerge through analyses of material culture. The primary advantage of such an interpretive lens is that it is necessarily historical and is always already situated within a framework of struggle. Consequently, dialectical analyses not only always result in personal transformation but also provide a crucial foundation upon which one may ground social transformations.

The next several chapters demonstrate how the grammar of gameworks may be used to interpret the content and mechanisms of a variety of dialectical struggles currently being engaged in and around the computer game complex. To demonstrate the method's pliancy, each of the following three chapters draws on different combinations of the elements that together comprise the grammar of computer games. In chapter 3 I examine the techniques of computer game development, focusing particularly on how game designers articulate their objectives, assumptions, and motivations. In chapter 4 I look at how game audiences respond to games as a community by studying both formal and informal computer game reviews. Finally, in chapter 5 I examine one particular game—*Black & White*—from an economic perspective. By "economic" I don't only mean "monetary." Instead, I refer to systems of value and exchange and to how those systems are substantiated, propagated, internalized, and resisted.

Two final notes on these next chapters: first, since they each attempt to demonstrate how the grammar of gameworks may be applied in different contexts and using different elements, they need not be read sequentially. If readers have a particular interest in the economies of computer gaming, for instance, they should have no trouble jumping straight to the last chapter. Second, like the method itself, these three chapters necessarily make manifest points of conceptual overlap as well as occasionally conveying the impression that the methodological elements I've selected for my analyses are the best ones. I cannot overstress the importance of understanding this method as a highly flexible system of relations bound together by the ways they influence meaning-making in local and general contexts. The computer gaming complex is a network that draws on human beings' innate desire to play, and it intermingles that desire with a host of ideologies that reproduce themselves through the medium of the game. This creates a situation where it becomes entertaining to be subject to a variety of rhetorics. True to the grammar of gameworks' design, these next three chapters explore this situation from multiple perspectives.

3

Capturing Imaginations

Rhetoric in the Art of Computer Game Development

"Are you sure?" David asked without looking up from his blue Game Boy Advance.

"Yes, I'm sure. I read about it on the Web last week. Besides, I saw it with my own eyes when I evolved it on the weekend." Maria and David were standing stock-still in the school hallway.

"I thought the Spearow would stay normal. What does it look like evolved?"

"It turns into a Fearow and it's huge. Not bigger than the trainer, but still. . . . " For the first time since class had let out, Maria and David glanced up from their games. Maria held her hand up to her shoulder. "It comes up to at least here."

"Geez. Any *Spearow?" Their eyes were back to the tiny LCD screens that showed them a seemingly endless world full of creatures to be discovered, trained, evolved, fought, and traded.*

"Yep. If you can keep it alive long enough, which I doubt you *can."*

"Shut up. At least I got a Poliwrath."

"Only because you stole your sister's water stone."

From a nearby doorway, a woman shouted, "Let's go, Maria!"

"I gotta go. My mom's waiting for me. Hey, did you hear about the Pokerus?" Maria clicked through the Game Boy's menus, saved her game position, and switched it off. "It's a new virus going around."

David turned his Game Boy off too, since Maria was leaving. "No, what's it do?"

"It doubles a Pokemon's stat experience after a battle. I can't tell if I got it though. I did some trades off the Internet, so maybe I do."

"Awesome! Will you infect me if you find out you have it?"

"Why should I?"
"Maria! I said let's go!" Maria's mom was walking toward her rapidly.
"Because we're friends."
"Not that good of friends," Maria smiled. "See ya."
"Fine. See if I help you with Ms. Moeller's fractions homework!"
"Oh, all right," Maria called over her shoulder. "You can have it if I get it."

~

If we were to go by the mass media's representation of video games—which often report that they are instruments of addiction and sociopathic behavior—we could only conclude that game developers must be among the most morally bankrupt craftspeople in history. Even before computer gaming was made one of several scapegoats in the Littleton school shootings, it had been on the receiving end of a steady barrage of criticism from a broad spectrum of society: fundamentalist and conservative Christians who had previously lobbied against games like *Dungeons & Dragons* and rock bands like the Eagles and Pink Floyd (not to mention, of course, the entire rap, metal, and punk rock scenes); concerned parents' groups that had lobbied for a movie rating system years earlier; and progressive media critics who thought poorly of most mass culture multimedia, especially film and television.

One of the earliest critiques of computer games—published in 1969—is entirely speculative and accidental. Perry London, in his book *Behavior Control,* writes about Joseph Weizenbaum's computer psychotherapist software program named ELIZA. This program, which mimicked a therapist's technique of mirroring patients' remarks back to them, is discussed by London as an emerging and dangerous technology: "If it were possible for a machine to act *in loco therapeutis* by making those responses, a great economy of human resources would result" (98). As a result of this economy, argues London, people could become too dependent on machines and lose the ability to connect with human beings, an idea that has now fueled more than a dozen psychological studies into the impact of computer games. And unlike many later commentators, London does not optimistically conclude that this sort of neurosis is unlikely to develop: "Other factors . . . might also make it hard for some people to really 'warm up' to a computer, even a smart and loving one. Sooner or later, however, they probably will" (99).

London's critique is speculative because of his rather grim resignation that "sooner or later" everyone will succumb to what he sees as the inhuman charms that computers of the future will wield. His critique is "accidental" because London, like many others who retold the story of the "artificial intelligence psychotherapist" built by Weizenbaum at MIT, did not know that Weizenbaum had not set out to build an AI but rather had set out to show how gullible people are. He wanted "to show just how much apparent intelligence one could get a computer to exhibit without giving it 'any semantic endowment at all'" (Dreyfus et al. 71). In other words, Weizenbaum's ELIZA program was not a therapist; it was a computer game of sorts. London's critique of ELIZA, therefore, though intended strictly as a critique of modeling human behavior on a computer, was a warning that computers would someday be powerful enough to cause users to confuse them for friends and playmates.

By the mid-1990s, when the computer gaming industry began to close in on the movie industry's share of the entertainment market, critiques of computer gaming turned toward the responsibility of the developers. This shift, from blaming gamers to blaming game makers, is now more vital than ever. To a considerable degree, this shift is due largely to media critics' recognition that computer games are now rarely developed by small software companies but rather are products of international media conglomerates.[1] In 1999, for instance, MIT Press published *From Barbie to Mortal Kombat: Gender and Computer Games,* an anthology of essays about the dearth of computer games for girls and women and the possible correctives that the industry might take to change this trend. The book's essays include numerous references to corporate giants like Mattel, Nintendo, and Sega, many of which contain indictments along these lines: "None of the warriors is female. As the player kills off his opponents, he is rewarded with more fighting powers. In some cases the warrior rescues helpless damsels, but no women play active roles. The pace is rapid, and the game is accompanied by graphic images of spurting blood and exploding bodies and the vivid sound effects of blows. Top-selling games of a similar style are the 'Virtua Fighter' series from Sega . . . and the 'Street Fighter' series from Nintendo" (9). As game development has become big business, the principles of big business kick into high gear: the marketing department says that boys buy more computer games than girls, so the company decides to target its development strategies toward that larger consumer base. And so a biased trend becomes worse.

Despite these critiques, however, one might reasonably ask how game developers themselves describe the work they do in relation to society and culture. Do they see themselves as media artists in the vein of independent filmmakers, living and working at the fringe of a billion-dollar industry and doing their art uncompromisingly?[2] Are they adults who have stumbled into a profession that allows them to play for a living, like kids who fantasize about inventing toys or new kinds of candy or perhaps becoming professional athletes or musicians? In the wake of so much criticism of the violence of computer games, it is indeed a question why many developers continue to work on titles that revel in brutality and murder. It would seem that despite such bad press—perhaps even because of it—many computer game developers continue successfully to make and sell "objectionable" games. How do they justify this? Why is it that such outspoken criticism by the likes of Senator Joseph Lieberman and retired West Point psychology professor Dave Grossman have had relatively little effect on the industry and the material it celebrates in advanced 3-D graphics games like *Soldier of Fortune* and *Max Payne*?

Actually, there is considerable debate about the ongoing popularity of violent games. In 2000 the top four best-selling console games (i.e., games for the PlayStation, Genesis, etc.) were *Pokemon Gold, Pokemon Silver, Tony Hawk's Pro-Skater II,* and *Driver 2*.[3] For PC systems (i.e., multipurpose desktop computers) the top-selling games were *The Sims, Who Wants to Be a Millionaire, Roller Coaster Tycoon,* and *Diablo*.[4] Notably, none of these games is a first-person shooter or third-person oblique fighting game, the two game design styles that most represent the "violent game" designation. In addition, many of the newest arcade games are decidedly nonviolent. In *Dance, Dance Revolution* players attempt to keep time to increasingly up-tempo soundtracks by dancing on a small stage connected to a video screen that displays where each foot must land on each beat. Other games have players riding a mountain bike down a virtual mountain, snowboarding in Utah, skateboarding on a university campus, and riding a magic carpet through rocky canyons. In fact, all industry analysis companies agree that the most popular game genre is Adventure/Role-playing, which outsold the Action genre by nearly one million units (PC Data, Inc., in *Wired,* 151) or 4 percent *(Interactive Entertainment Industry Overview* 16). Indeed, of the top twenty best-selling titles in 2000, the most violent titles were *WWF Smackdown,* a pro-wrestling game listed in the fourteenth position, and *Madden NFL 2001,* a football game listed in the seventeenth position. According to the NPD Group, not one of the top five best-selling games of 2003 had graphic violence as part of its gameplay ("Funworld: Industry Trends"). Thus, while "objectionable" games are dramatic, they're not actually where the big money or primary audiences are.[5]

This fact indicates just one of several contradictions with which developers must contend regularly—and it's not even the most formidable contradiction they must negotiate. Scholars of the computer game complex need to be able to identify such contradictions and address them in their analyses. One effective way to approach these contradictions is to recognize that industry insiders often talk about computer games as a newly emerging art form even as they also see them as a new kind of multinational business. Furthermore, many game developers struggle with the fact that games are increasingly expected to conform to mainstream consumer tastes. Together, these two interrelated struggles constitute a major part of the foundation upon which many other struggles on the production side of the computer game complex stand.

By way of example, consider that at the 2001 Electronic Entertainment Expo in Los Angeles game developers from all over the world met to release new products, discuss industry trends, and get a look at their competition. At a workshop titled "The Future of Games and Gamers," Martin Davies, cofounder of Digital Anvil and a veteran game company executive, observed, "everyone who works on a game is an artist." Davies meant by this that each person on a game development team is a skilled craftsperson working with limited resources to create a unique artifact. While it is commonly accepted among computer programmers that their work is an "art," those outside the profession often don't see it that way. People find it easier to judge something "art" when they can see it. Computer code is decidedly invisible. For this reason, those with narrow definitions of "art" see programming more as a technical process, no more viewing it as art than they would the process of generating a topographic map out of field survey data, or writing down a recipe for apple-raisin pie.

The "real" artists in the game development field often have it only slightly better. Like other commercial artists—graphic designers, advertising illustrators, wedding photographers, and the like—game artists, the people who create the 2-D and 3-D models and textures that comprise computer game worlds, are often viewed as having sold out or as being computer geeks who couldn't make it as fine artists. The host of other finely honed skills that people practice in developing the current generation of computer games—level designers, rule system experts, specification and resource trackers—rarely even receive the trouble of having their artistry questioned, since very few people indeed have *that* broad a definition of "art."

While all of these professional activities could arguably constitute forms of artistry, such an elevated designation tends to become more difficult to bestow when the arts are practiced in the interest of making money. This phenomenon has certainly been critiqued by such artists as Andy Warhol and Roy Lichtenstein, both of whom built substantial art careers out of the contradiction that is mass media art. When a programmer must complete a game engine quickly in order to keep a project on schedule for a Christmas season release, is she still an artist? What if she must cut corners, kludging together pieces of code from other projects she's worked on and forgoing standard optimization reviews that would make the game more stable or more efficient? What if the graphics artists use a 16-bit color palette instead of a 32-bit or greater one to minimize production costs and end-user system requirements? What if the rule system is no more complicated than that of the game of checkers? What if all of these people are working under production constraints so strict that it is commonly understood that the game will ship on schedule no matter how buggy it is? Or what if the working conditions for these people are more like a sweatshop than a studio? These are the kinds of questions that many current game developers must negotiate as they inhabit the contradiction of being artists in collaboration with big business.

Another contradiction that computer game scholars will quickly discover is that developers must cope with the expectation that their games be "realistic" enough that players understand them almost intuitively, but not so realistic that they're frustrated or driven to tedium by them. Stephen Poole, in his book *Trigger Happy,* discusses this subject at length, as does Chris Crawford in *The Art of Computer Game Design.* Poole offers as an example the phenomenon of laser weapons:

> Firing laser beams is not like skeet shooting, because lasers are made of light, and light travels very, very fast, at 300 million meters per second. At the short distances modeled by videogames, where fighting spacecraft are never more than a mile or two apart, lasers will take about a millionth of a second or less to hit home. . . . But what of your enemy? Say he's a nippy little xenomorph, flying at thirty thousand feet per second. That's about twelve times faster than Concorde. Unfortunately, even if he's two miles away, and flying directly across your sights (perpendicular to your line of aim) at that high speed, he will have moved a pathetic total of four inches sideways in the time it takes your laser beam to travel from your guns to his hull. (45–46)

Poole goes on to note that if computer games involving the firing of laser weapons were truly "realistic," a player would simply have to line up the sights with the target and fire—not much sport in that. So instead, developers treat lasers more like conventional guns, requiring players to lead shots at a moving target and thus making the game more challenging and fun.

Such decision making is difficult because "fun" and "realism" are important terms for game publishers' advertising departments; a brief review of game packages, game ads, and game reviews proves this. Yet, if Poole and Crawford are right that after a point "realism" and "fun" enter into an inverse ratio with each other, then knowing where this point resides is what constitutes at least a part of the developers' art. Evidence of the importance of this art—from a sales perspective, at least—can be gleaned from a visit to any computer game store. Invariably, the dustiest titles will be simulations: flight simulators with no combat element; system simulators in which players build towns, countries, or electrical circuits; sailing simulators; driving simulators (not racing games, but simulations that allow players to take a 1998 Chevy Lumina out for a spin around the neighborhood at safe and legal speeds); and others.

One of my personal favorites of this genre is *Air Traffic Control Simulator.* In this title, the player chooses from dozens of airports around North America—from Dinkstown, Alabama, to O'Hare International in Chicago—then attempts to route safely the air traffic through that airspace during different times of the day using only the radar scope and a host of reference sources available to real air traffic controllers (ATCs). The learning curve on this simulation is so steep as to be nearly vertical: not only does one need to familiarize oneself with the moderately complex symbols and operation of the radar scope—arriving and departing flights, flight strips, VORs, VORTACs, range marks, LA/CA systems, airport and aircraft information, holding patterns, safe altitude grids, facility frequency changes, clearance codes, and all the radio chatter jargon that attends all these features—one must learn to process all of this information for numerous aircraft simultaneously. Or not. In the real world, between the hours of 7:00 A.M. and 9:00 A.M. Nashville International Airport receives perhaps one arrival and two departures. In playing this simulation with this particular scenario, a player would literally sit for two hours in front of the computer screen, watching the radar scope sweep its circle around endlessly empty skies for half an hour or more at a time, waiting for that next arriving or departing flight. Major airports, on the other hand, may involve processing close to one hundred flights per hour, which is presumably the aspect of the simulation that earns the software its motto: "experience for yourself the high-stress world of air traffic control!" Keep enough planes safely in the air, and you'll be promoted periodically. Crash a plane into another one or into the side of a mountain, and you'll be fired and your ATC game persona will be erased. No extra lives in this "game." And yet despite all this realism—realism to the point of tedium unless you're studying for the FAA's ATC exam—the developers still excluded certain aspects of the ATC experience: pilots who mumble flight data or mishear ATC directives, equipment failures in the tower or aircraft, and of course, labor disputes that may or may not result in strikes.

Developers, then, must somehow successfully negotiate at least three industry contradictions in their work: (1) computer games require art to be practiced under the constraints of big business; (2) computer games must be realistic enough to hook players with their intuitive interfaces, game rules, and physics engines, but not so realistic that they're experienced as tedious, frustrating, and as irreversible as real life; and (3) computer games can be disturbingly unsavory and still be popular among many gamers. This last contradiction suggests that developers must somehow discern and evaluate the qualities of "fun" among a very broad audience. Clearly, different audiences have different tolerances for viewing and participating in virtual violence, drug use, sexually themed narrative elements, and other game components. How is it that in the face of wide public criticism—some of which is even endorsed by major medical associations—and the complexities of negotiating these three ubiquitous industry contradictions game developers continue to flourish in their work?[6] One way to begin to answer such questions is to examine how game developers describe their art and trade to each other—particularly expert-to-expert and expert-to-novice. By drawing on the grammar of gameworks to ask how agent/developers use the different functions of rhetoric to influence the ongoing struggle over the connection between played violence and real violence, for example, computer game scholars can gain insight into the suasory mechanisms of that struggle—insight that subsequently can help scholars become agents in that struggle as well. In an effort to flesh out such an analysis, as well as to explicate further the grammar of gameworks, let us look at some of the ways game developers work to manage the meanings of their arts.

Rhetorical Functions Revisited

In the previous chapter I drew upon the work of Barry Brummett to show how the grammar of gameworks accounts for the "functions" of rhetoric within the computer game complex. When rhetoric is used to address specific questions and problems of an immediate nature, it is serving an exigent function. In such cases, agents such as game developers "know that they are specifically attempting to influence meanings" and the audiences of such rhetoric "know that someone is trying to influence them" (Brummett 40). One problem with this claim is that it posits that rhetor and audience are always aware that meanings are being "managed." However, this excludes a very common instance of exigent rhetoric, namely, what might be called "tutoring." The sixth grader who can't figure out how to multiply fractions and seeks help from a schoolmate, for example, certainly has a pressing problem that warrants a meaning-making response. Both student and tutor, however, would not likely automatically understand that suasory work was under way in their exchange of questions and explanations. Similarly, a lost driver who stops to ask a pedestrian for directions would not likely be consciously aware that in responding to the request the pedestrian is being intentionally persuasive. Nonetheless, both of these situations involve responses to pressing problems that do manage meaning quite pointedly.

When rhetoric functions exigently, then, it is more accurate to say that it is often apparent to both rhetor and audience, *but not always.* The reason for this has to do with rhetoric's conditional functionality, to which I'll return in a moment. For now, though, it is sufficient to understand that exigent rhetoric is not always consciously suasory and that in its unconscious capacity it is frequently made manifest in answers to questions that seek information: "How do I/we . . . ," "What is . . . ," "Why is . . . ," and so on. These are the kinds of questions that game developers ask with great frequency.

When rhetoric is used to address day-to-day matters and problems, it is serving a quotidian function. Since rhetoric serving this function is applied rather mundanely, using generally accepted concepts, ideas, and terms, it tends to be rather formulaic, helping its users—game programmers, for example—to resolve common problems by rote. This is not to say, however, that suasory techniques have a reduced presence or are less compelling than when rhetoric is functioning more exigently; rather, the results of prior exigently motivated suasory techniques have been accepted as valid and are applied to common problems with relatively less awareness of those suasory techniques than when the rhetoric is functioning exigently. The game developer who always writes a detailed design document—a sort of outline of the game—as a way of starting a new game because that's what she was taught in school could be viewed as participating in the quotidian function of rhetoric; design documents are not necessary for new projects, but they are generally considered to be a helpful step in the development process.

The third way that rhetoric can function is conditionally, which is to say invisibly. When rhetoric functions this way, few people realize that suasory techniques are working, because they are being applied unconsciously. Conditional rhetoric is deeply embedded in other systems of meaning-making, including logic, language, tradition, and protocol. It is completely accepted, not as "rhetoric" but as common sense, as what is natural or obvious, as the conditions by which we intuitively interpret the world. Unlike those functions of rhetoric in which some responsibility may be accepted for why things are done in certain ways, conditional rhetoric very rarely is recognized as having an agent and a suasory purpose. The assumptions and naturalized rules that found what is meant by terms like "real" and "reality" are sites where conditional rhetoric is actively at work, ceaselessly moving people to behave consistently and sensibly. In the case of questions that seek information (as in the problematical example of exigent "tutoring" rhetoric described above), the exigence of pressing problems like "I don't understand" or "I'm lost" demands a response that is unquestionably rhetorical but whose appearance as inherently suasory material is masked by the discursive conventions of asking for help from someone presumably more informed than the questioner. In such a case, rhetoric is still acting in an exigent capacity, but the nature of the rhetorical context has evolved such that any consciousness of how meaning is being manipulated or managed is masked.[7]

It is important to remember Brummett's injunction that these functions of rhetoric operate along a continuum and that their identification is not to be understood categorically: a particular text may be mostly quotidian but also somewhat exigent and will always be founded on a set of assumptions held together by the conditional function of rhetoric. From another perspective, all discourse within the computer game complex depends on the conditional function of rhetoric, and by specifically looking to reveal this function, the computer game scholar will begin to reveal its presence in a host of quotidian and exigent instances.

In looking at the ways agent/developers make and manage meanings within the practice of their art, then, the computer game scholar may begin by choosing several discreet texts and trying to identify where, when, and how these functions come into play. This will necessarily lead to an examination of the kinds of influences and manifestations that provide the content and context of the functions, which should also begin to suggest where important transformative locales—points at which rhetorical events generate ideological changes—reside. Before undertaking such an analysis, I want to describe in a more general way the possible relationships that other scholars could pursue between agents and functions. The purpose of this "contemplation of the possible" is to make the scope and utility of the grammar of gameworks clearer to readers who are interested in using the grammar in their own analyses. Following this I will use several examples drawn from the discourse of computer game developers to show how the transformative locales of a particular struggle can reveal to scholars how shifts of power made manifest in the contradictions that agent/developers negotiate may be linked to similar struggles in broader dialectical contexts.

Rhetoric in the Discourse of Game Developers

Computer game scholars can learn much about their subject by paying attention to the problems that agents within the computer game complex identify and address. Such exigencies are to be found in many places: agent/players who try to convince parents, guardians, partners, or themselves that their current gaming system is too old and needs to be upgraded; agent/marketers who argue at a production meeting that without a budget to run prime-time TV commercials the new game will be a failure; the parents' organizations that lobby to keep local schools from allowing coin-operated arcade games in cafeterias. All of these scenarios demonstrate the use of rhetoric to respond to particular exigencies raised as a consequence of the presence of computer games. But exigent rhetoric is at work in the computer game complex long before a new game or game system comes to market. Exigent rhetoric drives the process of game development itself. The very existence of game developers presupposes an exigence, namely, that new forms of interactive computer-based entertainment are needed. And since the computer game complex grows larger every year, it seems that addressing this exigency only increases its demand.

For the computer game scholar, this is a puzzle: How is it that despite all the time, effort, and money being expended on meeting this demand, the exigency is never sated? One way to begin work on this puzzle is to examine how computer game developers define the nature of their work and the nature of the exigencies that such work is meant to address. Developers are the people who first identify a particular exigence in the marketplace and set about responding to it, usually by creating other exigencies of their own. These self-imposed and self-defined problems require a wide range of cultural, professional, and personal significations to be negotiated so that as the game development process evolves, its participants can work efficiently and coherently toward fulfilling their objectives.

This process of negotiating how games mean during their production is the focus of this chapter. I have selected this focus as part of my explication of the grammar of gameworks not because agent/developers and exigently functioning rhetoric are the most important elements in the grammar but rather because a great deal of meaning-making power is imbricated by developers into the cultural artifacts they are working on at this point, power that ultimately influences decisions, interpretations, judgments, and dialectical shifts far beyond the workspace of level designers, illustrators, musicians, and programmers. In addition, the exigent rhetoric of agent/developers has the advantage of being fairly accessible to any scholar committed to critiquing the computer game complex. Other agents and functions of rhetoric in the grammar of gameworks play equally important but different roles in the computer game complex, of course, and I will touch briefly on those roles both at the end of this chapter and in subsequent chapters. This chapter, however, is meant to shed light on some of the meaning-making work that agent/developers do in order to transform their ideas into working games.

Whenever computer game developers explicitly ask for and provide help to each other on particular development challenges, they draw on discourses that mediate their understandings of exigency. Sites where such discourse is found include development workshops, Q&A sessions at professional conferences, and professional consultations and in-house project development meetings. Venues like these are rich with rhetorical language functioning in an exigent capacity, since in all of these situations developers are trying to overcome the myriad (and often unforeseen) technical, artistic, managerial, and business problems that arise in the course of making a computer game and getting it into players' hands. One drawback to depending on these venues for scholarly work, however, is access: because the computer game industry is so competitive, most game development is done behind closed doors and with numerous counterindustrial-espionage strategies in place. Fortunately, much of the discourse that could be recorded in those restrictive settings may also be found in more public forums like Usenet newsgroups and Web boards. These more public venues for game developer discourse, while typically frequented by less established or more open-source-minded professional and advanced amateur developers, can provide game scholars easy access to a highly focused professional support network.

There are some differences between private and public exercises of exigent rhetoric among developers, of course, but they are minor. The exigencies that arise at an in-house development meeting, for example, will often hinge on the idiosyncrasies of a customized game development tool, character model, or interface texture that was built in-house.[8] By contrast, the problems articulated on newsgroups and Web boards typically involve the idiosyncrasies or complexities of certain industry-standard game development software applications, device drivers, and hardware interfaces.[9] Similarly, agent/developers at in-house meetings tend to be more candid and conversational than agent/developers on the Internet; predictably, when such strangers ask each other for help, their discourse tends to be courteous and very technical.

Both of these minor differences—the focus on proprietary in-house material versus industry-standard material, and conversational versus courteously technical discursive style—influence how computer games develop not only because of the content of the discourse or its delivery but because in their responses to particular technical exigencies they have an impact on how games mean. To put it another way, because developers are working to solve specific problems, content and style don't matter all that much if the computer game scholar is simply trying to understand what function rhetoric is playing in the development process and why. The fact that in these particular situations game developers are trying to solve problems about their games suggests that the meaning-making techniques they're using during their face-to-face or computer-mediated conversations tend toward the exigent function. What remains, then, is to identify and characterize some of the techniques that developers use when working in this rhetorical mode and to discover how the use of rhetoric in these ways serves to promote certain interests over others.

An effective way to begin looking for how rhetoric is functioning in the game development (production) phase is by studying how agent/developers use it in decidedly overt conditions. This approach requires that the scholar first identify what developers see as their most pressing problems and ask what these priorities might suggest about how developers attempt to manage the meaning of their work within their professional community. By studying both what developers consider to be pressing problems and the techniques that are used by developers to articulate solutions to them, the computer game scholar can gain important insights into how certain kinds of values are assigned and reproduced in the industry and how agent/developers negotiate power within it. When, for example, developers raise problems that are primarily technical, and when the responses to those problems are equally technical, then the scholar might reasonably conclude that among developers, issues involving a project's ethical or sociopolitical implications are relatively unimportant. On the other hand, this observed technical focus might indicate that the project's division of labor is such that only particular members of the development team are responsible for considering the ethical and sociopolitical implications of the game and that the technical emphasis of exigent rhetoric under analysis does not originate with one of those members. This ambiguity underscores how rapidly even a seemingly straightforward rhetorical exigence can become complicated. It also shows how research and analysis must always work together when they are applied to the computer game complex.

For the sake of clarification, consider the latter of these two possible interpretations. Analyzing the ways rhetoric serves or prevents the resolution of exigencies helps to explain how different kinds of power are negotiated among the computer game complex's agents. Therefore, by looking specifically at how agent/developers tend to communicate those exigencies, the scholar can begin to sort out how a particularly pronounced public exigency—like the hue and cry over violent computer games—can have so seemingly little influence on the people who are meant to respond to it. If a game project's creative director and producer, for example, are mainly responsible for considering its ethical implications, then the project's nonmanagement staff will be more or less shut out of such considerations, at least within the project's official development framework. These artists' work, then, is constrained to the practices of their crafts, which may not include engaging in critique. If one supposes that it is simply the work of creative directors and producers to engage the ethical questions that a particular game project raises, just as it is the work of its programmers to engage questions of coding event triggers and collision algorithms, then a model of production emerges in which only those developers at the top of the management hierarchy are considered worthy or capable of making the decisions that will most influence the shape of a particular industry artifact—an artifact that constitutes in a material way a response to the public exigence decrying exercises in virtual interactive violence.[10] It also creates an internal class hierarchy, one that posits privileged groups of thinkers and underprivileged workers. What this hypothetical—though realistic and fairly common—situation reveals, in other words, is that when the computer game scholar finds rhetoric functioning in an exigent capacity, she or he will also find the external signs of deeper struggles, repairs, adaptations, and compromises. Studying how signs like this appear within the exigencies described by agent/developers will often reveal how ideologically determined contradictions within their work are masked, reinterpreted, reauthorized, and mystified. Contradictions like these permeate the computer game complex and inevitably connect back to comparable but more systemic struggles in the dialectic.

Agent/developers manage how games mean at many more points than when exigencies arise, however. When developers respond to a public outcry or the setting of a sales record, their rhetoric is fairly easy to track, because they tend to respond in the public eye: press conferences, open support or rejection of industry regulation, or the development and release of sequels. When agent/developers are simply doing their daily routines, though, their rhetoric is less apparent. Such routine rhetoric—that is, rhetoric functioning in its quotidian capacity—can be found wherever the efforts of game designers are not oriented toward overcoming major obstacles but are still guided by relatively conscious decision-making processes. Developers must regularly negotiate a host of innocuous issues, which, while absolutely crucial for the completion of a project, often feels to them like grunt work. It is in the execution of these development routines—making code more efficient, altering sound effects and animations based on the comments of the quality assurance department, and creating new textures for a level to make it less repetitive, for example—that rhetoric is used semiconsciously. If one were to ask a designer in the midst of such work if she were doing work aimed at manipulating players somehow, she would likely respond affirmatively, but without such a directed inquiry she would probably think little about the effects of her work on players and more about just trying to get her task done.

This kind of work is rarely discussed in online newsgroups or Web pages, and when it's discussed in face-to-face project meetings it is usually done in tones of complaint rather than with an effort toward problem solving. Consequently, rhetoric functioning quotidianly is most readily found in places where the routines of the profession are specifically under discussion. Such discourse is relatively easy to find in professional game development periodicals and at gaming conventions like the Electronic Entertainment Expo and the International Game Developers' Conference (IGDC). A careful reader or listener will also catch glimpses of this rhetoric in interviews with developers and in articles in which developers narrate the story about how they made their games. Typically, the anecdotes are brief because they relate to mundane tasks that most people—including the developers—find uninteresting.

The scholar can also observe meaning-management happening at the quotidian level of production by watching game designers go about their daily work routines. Here again there is an access problem, but if it can be overcome, an examination of what designers do all day long for weeks on end is extremely instructive to the analyst of the computer game complex. Because much of designers' daily work involves quotidian rhetoric, the scholar who is able to observe these routines will also be able to identify how computer games are developed through automatic behaviors that go largely unquestioned. Once a project is under way, there tend to be fairly long time spans (several days) between major problems that require an exigent rhetorical response. This means that designers are working on the myriad small tasks that comprise one of a game's major components, putting into action techniques they know well and have long since stopped analyzing.

In these glimpses of the mundane aspects of computer game development, powerful rhetorical events may be discerned that are on their way to becoming routinized and naturalized. As developers streamline their methods for turning game ideas into games on store shelves, they become more efficient producers but at the expense of carefully reviewing their work. Like metonymy, which allows communicators to radically simplify an issue for the sake of easy comprehension by others, quotidian rhetoric allows transformative work to be done without taking the time to consider the nature or implications of the transformations it promotes. An artist, for instance, may well have to grapple with a problem about how to animate a certain common sequence of events—opening a door, for example. This struggle may initially constitute an exigence and thus require rhetorical practices that construct it as such, but once a solution has been developed and accepted, subsequent door-opening animations needn't demand such pointed rhetoric, because the situation has ceased to be exigent. Instead, the known solution may simply be duplicated, perhaps changing a few minor details so that the door-opening sequence remains interesting.[11] In a game with dozens or hundreds of doors, rhetoric functioning quotidianly becomes a crucial time- and money-saving technique that eventually affects a project's bottom line.

More established game design companies now rely on quality assurance (QA) teams to counteract the problems that sometimes emerge as a result of day-to-day problems being resolved mechanically. Companies like Mattel, Ion Storm, Eidos, and Electronic Arts entrust these teams to identify a wide range of problems that develop because of misjudged design objectives, poor or misguided programming, and confusing art and interface design. Many of the problems QA teams discover, in other words, are the outcome of malfunctioning quotidian rhetoric. Game developers learned long ago, however, that it is usually cheaper to go back and fix several small problems that grew out of the assumptions of the original design than it is to track and test every new addition to the complex game system as it is implemented. It is more efficient, according to current design wisdom, to put in all fifty doors and then go back and fix the three that interfere with gameplay than it is to test the entire game system after each of the fifty doors is added.

How games are made to mean through the quotidian efforts of agent/developers has the effect of simplifying developers' work by freeing them from considering all the implications of common decision-making and meaning-management situations. Studying this process, then, involves identifying these shortcuts and surfacing their implications. Sometimes quotidian rhetoric is relatively innocuous when used infrequently, but it can have unintended consequences when it is used often. And even when used infrequently, quotidian rhetoric can have both intentional and unintentional cumulative effects: design trends that become design constraints, in-house legal protocols that become industry standards, and management techniques that are unwisely transferred, for example, from programmers to illustrators. By analyzing how rhetoric is used to address the day-to-day issues that face game developers, scholars of the computer game complex can also discover the processes by which certain once-exigent rhetorical events begin to enter discursive insurgences, going from the overtly persuasive to the subconsciously persuasive. It is at this point, too, where a careful analyst can begin to see where the quotidian completely disappears below the horizon of consciousness and begins to function conditionally, which is to say, invisibly.

When rhetoric begins to function so covertly that extremely few people are ever aware that transformative efforts are being intentionally expended upon them, it is working conditionally. For game designers, this would include the logic that dictates why they make games at all; what—for them—constitutes fun or entertainment; why computers are thought to be worth their time and talent; and what ethnic, gender, sexual, and class stereotypes they hold. Conditionally functioning rhetoric permeates everything a game designer does, since it is what makes language—including the visual language of imagery and the auditory language of music and sound effects—make sense. When they create virtual humanoids with large teeth and sharp talons as in the game *Thief*, for example, they are drawing on a horror trope thought to inspire enough anxiety in agent/players to elicit a fight-or-flight response. For the game *Half-Life*, agent/developers depended on the probability that scientists in white lab coats working busily at computer consoles would elicit curiosity and respect in players. And the impossibly buff, fatigue-clad warriors in *Rogue Spear* seem designed to elicit fearlessness in players—as long as the warriors are one's allies. Such characters are commonplace in computer games and play upon stereotypes that developers usually rightfully assume players will immediately recognize and connect with emotionally. To a limited extent, then, computer game scholars can arrive at some conclusions about the conditional rhetoric put to work by agent/developers by taking note of agent/players' responses and how visual tropes are relied upon to elicit particular player responses.

Developers use computer games' audio components similarly. They know, for instance, that musical scores that settle among minor and diminished chords or that depend on dissonance are unnerving—to most Westerners at least—and make players feel suspicious, reluctant, or scared. They also design sound effects like echoing footsteps, dripping water, and the clank of heavy machinery that they know—again, because they are tropes—can also have powerful emotional effects on gamers. Agent/developers build race car simulations that are accompanied by up-tempo rock scores with a driving bass line. They orchestrate ethereal soundtracks—lots of liquidy synthesizers and echoey transitions—to help keep role-playing gamers in a ponderous, imaginative state of mind; and they infuse flight simulators with numerous ambient noise effects to establish an authentic "mood" for sitting in the nose of a flying machine: the rush of wind over the cockpit, the chatter of the radio, the clicks and beeps of various instruments. Such choices of image and sound are designed to keep players stimulated and totally engaged, choices that are made by developers who depend on knowing what counts as frightening, grim, and victorious among the agent/players who are their audience.

Developers depend, in other words, on knowing how to tap unconscious meaning-making triggers—conditionally functioning rhetoric—in players.

But it is not simply that rhetoric functions conditionally in players' perception of scary images and music as such. What is important here is that scholars recognize that game developers rely upon their intuition and expertise to implement certain signs in a game that they believe will be interpreted by players in a way that will catalyze an appropriate transformation, say, from relaxed to tense or from confused to angry. In interactions like this, rhetoric is functioning conditionally in the agent/developer who somehow knows that players will be frightened by a large and dark underground chamber and also in the agent/player who in fact *is* frightened by the large and dark chamber. Neither of the agents may be able to explain why fear is effectively elicited in this scenario—it just is. Game developers depend on this conditional function of rhetoric at every turn in the development process. And when their dependence is modeled into computer games that are played by thousands or millions of people, it becomes clear how rhetoric both influences and is influenced by mass media and mass culture forces. Conditionally functioning rhetoric—social logics, for example—is drawn from culture, embedded in the artifacts that culture supports, and re-presented back to the culture that then reconsumes them; the entire computer game complex—games, gamers, and the industries that support them—becomes a mechanism designed to reproduce the values of the society out of which the complex arises and within which it thrives.

When it comes to trying to discover examples of this rhetorical work, there are at least three effective ways of approaching the task: (1) study game developers themselves (i.e., ethnography); (2) study game developers' creations (i.e., games); and (3) study how game developers are taught about their work. The first approach is a difficult one—as most ethnographies are—again, partly due to the access problem and partly due to the multitude of "human subjects" challenges inherent in this analytical strategy. The study of computer games themselves as part of a search for clues about how agent/developers' rhetoric seems to be functioning conditionally is necessarily speculative. Brummett writes, in fact, that when rhetoric functions conditionally it usually appears "like a ghost haunting the houses of 'real' texts, faintly seen assumptions and conditions hovering just beyond the clear and concrete signs and utterances of speeches and everyday life" (46). When meanings are managed in this manner, he says, they operate not in discrete texts—like computer games per se—but as "shadow texts . . . ever present, rarely if ever consciously noted, dependent on other texts for their existence, yet providing reassurance of the fundamental 'reality' of the meanings embodied in other texts" (46).

Searching for the use of conditional rhetoric in the processes of computer game development, then, requires scholars to gaze beyond the "look" of a game and examine its "feel." In playing a game, can one tell that it's supposed to elicit feelings of danger, claustrophobia, or panic? Games that require characters to swim underwater often have the effect, for example, of leading players—the people who are sitting there in front of the computer screen—to hold their breath. It is usually a combination of screen colors, music, and sound effects that elicits such feelings—but why do they have the effects they do? Often, even developers don't know why they work, they just know they do.

There are ambiguities here, of course, just as there are among instances in which exigent and quotidian rhetoric are used. Dark and shadowy backgrounds are scary to many people but comforting to others. Characterizations of gun-toting white men in uniform will also elicit a variety of feelings among different people, even though those people may share a geographic locale. We might expect, for example, that the children of U.S. Border Patrol agents and the children of undocumented workers in southern Arizona will be differently affected by a virtual soldier unholstering a sidearm. Studying the way game developers seem to be trying to affect their audiences, then, gives gamework scholars clues about how agent/developers conceive of what makes sense and what can be taken for granted. This is, to put it another way, the study of how agent/developers unconsciously use the conditional function of rhetoric to prepare the ground for the agent/player transformations their work will inspire. This is also the study of what interests those transformations do and do not serve.

One might reasonably argue that an examination of the "feel" of a game says nothing about the developer and everything about the player: what feels scary to one person might seem campy or dumb to another. But part of the work of a gamework scholar is to study how people are transformed by language (of one sort or another) in ways that serve to influence different interests and dialectical struggles. Despite a number of purist theories that argue for total experiential individuality, most people would agree that within certain communities and cultures, certain types of experiences elicit similar responses in everyone. Mass media, of course, depend on this phenomenon. Computer game analysts should also take note of the fact that when people become numbed to certain tropes, they become more or less immune to certain rhetorically driven elicitations: familiarity with horror movies makes them less frightening, and familiarity with adventure or mystery plots diminishes one's intrigue at them. I will return in more detail to this phenomenon in the next chapter, which focuses on game reviewing, but for now it is enough to acknowledge it as a relatively common experience that game developers routinely try to overcome with new techniques and technologies.

So far, I've discussed only the first and second approaches to discovering examples of agent/developers' use of conditional rhetoric. The third approach, studying how game developers are taught about their work, seems to me to hold the greatest promise for gamework scholars intent on understanding how agent/developers make and manage the meanings of their games. Studying what agent/developers say about the work they do—how they do it and why—is a particularly good way to discover how rhetoric functions in the computer game complex, because there are fewer restrictions on access than in the other two approaches and because such work tends to be definitive. There is, for example, a wealth of firsthand material available to people who do not have easy insider access to the spaces where computer game development takes place: there are thousands of documents on the Internet and dozens of books and magazines that treat the subject of the art of game development. These materials have the advantage of being methodical explanations of how practicing game developers understand what makes an effective game.

To explain these understandings, developers must suddenly bring into the light their assumptions about the industry, about the nature of play and entertainment, about running a business, about game players, and on occasion, about what roles computer games serve in society. In addition to these is the advantage that the agent/developers have gone on record about their assumptions, making the interpretation of game developers' rhetorics a somewhat less speculative or intentionalist exercise than other approaches sometimes require. Documents in this vein often make claims about what players are like, as if such generalizations count as valid evidence (which they do under certain circumstances). Good game designers, like good advertising agents, are particularly skillful at knowing intuitively what will capture their audiences' attention. While providing an objective to a gamer—say, to destroy all the blue robots—may be enough to gain his or her attention for a few minutes, such an unadorned objective will be unlikely to hold players' attention for the twenty-five or more hours that gamers say a title must remain interesting in order to be worth the money they paid for it. Instead, developers adorn games with plot details that depend on rhetoric functioning conditionally: A princess has been kidnapped by the Blue Robots—she must be rescued! After centuries of enslavement, the Red Robots are trying to throw off the chains of oppression fashioned by the Blue Robots—liberty or death! The Blue Wizard has broken away from the Rainbow Magic Clan and is now amassing an army of powerful magic Blue Robots in the craggy Northern Steppes—conquer the Blue Robots and capture the Blue Wizard before he consolidates all the power of the Rainbow Magic Clan for himself! Clearly, these imaginary scenarios tap into assumptions about freedom and justice, assumptions that are not universally applicable. Such scenarios also offer superficial exigencies to players, exigencies that really only serve to summon the more compelling responses that the conditional rhetoric empowers.

Gamework scholars, particularly those trying to understand the dialectic more thoroughly, will find it particularly helpful to identify how meanings are made at the conditional (unconscious) level because quotidian and exigent rhetorics typically are born out of it. Moreover, quotidian and exigent rhetorics can, over time, become so naturalized that they themselves become conditional. The idea of calling someone on the telephone to set up a meeting, for example, today seems utterly commonsensical—even if that person's office is just a few doors away. But this was not the case one hundred years ago. Eventually the telephonic revolution became a dim memory and, by the 1970s or so, wasn't even that for most people in industrialized societies. Studying how rhetoric functions conditionally in a given context adds a new level of complexity to one's understanding of that context and of the dialectical struggle in which it is embedded. More than that, however, studying conditional rhetoric means revealing systems of logic and common sense that typically go unacknowledged and unquestioned. The effect of such analysis is necessarily transformative to all of those who are exposed to it: certainly the veracity of the analysis can be challenged—even rejected—but even in the wake of such dismissal, transformations have occurred.

In many ways the most difficult part of the process of examining and then explaining the machinations of conditional rhetoric is not persuading people that the examination is sound but discovering the conditional rhetoric in the first place. Because scholars of the computer game complex have often themselves accepted the truth or obviousness of the conditional rhetoric under examination, locating such subtle instances of the control of meaning involves a struggle against oneself and against the means by which the conditional rhetoric hides. Like proofreading one's own writing after having just written it, revealing conditional rhetoric can be only partially successful; otherwise, the supportive systems of logic that help construct meaning for the examiner would themselves collapse. Thus, analyses of how the agents in the computer game complex manufacture artifactual meanings must necessarily proceed by situating such analyses within an understanding of the dialectic in which such rhetoric is at work. Consequently, revelations about conditional rhetoric's operation emerge slowly and in iterations that draw always on preceding observations and challenges. Studying one main function of rhetoric (e.g., quotidian) in the computer game complex necessarily entails studying the other two (i.e., exigent and conditional); this is the nature of the dialectic.

In the remainder of this chapter I will examine three particular sites where agent/developers make manifest the different functions of rhetoric and will conclude by proposing what these analyses suggest about the relationship of the computer game complex to larger struggles being contested through rhetoric in the dialectic itself.

Exigent Rhetoric in Game Developers' Discourse

A subject line in a message posted on an Internet public forum not long ago read: "Help! I can't read bone orientation in world space." This exclamation immediately suggests the kinds of exigencies that are being discussed in game development discussion groups and have been for many years. I hope that it is clear by now how a study of exigent, quotidian, or conditional rhetoric can help scholars use the elements of the grammar of gameworks to critique how agents within the computer game complex make and manage how games mean in local and broad contexts. In the short analyses that follow, I demonstrate how several recurring technical struggles shape and are shaped by nine different characteristics of exigently functioning rhetoric as described by computer game developers.

For the most part, these nine characteristics are not unique to the computer game complex. Such features (found below) as "Exigent Rhetoric Reveals What Kinds of Power Are at Stake" and "Exigent Rhetoric Constructs Disciplinary Identities" could be applied equally well to analyses of intellectual property law or narratives of the history of bluegrass music.[12] I use them here primarily to emphasize the fact that even so complex a subject as the technical discourse of computer game developers can be understood as exercises of rhetoric that exhibit certain common meaning-management features. Taken together, these sections specifically exemplify how analyses of the rhetorical exigencies used by agent/developers in electronic support groups reveal how agent/developers mutually determine the value of their work, how they negotiate impositions of power within their industry, and how they define themselves within existing social and institutional parameters.

My sources for this discourse are the newsgroups under the comp.games.development.programming rubric, including comp.games.development.

programming.algorithms and comp.games.development.programming.misc. Contrary to popular opinion, newsgroups—a technology that long preceded the World Wide Web—remain extremely active in many subject areas, including technical ones. Technologically speaking, newsgroups are not very flashy or sophisticated; they consist of e-mail messages posted according to theme on a network of servers all over the world. On any given day, the eight major computer game development newsgroups list more than eight thousand messages.[13] Additionally, message boards on the most popular game developer Web sites receive roughly three hundred messages per day. This amount of communication traffic, though tiny in comparison to all Internet or even all newsgroup traffic, is indicative of game developers' reliance on their colleagues to respond to pressing technical problems.

When dealing with forums such as open newsgroups or Web-based chat boards, it is best not to make rigid claims about the categories into which their messages fit. Like most newsgroups, for example, the comp.games.development.programming.misc discussion group contains messages from people with a range of interests in game development running from intense (as exhibited in the title to this section) to nonexistent.[14] A significant percentage—about 5 percent—deal with professional opportunities, while another 2 to 3 percent of the messages describe new games or game development tools. Most messages, though, do fit the specifically designated technical theme. The average number of messages sent to the comp.games.development.programming newsgroup—the forum to which I will mostly restrict this analysis—was about ten messages per day during the time I was studying it for developers' uses of exigent rhetoric.[15]

In newsgroups like this one, as well as on the discussion boards of game development Web sites like Gamasutra.com and Gamedev.com, developers log on to receive and offer help on particular problems various members are experiencing at the moment. Since such groups typically have an active core membership, replies to most messages arrive within twenty-four hours and often within twelve. Admittedly there are relatively few people who can field questions on "bone orientation," "Navier Stokes algorithms," and "collision/intersection points of 2-D polygons," but it is perhaps for this very reason that such communication channels are so heavily used: the only people who can answer such questions also frequent these newsgroups and Web boards.

Two other points are worth noting. First is simply a reminder that the multiperspectival nature of the grammar of gameworks dictates that gamework scholars attend with equal diligence to the technical aspects of computer game production as they do to game content and audience reception. Just as cinema scholars have recently become accustomed to learning about the technicalities of film production—lighting, blocking, camera angles and optics, and so on—so must gamework scholars begin to familiarize themselves with technicalities of game production such as level design, 3-D modeling, and physics engines. To do otherwise is to dismiss the importance of the specific kinds of work that game developers—artists all—do.

Second, the participants in online game developer discussions range from beginning amateurs to highly regarded professionals. And while the majority of these participants are male, the number of female participants has slowly grown in the four or so years I've tracked such communications channels. This informal finding is consistent with a recent survey done on behalf of the International Game Developers Association, which found that the number of female game designers rose almost 12 percent between the years 1990 and 1999. It is in the context of this changing electronic population—coalescing around the exigencies of computer game development—that I turn now to an examination of how agent/developers try to control how their games mean.

Exigent Rhetoric Reveals What Is Valued (and what is not)

It stands to reason that when agents make the effort to define a problem or pressing need, they care about getting that problem solved or that need fulfilled. The suasory work done to convey or respond to such problems and needs (i.e., exigent rhetoric) can therefore be said to indicate some of those agents' values. Exigent rhetoric also carries with it—almost inherently—a value on action, because exigencies demand responses of one sort or another. These values, once identified, can be further examined for their contextual implications: How are they functioning to influence certain kinds of struggles in which agent/developers, for example, are engaged? The implications of these unspoken values may relate to matters concerning a developer's sense of personal or communal utility, their political affiliations, their historico-material context, or other situations that will be affected by the outcome of an exigency's redress. I do not mean to imply that *all* the values embedded in a text or artifact can be identified and analyzed by the gamework scholar but rather that *certain* values will be apparent on the surface of the artifact or text, and from these apparent values the scholar may tease out other, less discernible values at work in the shadows. But even this set of apparent and discovered values does not represent the fullness of whole value systems at work in, for example, a programmer's query to a newsgroup. As communications theorists are quick to point out, audiences regularly exercise aberrant readings of texts (and artifacts), gamework scholars notwithstanding.

For example, on August 14, 2001, a contributor to the game algorithm newsgroup posted this request:

> I need a *fast* algorithm for calculating the shortest path from A to B in a 11×11 grid. I've been looking for a sample using google but haven't had success. If someone knows any good references of a sample in pseudo-syntax/pascal (I use Delphi so my C++ skills aren't very good) please let me know! (Harzel)[16]

Apart from this initial message and a thank-you note, Harzel was a stranger to the group, yet within two days he had received six replies. Not only did these replies contain detailed solutions to his problem—"On an 11×11 grid, you might consider a brute force method. There are numerous ways to do it, a variation on a pixel-fill algorithm for example, or a plain breadth-first search (they are very similar)" (Summerhayes, July 15, 2001)—but also personal stories ("Last time when I've used this it was in simple game, on very slow environment (compared to Pentium it would be about Pentium . . . 1kHz, or even slower :) and for 14×14 grid most complex path didn't take more than 2 secs . . . ") (Burzynski). Follow-ups to the message contained corrections and modifications ("I misunderstood problem :) I thought about simplest thing: Euclidean distance d(x,y)=sqrt((x1−x2)^2+(y1−y2)^2) :) Reading too fast and too careess [*sic*] probably :)") (Burzynski). Additionally, one respondent engaged in a debate with another respondent (not Harzel) over his proposed solution:

> Why float? How are you getting the shortest path from this data storage? How many different maps, starting and ending locations is this allocation capable of storing at once? It appears to be one map only, starting and ending locations indexing to . . . path length? Ignoring eliminating duplications from rotations, reflections, etc. and going for a 0 as passable and a 1 as non-passable makes the total possible grids 2^(11*11) and this is a very simple representation. (Summerhayes, August 16, 2001)

Several technical characteristics are discernibly valued in this exchange, some stated and others implied: speed, ease of implementation, low resource requirements, and syntactic applicability (e.g., Pascal, not C++). Not surprisingly, given that this is a game programmers' newsgroup, the agents here value features that enhance efficiency. One way to interpret this is according to a business model that evaluates success according to speed: speed in debugging, speed in application run times, and of course, speed to market. Another way to interpret this emphasis on efficiency, however, is according to the art of programming itself: elegant algorithms, simple procedures that do complex functions, and the ability to create working programs rapidly are all signs of one's fluency in computer languages. In this particular exchange it is never explicitly stated whether business or art is the greater determining factor, but without examining the exchange for the values that stated exigencies make apparent, the gamework scholar might easily overlook the very presence of these important subtexts.

Noteworthy, too, in this exchange is that the rhetoric used throughout is responding specifically to a technical exigence, but the variety of responses within which the exigent rhetoric is couched is considerable. By identifying within the context of their exigent rhetoric what game developers value, the gamework scholar can also see how phenomena such as membership, discipline, mentorship, and collegiality are negotiated or enforced. This is an important foundation for any further understandings of how the dialectical struggles to which the computer game complex is linked may be shifting and being shaped by those agents participating in it. This early stage of the analysis of exigently functioning rhetoric reveals points of sensitivity, then, where transformative experiences are not only possible but expected—even though they are not stated outright. In this regard, the values defined by exigent rhetoric offer many clues as to how meanings are made in quotidian and conditional contexts as well.

Exigent Rhetoric Reveals How Value Is Assigned in Particular Domains

A more subtle analytical point than *what* values are revealed by an examination of agent/developers' exigent rhetoric is *how* those values are assigned. In other words, once it is clear what is valuable to developers, the gamework scholar may more easily pursue the question "How has what is valuable become so?" And although it may sometimes be less historically grounded, a related question—"How is that which is valued among agent/developers maintained as valuable?"—can also shed light on the ways suasory work motivates dialectical struggles.[17]

On August 10, 2001, for example, a thread was initiated that began "Hi, My source bellow seams [*sic*] correct but I'm not getting the effect I want, when it toggles to no frame the window caption remains" (Oti, August 10, 2001). Following this was an excerpt of source code (about fourteen lines) designed to control an application's window—the frame around a program.

The code was well documented, which is to say that the programmer had added many internal comments that explained what each line of code was supposed to do. Two days later, the same person posted this note after receiving no responses:

> Hello,
> I'm thinking of changing my name. It seams [*sic*] that people are more inclined to respond to other requests regardless of how obscure they may be :(Really, has nobody had or solved this window frame problem???
> Any help please. (Oti, August 12, 2001)

A few hours later, a response arrived. In its entirety it read: "WS_CAPTION" (Liimatta). Compared to most other responses to questions posed in the newsgroup, the brevity of this one is striking—but to be expected. The poster of the first message had overlooked an obvious solution to the problem, a mistake that many programmers consider annoying and rude. After the second plea, Jukka Liimatta finally broke the silence and gave away the easy answer. In this particular newsgroup, convened primarily by advanced amateur and professional programmers, there is nothing but appreciation for difficult problems and little sympathy for carelessness.

As evidence of this appreciation for complexity, consider a message sent just a couple of days earlier that asked about how one might build a pattern recognition algorithm for mouse movements—a technology made popular by the game *Black & White.* This question elicited eight responses, each of which is highly engaged with the posed problem and with other respondents' answers. In response to one programmer's solution, for example, another participant wrote:

> Eek, NO!. That method is not well known because a better method has been developed. Instead of ensuring the same number of points in the gesture. We calculate values of features (absolute length, curvature, start-end difference, angularity, linearity, etc.) then apply a hyperplane intersection to the vector over a matrix of trained gestures to get the score result and the mahalanobis distance for certainty.
>
> The time loss for the matrix over vectior comparisons is made up by the versatility in direction, size and the removal of a need to interpolate any points. With an overall gain in recognition of 7% to 98% for grafitti text and 99% for geometric symbols. Although it is highly dependant on the chosen feature sets.—AJ (Jeffries)

In this newsgroup there clearly exist categories of good and bad questions. But unlike some other newsgroups in which bad questions are rewarded with a cacophony of flames (irate messages), standard operating procedure here is the cold shoulder, or at best, a curt answer. New participants to this and other game developer discussion groups are quickly disciplined—either directly or indirectly—so that they know and obey the protocols of the discussion. In many game developer newsgroups and Web boards, this discipline rewards obedience and punishes violation through discursive copiousness and isolation, respectively.

The question of how value is placed and perpetuated is one of the most important questions that gamework analyses can answer. It is by such answers that counter-rhetorics may be developed, rhetorics that can help scholars devalue preexisting standards when necessary. It is also by such answers that newer and more fitting rhetorics may be inserted into ongoing struggles. If technical language or evidence of an interesting project are prerequisites for gaining an audience's recognition, then it seems that not *all* exigent rhetoric is deemed worthy of response. Rather, only that exigent rhetoric that conforms to the disciplinary boundaries established and enforced by empowered agents is granted legitimacy. Values are assigned in this discursive community, then, through disciplinary actions that are at first imposed by those who have already accepted the community's strictures, and later are self-imposed through internalized notions of professional propriety. The scholar can see in this dynamic that when the discourse by which game development exigencies are disciplined, so too will be the other functions of rhetoric that mediate daily and commonsensical meaning-making activities.

Exigent Rhetoric Reveals How Power Is Negotiated in Particular Domains

When pressing problems are communicated to an audience, then taken up by that same audience in an effort to solve them, power relations are often brought into stark contrast: newbies versus experts, amateurs versus professionals, trend followers versus trend setters, and from a simple materialist perspective, the minimally equipped versus the well equipped. This is because the problems themselves are manifestations of existing power relations and indicate instances where a set of powers existing in a state of equilibrium (which is not to say equality) is considered to be unsatisfactory. Problem solving, then, is a way to break the equilibrium and reestablish the power relations in a different—and presumably more advantageous—configuration. The mechanisms of these negotiations are various and complex: a fourth-grader's math "problem" is of a different sort than the hydrodynamic engineer's problem of controlling a supercavitating object, yet both involve applying certain forces to gain a new level of control—and hence, power.

The examples above demonstrate this phenomenon well; inquirers' questions are taken up or not and are evaluated as cutting edge, outmoded, interesting, or dumb. As pressing problems are expressed and solved, the gamework scholar can identify the movements of power that establish authority, control the direction of particular discourses, and produce certain expectations about the nature of future problems. If exigencies are addressed technically and definitively by experts, then the negotiation of power may be based on a fairly restricted merit system in which power is not shared but taken. On the other hand, if exigencies are addressed holistically so that solutions are arrived at gradually and with guidance by more knowledgeable participants, then the negotiations may tend toward an open exchange and sharing of power.[18] Outside of institutional educational systems, power among agent/developers seems to be negotiated more on the former model than on the latter. This is likely because in the game development industry, production of a commercially viable product is the top priority, not the training of its producers to work for some form of universal social justice.

Exigent Rhetoric Reveals What Kinds of Power Are at Stake

"Power" is a nebulous term and comes in many forms: intellectual, cultural, mechanical, political, and so on. Economic power often supercedes or intervenes in these other types of power, a phenomenon that explains how economically powerful nations are able to dominate weaker nations without the use of military force. Studying exigent rhetoric can reveal which kinds of power are being wielded and resisted, providing the gamework scholar with a useful way to recognize why a dialectical struggle seems to take the shape it does and how it might be related to similar power struggles at a more local level (e.g., within the computer game complex). A worker's struggle to be fairly compensated for her labor in a factory that manufactures computer game cartridges, for example, may overtly concern an economic struggle but may less obviously, though just as importantly, involve a struggle against male power and its attendant workplace privileges, or the exploitative practices stemming from U.S. imperialism.

I have already provided several examples of how technical power is wielded in the comp.games.development.programming.algorithms newsgroup, noting in particular the way it is used to mind the gate of this forum.[19] But there are other struggles here. On August 10, 2001, a company called PocketView Broadcasting posted a request for games that it could take under contract and develop into commercially viable products. The request included a number of specifications for submitted games but did not include any information about the terms of agreement between potential developers and the distributor. This invitation, compelling to the less experienced developers in the forum, raised the ire of more experienced participants, many of whom had stories about amateurs whose ideas and prototypes had been stolen by distributors using just this kind of approach. Within a day and a half, a developer responded to PocketView's call with this message:

> Wha[t] would happen to my labour of love if I were to submit it to you? Would you then own it? give me nothing and take all the credit? Or would I actually get something? How well would you market my game? Would I have a say in strategies, ideas etc? What are my options. Of course, I'd love you to publish my games, but on good terms ;)
> Cheers—Moe (Moses)

Moe understands that his technical power is precisely vulnerable at the point where the development process becomes determined by money rather than 3-D art, audio tracks, and the idiosyncrasies of game engines. It becomes, in other words, a project about wielding market power in a highly competitive industry rather than wielding technical power over a "labour of love" in a field of one's professional compatriots. At the same time, however, Moe seems to want some of that market power, as we see in the final sentence: "I'd love you to publish my games, but on good terms." This is a transitional moment for Moe, and even though these two discussants took their conversation off the list and into private correspondence, it is clear that technical, artistic, and economic power are all vying for representation in this relatively simple newsgroup exchange.

Among game developers, then, several types of power appear to be at stake. Most apparent is technical power, which gives its wielders control specifically over computers, making them do the things programmers want them to do. Matters such as how to increase the display rate of polygons and program force-feedback devices are, on the surface, about controlling particular technologies. If we inquire into why such power is important to attain, we quickly see other forms of power are at stake. To control computer technology at the level of sophistication that game developers require is to wield both professional and artistic power, each of which can in turn be used to gain and wield economic power. And as in any other situation in which economic power has been achieved, game developers in this position gain access to tremendous cultural power, the power to shape the consciousnesses of millions of game players and the face of mass culture itself. The creators of games such *Doom, Tomb Raider, Myst,* and *Deerhunter,* for example, not only enjoy the economic power that has come with the success of their games, but they also enjoy the power to wield their ability to shape other forms of mass media. Recent car advertisements, for example, capitalize on the popularity of the absurdly proportioned adventurer Lara Croft, on the eerie *Myst*-inspired landscapes waiting to be conquered by the latest sport utility vehicle, and on the popularly accepted myths about the psychopathologies attributable to *Doom.* This power also garners sufficient respect by the armed forces that they use computer games to recruit and train new soldiers, and by stock brokerage houses whose ads imitate the wait-then-shoot mentality and interface of *Deerhunter.* Ernest Adams, in his "Dogma 2001: A Challenge to Game Designers," actually attempts to deprivilege economic power by advocating instead for creative power. The drive to get rich from game design, he says, has mostly ruined it as an art. His manifesto defines a new set of professional values that emphasize creativity in both the technical and plot elements of games, even if it must come at the expense of not using the latest technology or drawing on the latest media trends and fads. When developers express and address specific professional problems and needs, they simultaneously reveal what kinds of power are at stake for them. For "Moe," Ernest Adams, and many other developers, the struggle between computer game development as an artist's labor of love versus a businessperson's project designed to tap into mainstream high-revenue media genres and cutting-edge technologies is an ongoing one that is consistently reflected in their uses of rhetoric to foreground particular exigencies.[20] These articulated problems and responses can often reveal to the gamework scholar what kinds of power are at stake (e.g., social, professional, creative) among particular agents, as well as who wields that power and confers it on others.

Exigent Rhetoric Reveals How an Artifact's Contradictions Are Masked

Although the expression of a problem always occurs within the dialectic as part of a particular dialectical struggle, the nature of this struggle is not always readily apparent.[21] This is the case because the contradictions—the core disagreements—of dialectical struggles are often masked by a number of other meaning-making events that have been offered up in service to one position or another over time. In the computer game complex, for example, the art versus business contradiction is often masked by such debates as whether or not commercial art is "real" art, whether or not programming can be considered "artistic," and whether or not certain gaming platforms give developers more creative freedom than others. These events, some of which may be only semi-relevant, act as signs that form a matrix around the contradiction, making it difficult to identify. Exigent uses of rhetoric can often help the gamework scholar reveal these underlying contradictions, however, by pointing out the most important elements in the surrounding matrix and by showing which key words constituting it are particularly ambiguous. An analysis of exigent rhetoric, in other words, can help clarify which elements and terms in the masking matrix are under the most tension and therefore are most likely to be near the contradiction under investigation.

Without clear exigencies to provide gamework scholars with markers about which elements in the dialectic are most important, they are in the unenviable position of having to decide the importance of various signs for themselves. Such a position forces scholars to interpret dialectical contradictions according to their own definitions—certainly not an illegitimate critical enterprise but one that runs a greater risk of missing or misidentifying those contradictions. In analyzing gameworks, it is time well spent to find examples of exigent rhetoric that may have served to shape the masking matrix of signs surrounding them. Such signs can reveal telltale contradictions that, in part at least, contribute to how gameworks are imbued with certain values and influence how they are able to make meanings in their users.

Exigent Rhetoric Reveals How Internal Contradictions Can Be Reinterpreted, Reauthorized, and Mystified

The previous section describes an analytical technique by which the central contradiction in a dialectical struggle may be identified by examining an instance of exigent rhetoric and the responses to it. In that case, exigent rhetoric offers signs, via the contextualizing details, indicating which struggle among several is where the central contradiction lies. One needn't always examine exigent rhetoric in order to exclude misleading signs, however. It is sometimes useful for the scholar to examine as many of the signs as possible that are offered through a particular exigency. Typically, this critical exercise is most fruitful when the central contradiction has already been discovered and the gamework scholar wants to begin to understand the history of the dialectical struggle itself. By not disregarding any related exigent rhetoric and by noting how each such rhetorical event gives shape and direction to the dialectical struggle, the scholar can begin to understand how these different signs contribute to the struggle's evolution. In documenting this development, the ways these signs have worked to influence the appearance of the primary contradiction—intentionally or coincidentally—will be gradually revealed and the discursive moments when the contradiction was reinterpreted, reauthorized, or mystified will thereby be discovered. Such revelations also suggest something about the different participants (or entire contingents) in the dialectical struggle, because each will define the struggle and value its various aspects differently.

Although the discursive sample in the comp.games.development.programming.algorithms newsgroup is relatively small—twelve hundred messages or so sent over several months—it is plain that as game developers in this venue help each other solve a host of technical problems, an additional contradiction haunts the art of computer game development: designing systems of play that make manifest the developers' creativity requires workers to regularly forgo creativity in order to deliver a product on time to an audience that has little tolerance for products that don't fit neatly into certain well-defined categories. This contradiction is either simply ignored (in favor of a concentration on technical issues) or is recast as a challenge: try to be creative within the constraints of efficiency and standardization. By attending to the exigent rhetoric in a case such as this, computer game scholars open a door to the mechanisms of conditional rhetoric and to the vast network of underlying assumptions and ideologically determined decisions that make computer games the potent purveyors of mass culture that they are.

Exigent Rhetoric Constructs Disciplinary Identities

Earlier I described how a study of exigent rhetoric can help gamework scholars discern how value is assigned in particular discursive domains and cited as an example the role discipline plays in enforcing the maintenance of such values. A related characteristic that scholars should be aware of is that exigently functioning rhetoric works to construct disciplinary identity itself. One of the first observations one makes upon examining the construction of exigence among computer game developers, for instance, is that it is socially definitive. Even as different agents are employing different rhetorical techniques in order to ask and answer pressing questions within their field, the expressions of these exigencies themselves are constituting boundaries that define what can count as a valid problem or need.

For example, the very first message of the comp.games.development.programming.algorithms newsgroup was posted on July 22, 1998; its subject line was "First Draft." In that message the author requested that people submit lists of links related to game development algorithms. In what surely had to be a disappointingly inauspicious beginning, no one replied to the message. It was not until two days later, when someone posted the following message, that responses began to be posted and the list began to develop its disciplinary character:

> I'm looking for a good line intersection algorithm, That is, given x1,y1 and x2,y2 (end points of 2 lines) I need to know if these lines intersect. I know (on paper) how to do the calculations but these have divisions which will be slow (I need to do quite a lot of calculations per frame). (Leone)

Four detailed responses were submitted in response to this query, which was both a well-defined exigency and the first post on the newsgroup to elicit a response. Over the next week, nearly sixty messages were posted, most of which were replies to other game developers' exigencies. Messages that didn't specifically address the topic of the newsgroup or that did not clearly state the nature of the algorithmic problem were ignored or rebuffed. After one poster asked a "which do you think is better" question about different game engines (in a way that revealed no particular exigence) (Waits), a respondent wrote: "Nice to see a post in this new group. But, I hope this group at least can be for serious discussion on the industry" (S. Williams).

In this way, rhetoric—language designed to make and manage meanings and thereby motivate change—when functioning to address exigent matters, may in the course of time inadvertently serve to assist in the construction of group identity. In the case of computer game developers, their questions and answers to each other are not only instances of how agents fashion persuasive responses to peers but are also instances of how protocols for correct behavior within a group can be informally established yet rigorously policed.

In the above analyses of how agent/developers work to determine how their games mean by identifying and addressing exigencies in the production cycle, I have tried to describe how particular technical game development problems may have shaped and been shaped by the discourse used to describe and privilege them. In this capacity, the suasory work that such exigent rhetoric does—even in the complex technical discourse of computer game developers—is clearly involved with the management of meaning, not only of particular problems but also of all the social relations present in the computer game complex: how agent/developers mutually determine the value of their work, how they negotiate impositions of power within their industry, and how they define themselves within existing social and institutional parameters.

It seems unlikely, perhaps, that the most overt aspects of rhetoric's functions can be useful for understanding the full complexity of a localized dialectical struggle. It may also seem counterintuitive that the surface features of discourse, for example, can be helpful both in constructing an interpretation of a range of texts and artifacts and in opening up the context of those texts and artifacts for a deeper analysis of a dialectical problem and its underlying contradictions. Yet, examining how many of a game's meanings are established through its agent/developers' defining of exigencies accomplishes both of these purposes and simultaneously clarifies what these agents consider important and valid work. Such examinations also establish a solid foundation from which to launch further inquiries into agents' uses of and dependence on quotidian and conditional rhetorics. It is toward these subtler influences within the computer game complex that I now turn.

Quotidian Rhetoric in Game Developers' Discourse

Learning to play computer games these days is hard work. In the game *Splinter Cell*, for example, players must memorize the button combinations for a dozen or so movements, keep an eye on health and stealth meters, and stay aware of which weapons and ammunition are being carried, all while focusing on the current mission's objectives, navigating unknown surroundings, listening to information coming in over the radio, and strategizing about how to surmount immediate obstacles. Learning to play games like this is akin to learning how to drive a stick shift during rush hour in Manhattan while the radio is playing and a chatterbox is sitting in the passenger seat. But eventually all these details fade into the subconscious and playing the game becomes natural.

For the most part, learning to play today's complex and immersive games serves as a good example of how the work of meaning-management (rhetoric) traverses the continuum of rhetorical functionality from the exigent through the quotidian and into the conditional. Certain features of gaming never quite make it to the conditional end of the continuum: setting up the console, inserting memory cards, selecting saved games; gamers do these things repeatedly, but because they recur only occasionally, they never quite become second nature for most players. Such tasks are comparable to rhetorical events that function quotidianly, that is, suasory events that address what may be called micro transformations. When rhetoric functions at the quotidian level, it makes possible the completion of mundane tasks in a more or less careful, but not very thoughtful, way.

A new computer game begins with an idea, arguably a rhetorical exigency: "How can we build a great Formula One racing simulation?" From there, developers draw up a design document that details everything that can be determined about the game in the preproduction process: look and feel, storyline, major and minor characters, platforms, technical specifications, budgets, milestones, production schedules, and personnel hierarchies. Drafting this document requires almost nothing but exigent rhetoric: staffers argue out each of these things one by one, bringing to bear in the meetings everything from personal anecdotes and eccentricities to market research data and technical constraints. But once this document is complete and the project is begun, the rhetoric of game development mostly shifts away from exigent functions and begins to work more quotidianly. The next milestone may lie three months out, and the intervening days will be spent doing routine tasks punctuated only occasionally by an unforeseen technical or management problem.

When the ways that games mean are being managed quotidianly, discovering and analyzing those ways can be challenging. This is because quotidian rhetoric is perceived not so much as pressing and transformative as necessary: in order to begin rendering animation sequences, an artist must first get all the models built. Assuming that the artist knows how to use the modeling software and assuming that the game characters, objects, and environments have already been sketched out for the design document, the artist's only remaining task is to build those models in a 3-D graphics model application like LightWave, Maya, or 3-D Studio Max. There will, of course, be small hitches in this process—tweaking the lighting, creating fog effects, or shading individual pixels for better visual effects—but even these small challenges are all in a day's work for the game artist. Solving these problems requires a bit of trial-and-error work, but they're not really exigencies because they're not urgent and because failing to resolve them will not bring the project to a halt. Asking an artist working at this stage of a project about what she did that day is more likely to elicit a response along the lines of "same old, same old" than "I finally figured out how to. . . . "

And yet game development projects would never get finished if it weren't for rhetoric functioning quotidianly. Moreover, many exigencies would never emerge if a host of smaller quotidian rhetorical events had not paved the way for them. Consider, for example, the process of "asset management." This aspect of game development is an unsung art, yet it is crucial for virtually all large-scale game development projects. In a nutshell, asset management is the controlling and tracking of all the objects in a game: models, textures, sound effects, music clips, animations, and script elements. Asset management is important because teams of developers often work independently, even while they are working with the same assets. Without asset management, an animator might tweak an existing animation to make it more lifelike, while a programmer down the hall builds the old version of the animation into the latest working version of the game. As a result, the artist's time is wasted, and so is the programmer's when she discovers that she has to go back and rebuild the application with the updated animation. In the early to mid-1990s, asset management was hit-or-miss, and many companies established formal protocols that required everyone to notify everyone else about the current status of all "under construction" assets. Needless to say, these protocols didn't always get followed. Asset managers, first as people and later as software applications, stepped in to accomplish this task more consistently.

Herb Marselas, in an article in the November 2000 issue of *Game Developer,* discusses the importance of asset management, noting in particular how his company, Ensemble Studios, was suddenly faced with the fact that the daily routines for tracking assets had become so problematic that it had become an exigency:

> *Age of Empires II: The Age of Kings* consisted of more than 40,000 game and production assets, ranging from bitmaps and textures to 3D models, sounds and music, and source code files. However, with the exception of the source code, managing game assets at Ensemble Studios has largely consisted of editing, copying, and renaming files on local and shared network drives. This process has sometimes resulted in a number of problems, including misplacement, corruption, or accidental loss of game assets. All of these problems result in effort that must be spent finding or re-creating missing assets. (40)

According to Marselas, the exigency that demanded "about eight full-time man-weeks of programming" away from the game development schedule (not including testing or upgrades) to build a software-based asset management application was a direct result of inadequate communication among team members and the machines upon which they worked. Once their asset management software was up and running, however, the team members found themselves in a new routine and were again distanced from those rhetorical events that were functioning exigently. Although Marselas does not dwell on how the asset management software his team built from scratch was planned—let alone first considered—he does note that it was a collaborative effort (48), and he includes the list of requirements for the system that was drawn up at a series of planning meetings (41). The asset management software was, in other words, the product of a combination of exigent and quotidian rhetoric.

This example of the failure of quotidian rhetoric at Ensemble Studios—the failure that led to the creation of the asset management software—illustrates the dynamic nature of rhetoric's functions along a continuum: when routine meaning-making processes break down, exigencies that shape meanings in more overt ways emerge. As such, this example is helpful for its portrayal of how quotidian and exigent rhetoric shift one into the other, but it does not shed much light on the nature of quotidian rhetoric itself. Let us consider another example, then, that does.

In the September 2001 issue of *Game Developer*, animator David Stripinis recommends that graphic artists learn basic programming skills. His argument is simple: "You may wonder why, as an artist, you should invest the time to learn some obscure collection of ifs, fors, and thens. The answer is simple: Scripting makes your life easier. Whether it's automating a repetitious task, doing something the computer is better at than a human (such as creating anything random), or adding new functionality that your program lacks, a clever artist can accomplish all this, and more, with scripting" (40). Throughout the article, Stripinis repeatedly emphasizes the expediency of programming for artists, usually by calling attention to the tedious aspects of making game art: "The life of a game artist is often filled with repetitive tasks" (42); "the power of scripting for the artist is in accomplishing mundane tasks" (43); "Now we can do all those modifications and exports in a minimal amount of time and without error" (43). Perhaps anticipating a skeptical artist's criticism that scripting is merely the replacement of one set of mundane practices for another, Stripinis observes that the advantage of scripting is that you have to create a script only once: "You don't want to rewrite a script every time you need to perform some common function you need. So let's create a command that we can execute from either a button or the Script Editor" (42). The operative concept here—and in virtually every other part of the industry that addresses the matter of mundane professional tasks—is that they must be made more efficient, quicker, or altogether invisible.

These two examples—asset management and artists as programmers—reveal several important points about quotidian rhetoric that the gamework scholar can use. First, although there is general appreciation for people's methodical detail work, in the game industry at least, it is respected only to the point that it is absolutely necessary. As a consequence, the routine of a profession, despite its necessity, is seen as the work of "grunts," or as they are called among programmers, "code monkeys." The eagerness with which people try to develop shortcuts is a sign of the tone that often accompanies quotidian rhetoric, namely, boredom and some amount of embarrassment. This also explains why gestures toward the exigent are so common from a scenario in which quotidian rhetoric rules, and also why conditional rhetoric can develop so freely from it: few people want to pay attention to the same thing repeatedly, no matter how important that thing is.

In terms of the dialectic, an examination of how games are given meaning through the exercise of routine processes and decisions reveals stasis points at which the dialectic is in an even tension. At such points, transformation *could* happen, but it's not happening at the moment. When people like Marselas and Stripinis call attention to those stasis points, it is usually to advocate for change. In their advocacy, ideologies become apparent: automating collaborative processes is good because then people need no longer endure the mistakes of others and blame can be shifted to technology (asset management); if artists would learn to program they'd be better off, because then they could just let the computer do all the tedious work for them and concentrate on being creative. When a computer game scholar looks at moments when rhetoric is functioning quotidianly, she or he is looking precisely at a site of ongoing struggle, subtle though it may be. Rather than dismissing the small meaning-making events enacted by agents, then, game scholars interested in the dynamic of the dialectic would instead be wise to pay special attention: What transformations are in the works? What dissatisfactions are being fomented or are naturally evolving that will inspire a transformation? What techniques are being implemented—or could be implemented—that would shift the meaning-making work from being quotidian to exigent or conditional, that is, indicative of crisis or common sense?

Answers to questions such as these will suggest to scholars of the computer game complex ways that powers are balanced against one another in both antagonistic and nonantagonistic relationships. Often, as in the case of computer game development, these answers can be discovered through an examination of those places where quotidian rhetoric is given voice: the tips and tricks of the trade sections of newsletters or professional publications, job descriptions, project specifications, and analyses and descriptions of tools of the trade. I will return to this latter point in the next chapter, where I examine the rhetoric and dialectic of game reviews. While games *are* the trade rather than tools *of* the trade, many reviews—as we will see—are built upon reviewers' insider knowledge of the game development process, including the ways designers rely on particular tools such as licensed game engines, character modeling packages, and music editing software. Before proceeding to that analysis, however, there remains one more function of rhetoric that warrants discussion.

Conditional Rhetoric in Game Developers' Discourse

There are basically two kinds of books for learning about computer game development: those for amateurs and those for professionals. There are some overlapping subjects in each, but in general these are the two audiences that publishers have created. Both kinds have educational ends and yet they are clearly distinguishable, usually by the look of the covers alone. Books for amateurs tend to have covers that look like games: flashy fonts, lots of colors, sometimes even computer-generated humanoid figures and eerie landscapes. These books also tend to be of moderate length—four hundred pages or so—and have titles like *Game Design: Secrets of the Sages* and *Awesome Game Creation, No Programming Required.* Books for professionals, on the other hand, look like giant technical manuals: the covers use simple but imposing typefaces over backgrounds of matrices, sine waves, or microcircuits. These books, which are just as often hardcover as not, usually run to eight or nine hundred pages, have full-color signatures bound into the center of them, and have titles like *Game Architecture and Design, Game Design: The Art and Business of Creating Games,* and *3-D Game Engine Design: A Practical Approach to Real-Time Computer Graphics.*[22]

Despite these and other differences, however, there are many similarities, especially as one begins to discern how agent/developers influence how other developers make sense of the ways games mean. Nearly every book on computer game design, for example, contains a chapter on the history of computer games, all of which are more or less the same except for slight differences that highlight the theme of the book. A general book may focus its historical overview on a simple chronology, from *Space Wars* to *Neverwinter Nights.* A book on 3-D game engine design may focus on major innovations in physics simulators as represented in those same games. Except for the most technically specific texts (e.g., *Mathematics for 3D Game Programming and Computer Graphics*), most books on computer game development summarize the major game genres, offer advice on what makes games fun, and describe how to put together a design document. Many of the books explain important terms like "vector," "sprite," "texture," "voxel," "API," and "DirectX."

One of the most effective ways of discovering conditional rhetoric, that is, the underlying logics and assumptions, among agent/developers is to examine the processes and techniques that they posit are "best," "correct," or "natural." Certain decisions—like a book's target audience—necessarily shape some of the details of these descriptions: *Awesome Game Creation,* for example, doesn't contain lengthy treatments of "software factories" and "architect groups," as *Game Architecture and Design* does, since most amateurs aren't much concerned about production schedules and aren't managing large production teams. The following table summarizes the production processes proposed by four major texts that were simultaneously available in 2002. In general, all the books suggest a mostly self-evident procedure: come up with a good idea, write down the details of that idea, turn the idea into reality, and

Table 1: Production Processes According to Major Game Development Texts

Game Design: Secrets of the Sages	*Awesome Game Creation: No Programming Required*	*Game Design: The Art and Business of Creating Games*	*Game Architecture and Design*
Choose a genre	Choose a genre	Concept development	First concept
Create the characters	Write the game idea	Project proposal	Core design
Create the storyboard	Write the game treatment	High concept	Game play
Write the design document	Determine technology	Features summary	Detailed design
Design the puzzles	Identify audience	Story	Game balance
Design the levels	Select a team	Game play mechanics	Look and feel
Design the mission	Write the design document	Profit & loss statement	Team building & management
Programming	Make the game	Risk analysis	Technical design
AI		Proof of concept	Development
Artwork		Game design document	Run-up to release
Animation		Art bible	Postmortem
Sound/music		Production path	
Game testing		Technical design document	
Customer support		Project plan	
Marketing		Prototype	
		Development	
		Alpha	
		Beta	
		Code freeze	
		Release to manufacturer	
		Patches	
		Upgrades	

sell the reality. A table such as this, though, makes it easy to begin asking questions that get at conditional rhetoric.

With one exception (*Awesome Game Creation*), for example, none of the texts discusses the question of audience in detail. This immediately suggests that there are a host of unwritten assumptions about agent/players that warrant investigation. And knowing that one text raises the issues of gender, age, and economic privilege, it becomes a straightforward task to examine the other texts for the subtle ways in which they construct agent/players. In *Secrets of the Sages*, game designer Bob Bates writes: "When people ask me what it takes to be a game designer, I tell them the single most important skill is what I call 'player empathy.' You need to be able to put yourself in the player's shoes. To anticipate what he's thinking, what he's feeling. To know what he'll want to try and to let him. To know what he or she will think is exciting. To know what will feel boring and to cut it out" (Saltzman 55). Aside from the overwhelming use of sexist language—a choice that Bates actually defends in his own book on game design[23]—we see here a concept that has wide industry acceptance: game developers believe they have a window into the consciousnesses of "game players." They don't often advocate market research in these books to see what game players are like and what they want; game developers are just supposed to know. How? By playing games themselves: all four books offer the advice that if one wants to design games, one must also play them a lot.[24] Chris Taylor, of Interplay, advises: "Always, always, always be playing games. You can't design for the market if you don't know what the market is doing" (Saltzman 48). There are, no doubt, some advantages to this, but I contend that when an industry in general fails to demonstrate a progressive sense of audience awareness, and when that failure is subsequently built into the educational materials for developers, then those failures—which emerge out of developers' assumptions (i.e., their conditional rhetoric)—are going to be endlessly reproduced. The same can be said about the failure of many game developers to invent new games that respond to the public's concern over representations of violence: if new developers are encouraged by their mentors to pay more attention to what already exists and to what sells well than to the concerns raised by scientists, social activists, and perhaps even their own ethics, then it can hardly be surprising that computer games evolve far more rapidly on technical fronts than on moral or ethical ones.

Another similarity among the books is that they all work to help game developers improve their abilities to negotiate the marketplace. None of the books questions the ethics of the marketplace, a fact that is not that surprising until we recall the contradiction noted earlier about game development as a business and as an art. Except in passing, none of these books—including the ones that overtly refer to game development as an art in their titles—genuinely treats it as an art. Game development is an art, these texts imply, insofar as it is complex and dynamic; it is not an art, however, in the more traditional sense that it is has an aesthetic designed to elicit reflection, inspire revolution, or represent "beauty." The artists in these projects are assumed to be commercial artists, wielding mouse and pen for a steady paycheck, not to teach or transform society. Bates writes, "If you are an artist, you must constantly keep up with your craft and be ready to adapt or die" (170). Ethics are for chatting about over pizza and beer in this business, and the seeming contradiction between art and industry servitude is for the most part an empty one. A story in *Game Architecture and Design* puts it most starkly:

> I once went to the European Trade Show, paying the extra for a Premium Club ticket (which allows you access to a private room where all the top management hang out and discuss their latest deals), and stayed for a while listening to the various conversations. The topics varied wildly, but one theme was common: the employees of the software companies were all discussed in terms of how they could be exploited. They were viewed as cattle, to be milked. This was something I had jokingly suspected for some time, but to actually hear it openly discussed was a bit of an eye-opener. It gave me some new insight on the industry. There were the few, living off the back of the toil of the many. For your average Joe Programmer, the industry is not a fair place, and the distribution of wealth is weighted heavily against them. Revolutions have been started for less. . . . This is not to say that I am advocating for all programmers to overturn their desks, smash their monitors, and storm the management offices. I am just making an observation that the games industry cannot continue in this fashion if it is to become a mature and stable industry. (Rollings and Morris 346–47)

Here, then, is a case in which a little bit of investigation into the conditional rhetoric of a popular contradiction reveals that the contradiction has been more or less accepted. The game industry is a business like any other under capitalism, operating at best according to principles exemplified by the Microsoft term "coopertition" (Rollings and Morris 167), a concept that involves everyone competing against everyone else—including one's peers—just as long as the company (i.e., the executives and shareholders) benefits in the end.

A gamework analysis here, done for the sake of better understanding a larger dialectical struggle, suggests that unspoken assumptions about the evolution of game development from art to industry are tolerated more than appreciated, if only because the logic of late capitalism—some people are rich and some aren't—is a truism. Rollings and Morris observe (wrongly, I would argue) that revolution is not really an option, even though they know well enough that the situation warrants it. So even in an industry that prides itself on progress, that progress is to be strictly technological and ought not to have aspirations to transform society to make it a more just and equitable place. The realities of the present world, it would seem, are so entrenched that even people who imagine alternative worlds for a living—agent/developers—cannot envision that their craft could have radically transformative effects (for better or worse) on society. With very few exceptions, game industry professionals seem to have resigned themselves to the "fact" that their work can merely be part of the background noise of societies as their games play out the logics that determine them.

Conditional rhetorics provide guidance to the development of hundreds of games every year, which are then played by millions of people. These games' effects are dismissed by most, despite the fact that a huge industry—the game review industry—is dedicated to considering these effects and the technologies that inspire them. I will examine this industry in detail in the next chapter by using the grammar of gameworks to see the relationships among agent/reviewers, agent/players, and influences like mass media and instructional force; part of this analysis will include attention to people like Ernest Adams and Dave Grossman, both of whom openly and articulately oppose some of the gaming industry's practices. Before shifting to that analysis, however, I want to round out this discussion of rhetorical functions and agents by briefly suggesting how the other components in the grammar of gameworks might evolve from here if they were to be pursued in a thoroughgoing gamework analysis.

Working Through the Grammar of Gameworks: Agents, Influences, Manifestations, and Transformative Locales

Having touched on some of the ways knowledge of rhetoric's functions (conditional, quotidian, and especially exigent) can be used to understand better the discourse of game developers, I want to propose briefly how this analysis might continue to play out if it were pursued throughout each of the other elements in the grammar of gameworks. The first of these elements involves agents: Who is doing the acting? Under the circumstances of the current analysis, the answer to this question has been relatively straightforward: the developers. Recall, however, the emphasis that many developers place on the importance of playing games themselves. What this means, in effect, is that agent/developers are also agent/players, and so the cycle of ideological reproduction, as I noted earlier, is well established even in the anecdotal professional lore. Additionally, those educational texts that focus on the business aspects of game development insist that programmers and artists must not be removed from the work of agent/marketers if the product is to be a best seller. Arguably then, one of the features that is beginning to mark all of the agents involved in the computer game complex is that the differences among them are becoming less distinct.

For computer game scholars who, rather than focus on agent/developers as I have done in this chapter, choose to focus on the work that agent/players or agent/marketers do within the computer game complex, the details of their analyses will likely be quite different from those I've presented. Despite this, however, I believe that the observation that the differences between agent types are becoming increasingly blurry will still hold true. This is largely attributable to the fact that the logic of late capitalism depends on the reproduction of certain ideologies—the value of profit, efficiency, and generic individualism, for example—that permeate developers, marketers, and players alike and on a global scale. It becomes less surprising every day that agent/players not only advertise games but also build them, that agent/marketers play active roles in game development and in game testing, and that agent/developers spend more and more time crafting marketing schemes and sizing up the competition by playing their products.

The grammar of gameworks element referred to as "influences" impinges on this chapter's study of the dialectical struggle between game developers as artists or businesspeople in dramatic and complex ways as well. Mass culture and mass media are particularly influential on how agent/developers get their ideas and on how they bring their ideas to life in playable computer games. Many developers acknowledge that TV and movies teach them what's marketable, while what's in shopping malls teaches them what the public wants to spend time doing. Games ride these mass trends closely, and the influence of these trends is readily apparent in many game designs. The recent game *Deus Ex*, for example, uses a half-dozen different cultural references on the cover of its box alone, in part at least to provide as many points of access to consumers as possible.[25] Among the "hooks," as they're called in the industry, are references to such films as *The Matrix*, *Terminator*, *Blade Runner*, and *Escape from New York;* such culturally established references as the ascension of Christ and alien abduction; and such sci-fi genre clichés as "only one man can save the universe now."[26]

Psychophysiological forces, too, are certainly at work in developers' minds, sometimes consciously and sometimes not. Figuring out or intuiting, for instance, which sounds will produce which effects in players carries with it both exigent and conditional rhetoric, and the quotidian functions of rhetoric sadly work only to reinforce some physiological standards that are widely known to be detrimental to players' health (for example, when shooting games generate repetitive motion disorders). Economic forces have already been touched on briefly in terms of working conditions, but much more could be said about them. Computer game industry professionals have a newsgroup devoted to such issues (comp.games.development.industry), and the International Game Developers' Association (IGDA) publishes an annual report on game developers' salaries in its journal *Game Developer.* Instructional forces continue to be largely ignored, despite the fact that the IGDA has a committee devoted to educational issues. Warren Spector—a legendary game designer and moderator of that committee—has said about the IGDA's commitment to educational outreach: "it's something we need to work on" (July 14, 2001). What neither he nor almost any other industry professional is prepared to say is that computer games are already instructional but that developers—unless they specialize in "edutainment" titles—do not devote any time in their design documents to consideration of that fact and its implications.

A treatment of the "manifestations" of game developers' rhetorics in the artifacts they produce deserves its own lengthy treatment. Briefly, though, the choices that developers make concerning issues of representation, conflict, interaction, and safety have powerful determining effects on how games mean and play, who buys them, how popular they become, and ultimately, what lasting cultural effects they produce. Some games, like *Half-Life,* successfully navigate the narrow course where hybrid games fit (strategy shooter with high conflict and high interaction), while other games subvert all conventional wisdom about how the different ratios among these four categories will (or will not) affect which titles become popular (e.g., *Deerhunter,* which has little interaction and minimal conflict).

Finally, there is the matter of the points at which local, communal, and societal transformations may be encouraged or squelched by the work of game developers. In general, developers don't consider these possibilities, preferring instead to blame any problems related in any way to gaming on something else: bad parenting, TV, movies, the poor economy—all are commonly cited. One of the points at which developers do see transformations happening is within their own community, at the homological level. Letters to the editor and critical essays about unfortunate turns of the industry often reflect developers' thoughts on the transformations of their discipline, though the effects of such discourses are usually less than one might hope for. These "transformative locales," as they are termed in the grammar of gameworks, figure importantly in my final chapter on computer games themselves. Apart from reminding readers of the contradiction that exists about the very existence of such transformative moments inspired in and by game developers—games have no significant effect on people versus games have so many and such lasting effects on people that society itself is being changed—I will leave a deeper discussion of transformative locales for chapter 5. I also want to remind readers that what the gamework scholar is after is to learn more about how computer games and the computer game complex are rendered meaningful and about how those meaning-making processes construct or reinforce farther-reaching understandings of culture, society, and the possibilities for transformation. With knowledge such as this, the gamework scholar can better understand the relationships that constitute the dialectical struggles that are linked to the computer game complex and that seem so intransigent when they are represented, for instance, in the media. The interpretations that emerge from such analyses put computer game scholars in a good position to make new arguments designed to effect industry-changing—if not culture-changing—action.

Having considered very specifically agent/developers and how they use and are mediated by the rhetoric of the computer game complex, let us switch now to an examination of how their products are received and described by those whose understanding of computer games is more sophisticated than the average player's but less technical than the average developer's. In particular, let us now consider how the grammar of gameworks' "influences" work to determine both interpretations of game content and game value, and also how such determinations can contribute to a deeper understanding of the contradictions of the computer game complex.

4
Making Meanings Out of Contradictions
The Work of Computer Game Reviewing

Sifting through the day's mail on the front porch, Melanie was glad to see at least one piece that didn't make her anxious: her kids' issue of Computer Gaming World. *She sat down on the steps and paged through the magazine, skimming the ads and reviews. Melanie had agreed to the subscription when, after studying several issues, she noticed that it didn't depend on the "sex sells" ploy as much as other gaming magazines seemed to. With the new subscription had come a new house rule: she got to read the magazine first. Partly she did this because she wanted the chance to get educated about the new games her kids were bound to ask for. More than once she had prohibited a game because of the magazine's detailed reviews. And more than once she had been able to make an informed recommendation to them for an alternative.*

Melanie's kids, of course, were on to her. They knew that the real reason she wanted to read it first was that she was an avid gamer herself and just liked to learn about the latest games before they did. She wouldn't deny this. Regardless, because of the magazine, Melanie had managed to get the whole family interested in The Sims, *a game where players try to lead virtual characters successfully through all the trials and tribulations of real life: making friends, setting up a house, working and playing. For several months, they'd all played the game together and were all neighbors on the same virtual block. Melanie smiled a little as she remembered how she had used the game to start coming out to her kids as a lesbian. When her character, "Ms. Crystal," kissed "Boots," a virtual neighbor, in public, people both in the game and in the real world were surprised. Melanie used the opportunity to explain to her kids that same-sex partners were just as normal as man-and-woman partners. It was only a matter of time—about two weeks, she recalled—before they asked her with the beautiful candor of childhood: "Mom, are you a* real *lesbian too?"*

~

Game reviewing, like other kinds of rudimentary media analysis, both evaluates its subject according to certain criteria and establishes those criteria as valuable. Every month, dozens of new game reviews are published, most in fan magazines and on Web sites, and a few in the popular press. Since 1999, for example, the *New York Times* has carried a feature called "Game Theory," a misnomer actually, since the pieces published there are simple "worth it/ not worth it" computer game evaluations. Similarly, *Time* magazine regularly publishes game reviews, mostly of titles that are adult-oriented but that are relatively inoffensive; to date, for example, the games *Hitman: Codename 47* and *Soldier of Fortune* have not been reviewed in *Time*, despite their popularity. The programs on G4, an all-video-game TV network, however, review even the goriest games and give viewers a chance to see the latest titles in action. Even many smaller markets carry computer game reviews: the *Arizona Daily Citizen*, the *Topeka Capital-Journal*, and *Morgunbladid* (an Icelandic newspaper) all regularly solicit game reviews from staffers and locals. As computer games have become ubiquitous in industrialized countries, so too have pundits interested in separating the wheat from the chaff.

Even more indicative of the ubiquity of game reviews is that the game industry itself is self-policing, albeit on a voluntary basis. Like Hollywood movies, computer games are now rated by an independent panel of reviewers called the ESRB, the Entertainment Software Ratings Board. The ESRB's rubric, which runs from "Early Childhood" to "Adults Only," is meant to function as a protective measure for consumers, giving them the chance to select or avoid titles with particular kinds of material. The ESRB attributes the increased popularity of computer games in the past several years in part to their rating system, which they claim makes parents especially more comfortable buying software titles that have been independently and consistently reviewed. Needless to say, such "protection" is not welcomed by everyone, and the ESRB has many critics both inside and outside the industry. Foremost among these critiques is the fact that the ESRB is the policing mechanism created by the Interactive Digital Software Association, a trade organization comprised of companies like Sony, Atari, Sega, Electronic Arts, and Nintendo. Critics argue that the ESRB has no real power to control how games are marketed and suggest that the ESRB is little more than a marketing ploy by the most powerful publishers to make computer games more appealing to those consumers who have reservations about interactive entertainment (Ruggill).

The ESRB's rhetoric and the responses to it are certainly worth examining, and contradictions are sure to abound in all the arguments over its independence and authority. The concern of this chapter, however, will be computer game reviews that are done less formally than those of the ESRB. In particular, I focus here on reviews published in the two most popular venues for such evaluations: online and print fan magazines. Since most active computer gamers also track upcoming game releases via these two venues—according to a 2000 survey by PC Data, Inc.—these sources can provide gamework scholars much information about what criteria are used informally by agent/consumers to influence their purchasing decisions and information about the sources of such criteria. The ESRB, for example, modeled its rating system after that of the Motion Picture Association of America, but most magazine, Web site, and newsgroup reviewers avoid such schemes, preferring instead a rather arbitrary five-point scale in which the numbers are replaced by icons (e.g., stars, facial expressions, or color bars), simple yes/no recommendations (also sometimes embellished with a gimmick like thumbs up or down), or no system at all, save for the arbitrary use of keywords like "awesome," "so-so," "rad," "lame," and so on.

In examining these reviews in the context of an analysis of the computer game complex, my main objective is to show how the grammar of gameworks' "influences" (mass media, mass culture, psychophysiological, economic, and instructional force) are brought to bear by agent/consumers to shape the market for computer games. This analysis is meant to clarify how the contradictions of the gaming industry described in chapter 1 are negotiated by agent/consumers. These negotiations within the computer game complex, I argue, mirror similar negotiations under way in the broader dialectic. Analyses of these negotiations, therefore, can help gamework scholars to understand better how the work of reviewers contributes to the interested public's awareness of the issues being contested in the dialectic. To begin, it is necessary to first cull from the print and online game review venues those evaluative criteria that are most common and to interrogate their implications.

Computer Game Reviewing Online

In the previous chapter I identified three major contradictions with which game developers must come to terms. First is the contradiction that game artists (including programmers, level designers, and the like) are often required to shun creativity in order to continue practicing their arts, that is, to stay employed in the game industry. The second contradiction is that developers must often make realistic games that aren't *too* realistic. The third and most commonly argued contradiction is that computer games are often unhealthily violent or disturbing yet remain extremely popular, even in the face of public disapproval by major medical, psychological, and educational organizations. While some gamers are aware of all three of these contradictions, only the last one is widely recognized by the average gamer. In the alt.games newsgroup for instance, there are roughly 190 threads (out of 64,000) that deal with the impact of violent or sexual representations in computer games.[1] By contrast, there are no messages in this particular newsgroup about the difficulty of being an artist in the industry[2] and only six or so messages about the delicate balance between the fun of realism and tedium of reality.[3] But regardless of the relative invisibility of industry contradictions to agent/players, I contend that good reviewers *are* able to identify developers' successful efforts to negotiate these contradictions. More specifically, in examining online game reviews for the game rating criteria they use, I have come to the conclusion that the contradictions game developers negotiate during the production phase subsequently are perceived as strengths or weaknesses by expert consumer evaluators. By using as analytical prompts the elements of the grammar of gameworks' "influences," gamework scholars can pose specific questions about how particular kinds of transformative moments seem to be initiated through fan-based interpretations of the negotiatory and meaning-making work done by agent/developers. Let us begin with an example.

In late June 2000, Greg Kasavin, the executive editor for *PC Games*, published his review of *Deus Ex* on GameSpot.com, one of the most popular game review Web sites in the world. GameSpot relies on three different subelements of review. First is the prose review, written using the modified conventions of entertainment reviewers everywhere: describe the concept/plot, evaluate the concept/plot, evaluate the characters, evaluate the graphics, evaluate the soundtrack/audio effects. The second subelement is a standard list of criteria that are rated on a scale from one to ten and weighted. GameSpot describes their scoring this way:

> *Graphics*—This category encompasses both the technical and the aesthetic quality of the game's appearance and presentation.
>
> *Sound*—This category encompasses both the quality of and the usage of sound effects and music in the game.
>
> *Gameplay*—This category encompasses everything from a game's interface, to its control, to its play balance, all to suggest how enjoyable the game is to play.
>
> *Value*—This category refers to a game's longevity [i.e., how long it takes

to play] and accounts for any additional features and options for customization in the game, as well as for the game's price point. Games with poor gameplay tend to have inherently low value scores. However, a game may be enjoyable, but otherwise very short.

Reviewer's Tilt—This category lets the reviewer sway the final score one way or the other to account for any disjunction between the four preceding categories. The reviewer's tilt is suggestive of the reviewer's overall experience with the game. For instance, a game that has good graphics but poor gameplay might have a low tilt. Meanwhile, a game that doesn't look or sound good or control well but that has a great story might have a high tilt.

The five categories are weighted differently in the final score; gameplay and reviewer's tilt are weighted more heavily than the other scores. (GameSpot)

The third subelement used by GameSpot is player voting. For each game reviewed by GameSpot, there is also a tally and comment board for everyday players. These players can vote in each of these categories themselves, and their votes are then tallied into a running average for the game. In effect, then, visitors to the GameSpot.com Web site get three reviews: a text version, the reviewer's numeric score, and the running average and textual comments of players who have logged on to the site. This presumably offers potential consumers a range of informed opinions about the game, with more and less detail to suit personal preferences. For analysts of the computer game complex, it has the added advantage of consolidating a variety of game review sources, often including hundreds of additional text reviews submitted by registered members of GameSpot.

Kasavin gave *Deus Ex*, a game with a multimillion-dollar development and marketing budget, a score of 8.2, which puts the title into the "Great" category—though just barely. Kasavin judged the game's "value" as excellent but its graphics and sound only average. "Gameplay" was only above average by Kasavin's estimation. The players' running survey, on the other hand, rated the game 9.4, a solidly "Superb" game. This tally was based on 843 submitted votes. Why the great disparity between the professional reviewer and the people in the field? To answer this, let's look at some of the comments written by these two distinct groups of agents.

Kasavin begins his review by noting that the game's producer, Warren Spector, is well known for his excellent games, of which he has made many. Perhaps too many, Kasavin implies, since this latest game "includes some . . . individual elements [that] are either overused or underdeveloped." After running down the basic features of the game—types of weapons, advancement protocols, and the like—Kasavin notes that the game is "quite long for an action-packed first-person game" and writes that the developers did a pretty good job of building in multiple ways of solving each of the game's puzzles and levels. Such "open-ended design," Kasavin proposes, is "certainly ambitious and for the most part successful." The amount of in-game detail is incredible, writes Kasavin, and includes newspapers, book excerpts, and e-mails, all of which are readable and provide relatively important background information and clues to the game. Finally, Kasavin describes the interactive elements of the game, saying that they are adequate, albeit a bit perfunctory at times.

The heart of the review, however, is when Kasavin makes this remarkable observation: "Unfortunately, character interaction tapers off in the game's middle third. . . . It's at these times, when you're closely attending to the means of accomplishing your goals, that you'll best be able to identify the game's weaknesses." This remark suggests that Kasavin has a method for analyzing games that is specifically designed to help him discover their weaknesses. Kasavin elaborated on this method through private correspondence:

> I identify a game's weaknesses by using my perceptions—touch, as well as vision and hearing. . . . Games have a feel—they're tactile in a way that other media are not. When I play a game that I dislike, it's often because something about it doesn't feel right. This has everything to do with the feedback the game gives me as a player. Are the controls not responsive enough? Was my effort not sufficiently rewarded? [. . .] I evaluate games based on execution. The first question is, what, exactly, is this game trying to let me do? The next question is, how well, exactly, is this game accomplishing its intent? (9/1/2004)

Kasavin also commented on the relationship between his gaming expertise and his knowledge of game production, knowledge that professional reviewers obtain through their regular contact with developers and that allows reviewers to make educated guesses about whether or not a game is in fact "accomplishing its intent." He suggested that speculating on production issues—on developers' budgetary and scheduling priorities, technical aptitude, or management skills, for example—in a game review was both problematical and inevitable. Kasavin explained that while his knowledge of game production "certainly affects how I think about games in general," he also recognizes the limits of his expertise well enough to know that drawing upon his game-production knowledge in a specific review could be unfair to developers (because he'd only be guessing) and irrelevant to consumers (whose concern is whether or not a game is worth buying).

Kasavin, then, "feels" how developers have negotiated the contradictions with which they have struggled in the making of a particular title through his practiced sensitivity to the kinds of feedback the game gives him while playing it. In the context of the general expectations that are elicited through a game's style, genre, and mood, this feedback helps Kasavin to pinpoint a game's "weaknesses," that is, moments when developers seem not to have adequately addressed the contradictions that faced them during production.

Not all game reviewers work so meticulously with their subjects as Kasavin, however, a fact that has routinely caused considerable controversy in the industry. At the 2001 Electronic Entertainment Exposition in Los Angeles, for example, the escalating tensions between professional game developers and professional game reviewers were deemed severe enough to warrant a roundtable discussion that would allow each side to voice its views. Robert Coffey, Assistant Editor at *Computer Gaming World,* was asked if reviewers used cheat codes[4] and other unseemly techniques in order to complete game reviews quickly and thereby scoop competitors. Coffey replied: "Yes, sometimes, but they shouldn't. But we have deadlines so . . . " (5/14/2001). Stevie Case, a game designer on the panel with Coffey, argued that such practices are "not fair on developers. It doesn't treat games fairly, because we spend years on the game, then you take less than a week to review it in order to scoop a review" (5/14/2001).

The main problem with drawing heavily on amateur or outsider understandings of a game's production process, say critics, is that unless reviewers have reliable insider information, they can only guess about which parts of the game were being fast-tracked, short-changed, or excised prior to release. Such guesses, continue these critics, will lead many reviewers to see problems where they *think* there might be some. Agent/reviewers, in other words, report on games not as typical players but as professionals working with all the pressures present in most other businesses: tight deadlines, desperate competition, long hours, and low pay. All the scientistic numbers tagged onto the reviews by GameSpot and other companies give them a quantitative element, but these numbers only reflect the biases articulated in the prose review and are necessarily subjective; it is difficult after all, even for experienced gamers to quantify such ephemeral characteristics as "game play." At the same panel discussion that Coffey and Case attended, Geoff Keighley, a reviewer for GameSpot before starting his own web-based game review site named GameSlice, responded to a criticism about using such numbers for rating games by mentioning that his company "used to review games like appliances but now we review them like art." At GameSlice, reviewers don't use number systems. They just write about games the way Pauline Kael wrote about movies. Consider this excerpt from Keighley's review of the game *Half-Life:*

> The nature of any software review is that it's somewhat subjective, but in the case of Sierra Studios and Valve Software's Half-Life, there is one indisputable fact: I played this game for four days straight; I was enraptured by the experience, deaf to the rest of the world, my emotions and senses honed in on the computer screen for umpteen hours on end. A review can be laced with superlative-frill to the ying yang, nit-picking the tinniest [*sic*] of pitfalls and aggrandizing idiosyncratic creative accents, but what's really important is the indescribable play experience—The pace, depth, uniqueness, and excitement that is ceded from the game to the player during their time together. Half-Life has an incredible play experience. That fact is indisputable.

Here, Keighley returns us to the point where this chapter began, with a search for the criteria that players use to evaluate games. What's notable here is that Keighley eschews the various complex rating systems discussed so far and instead offers a single criterion, which he argues is the most important: "the play experience."

Is there evidence that other players and reviewers share this criterion and that it's "the most important"? Yes, there is quite a bit, in fact. Back at GameSpot's Web site, a quick review of the amateur players' reviews of *Deus Ex* reveals that players will often forgive small imperfections if a game captures their imaginations. Lance Warhawk posted this, for instance, on June 3, 2001: "Wow, this game was absolutely fantastic, a complete joy to play. From the very first scene to the ultimate bitter-sweet ending this game held me in its grip and refused to let go. The Graphics and Sound, although sub-par compared to most other FPS/RPG games [first-person shooter/role-playing games], were adequate and made the world come to life." Hamdi Roumani, writing two months later, on August 26, 2001, seems to concur:

> Deus Ex is definetly one of the best games i've ever played. What makes it so compelling is that it is so different from other games, instead of focusing on the graphics which so many other games do (by this i do not mean the graphics are not up to par with other games of the same genre, only that they do [not] stand out in any way, the same goes for the sound) the producers made in what my opinion is the best story line for any game ever created, its plot is full of twist and turns which by the end of the game leaves you amazed.

There are many more messages like these, messages in which a game's drawbacks are overshadowed by the "play experience" it provides. Keighley seems to be correct in his assertion that playability is the most crucial criterion to players when they evaluate a game. Does the same criterion emerge as the most important in the print-based review magazines? I turn now to examine the reviews of *Computer Game World, PC Gamer,* and *NextGen Magazine* to answer that question.

Computer Game Reviewing in Print

It does not take long to realize that unlike their online counterparts, print-based game review magazines emphasize different criteria for evaluating games. This fact is perhaps nowhere clearer than in the monthly *Computer Games.* Each issue contains hundreds of color photos, most of which are screen shots of the creepiest, goriest, or most sexually provocative scenes of the games being reviewed. The accompanying reviews—and in this magazine, one has the strong sense that the text accompanies the photos and not the other way around—usually mention gameplay at some point, but they certainly don't dwell on it. By far the most important criteria for the reviewers working for this magazine are the technical aspects of the game: How detailed are the characters and environments? How smooth are the animations? Does the game make your hard disk grind away looking for files, or is it a quiet ride? How well does the game respond to the controls? These are the questions that dominate reviews in *Computer Games,* not questions concerning character development, plot, and the depth of the backstory.

In addition to the prose reviews, the reviewers also use a five-star rating system, though the criteria for awarding these stars seem to vary from one review to the next. In a review of a game in which players attempt to keep dinosaurs from becoming extinct, for example, the reviewer notes but does not particularly value the game's effectiveness at setting a mood and having a good soundtrack. Rather, the reviewer's bottom line is this: "*Dino Crisis* represents just a diversion of a few hours in this day and age. It's more of a walk down memory lane for lapsed Playstation devotees than a real game, though it can pack plenty of appeal for those so inclined" (Todd). Another review, this one of *B17 Flying Fortress,* is equally idiosyncratic, as indicated by the four-star rating (Excellent) matched to the headline: "Hasbro's serious bomber simulation is as flawed as it is good" (Berger). To the reviewer, both flaws and successes are measured only according to technological innovation and implementation. Playability, which is seriously impeded in *B17* by the overwhelming number of keyboard controls (over 130), is of little consequence; what is problematic is that the sound effects fade mysteriously and that "joystick key mappings don't seem to work" (77). So for this magazine the dominant criterion seems to be the effectiveness of a game's technology. Is it the same for more established review magazines?

PC Gamer, one of the oldest and best-selling game review magazines, uses screenshots more conservatively than *Computer Games* and implements yet another rating system, this one based on percentages. Percentages of what, readers are not told. The game *Homeworld: Cataclysm,* for example, received a "91%" and an "Editor's Choice Award" (Klett). Most reviews in this magazine are a full page, but this particular game warrants two; upon reading the review, one discovers why: this game has many "gush-worthy" features—eighteen different ships to command, twenty-five new technologies, a newly implemented "fog of war," and a time-acceleration feature. And gameplay? Yes, in this review playability does receive some attention, but it is far less than what is found on many online review sites. Steve Klett opens the piece by describing his waxing and waning appreciation for the latest games. Having settled on the fact that he is optimistic about the future of gaming, he writes: "And for that optimism I have to credit *Cataclysm* and the 20-plus hours I've spent so far lost in the Homeworld universe. . . . And 'lost' is indeed the most appropriate term to use. Playing *Cataclysm,* I took no notice of the phone ringing. . . . I had given up shaving and, sorry to say, showers. This game cemented my evolution into a *Game Geek Guy*" (Klett 130; emphasis in original). Apart from this rather exclamatory opening praise, the rest of the essay focuses mostly on the technical details; the only exception is when Klett observes that the "story is captivating" (130).

A less successful game, *Sydney 2000,* was awarded only 52 percent of the total number of *PC Gamer* mystery points and offers the readers almost exclusively a list of the game's technical shortfalls: "There are plenty of exercises in frustration, such as the barely controllable skeet shooting event. . . . And then there are the games that simply require you to mash keys like there's no tomorrow. . . . Unfortunately, *Sydney* has the feel of a quick port from the Sega Dreamcast, with console quirks in the menus. . . . Graphically, *Sydney 2000* isn't good or bad—it's just kinda . . . weird. The characters don't look like your typical polygonal athletes; they possess the odd texture of Claymation figures" (Williamson 151). In all of these examples from *PC Gamer,* we see that their reviewers are a bit more concerned with playability than most *Computer Games* reviewers seem to be, but only when the technical parts of the game are reasonably well designed. Such a review strategy is arguable I suppose, since it would be difficult to design a highly playable game without also designing the technical specifications well. Geoff Keighley, however, demonstrates that the playability criterion is sufficient even for poorly designed and implemented games, so why are these two print magazines opting not to treat it? Before proposing an answer to that question, I want to look at one more magazine, one that specializes in reviewing games for consoles like the PlayStation 2, Xbox, and GameCube.

NextGen, as a magazine devoted mainly to console systems, caters to a unique audience in terms of computer game players: their game equipment is dedicated to gaming alone. PlayStation users cannot balance their checkbooks on their system, and Nintendo system users can't type term papers on their controller pads. One might expect, then, that such a focused magazine would have the luxury of focusing on playability issues since most of the technical issues of the games are predetermined by the hardware manufacturers. Not so. *NextGen,* like *PC Gamer,* uses a five-star rating system that goes unexplained. Reviews here are shorter than in most other magazines, probably because there are so many of them. Console game sales outpace desktop computer sales by nearly three to one (Entertainment Software Association), which means that editors of magazines like this one have many more titles to deal with.[5] In *NextGen,* which reviews roughly forty games per month, most titles receive only 200 words of space. Better games may get 250 words, and the top-rated games get 300 words in larger than usual type. Photos are abundant but not overwhelming as they are in *Computer Games.*

Even to gamework scholars who are unfamiliar with console games it would be readily apparent that *NextGen* is as obsessed with technical details as the other print magazines described above. In a review of the widely praised game *Escape from Monkey Island,* reviewer Jeff Lundrigon writes that the game's "engine is lifted almost whole from Lucas Arts' last great adventure, *Grim Fandango,* and uses 3D characters over 2D pre-rendered backgrounds. When your character gets close to an object or person that can be interacted with, a list of possible options pops up, and the system works well enough" (85). In a long review of a (then) soon-to-be-released game titled *Twisted Metal Black,* writer Blake Fischer makes a gesture toward focusing on gameplay, then quickly settles back into its technical aspects: "Beyond the look and feel of the game, the team is really concentrating on maximizing every aspect of gameplay. . . . The most noticeable improvement to the gameplay is the simple upgrade to 60 frames per second" (25–26). While there is no question that frame rates impinge upon the playability of a game, it is unusual to bring such technical matters into a discussion of narrative and character development. *NextGen* is so focused on the technology that its reviewers rarely seem able to differentiate between gameplay and game specifications. To a degree this is to be expected in a game not yet released, since the reviewers were not able to sit down and play the game from beginning to end. But even the reviews of old standards—games like *Myst* and *Resident Evil*—are laden with technical details on frame rates and polygon counts rather than on elements of the story, types of interactivity, and the mood of the environment.

Print-based game review magazines, it seems, tend to be technology driven, while online game review sites offer more balance between attention to playability and technical matters. For the average agent/player, playability emerges as the most important criterion, whereas for professional reviewers the preference for one or the other of these aspects of a computer game seems to be determined by idiosyncrasy and editorial policy. Game developers are aware of the importance of playability to the success of their games, but it is a truth that, while well documented, seems to be forgettable. In all four of the book-length treatments on computer game design discussed in the previous chapter, the authors repeatedly emphasize that developers always need to keep the players' happiness in mind. Rollings and Morris, for example, spend an entire chapter on "game balance," an industry term for keeping games fun by making them challenging but not impossible, creative but not illogical. Ultimately, playability and technical innovation emerge as the main criteria used for game evaluation once a title ships. In the next section I will show how these criteria interact with influences like mass media, mass culture, and psychophysiological, economic, and instructional force to shape agent/consumers' understanding of computer games and the computer game complex. What will emerge is a sense of how the contradictions of the game industry make their way to the level of the consumer—or are actively prevented from doing so—and how these contradictions are expressed in the discourse of those whose self-appointed role is a deliberately suasory one.

Playing Up Influence to Influence Play

Agent/developers, as we have seen, regularly negotiate at some level of consciousness at least three contradictions inherent in the computer gaming industry:

1. Computer games are an art form based on mass production;
2. Computer games often seem to encourage unhealthy kinds of play;
3. Computer games require developers to design realistic games that aren't *really* realistic.

Developers' negotiations of these contradictions are inevitably instantiated into their games visually, auditorily, organizationally, and so on. When players play the games, they immerse themselves in the developers' negotiations of the contradictions and so are also confronted with them at some level of consciousness. I have also argued that online and print game reviewing emphasize two different criteria for evaluating computer games; the former emphasizes playability, while the latter emphasizes the technical aspects of games. Gamework scholars interested in discovering what roles industry contradictions play in these different kinds of reviews, then, need a way to focus their analyses along particular lines. The grammar of gameworks becomes particularly useful here.

Because the grammar of gameworks is multiperspectival, any examination of the computer game complex that draws on its elements and framework must necessarily account for processes of production, distribution, and consumption. One consequence of this is that any element of the grammar (agents, functions, influences, manifestations, transformative locales) can become a starting point for a gamework analysis. In the previous chapter, for example, agents and functions—particularly agent/developers and the exigent function of rhetoric—were the initial focus that eventually led to analyses of ideological reproduction within and beyond the computer game complex. I want to continue building on this previous work now by investigating how each of the "influence" categories may shape (and be shaped by) agent/reviewers, who, as will soon become clear, are a subcategory of agent/marketers. Through this inquiry, connections between the local cultural work of computer game reviewers can be articulated to dialectical work that is under way in broader contexts and that is having more far-reaching effects than those of the computer game complex alone. Such multiperspectival and relational analyses are meant to encourage transformative work in both the computer game complex and in the dialectical struggles with which it engages.

To begin, the gamework scholar must examine how, where, when, and why related transformations have taken place. Such study involves carefully observing how patterns of struggle evolve in material ways through history. Since computer games are among the newest (and arguably purist) forms of mass culture—that is, artifacts generated by a few specialists and designed to prompt voluntary consumption by thousands (or more) for a profit—they provide a unique opportunity to see such patterns, particularly in the relationship between how agent/developers negotiate the three industry contradictions noted above and in how those negotiations do or do not get identified later in online and print-based game reviews. By pointedly questioning how industry contradictions, game reviews, and the influences operative in the computer game complex interact, new patterns and opportunities for transformation begin to emerge. Below are five such pointed questions and some tentative answers for each.

How can an understanding of mass culture *help gamework scholars examine how game reviewers work on and through industry contradictions?*

Mass culture is essentially a widely and voluntarily shared experience constructed by a few specialists for profit. Since game reviews are specifically written for consumers, gamework scholars can surmise that reviews must somehow facilitate the process by which the shared experience of particular games is propagated and profits are maximized. Seen from this angle, game reviews are little more than in-depth commercials; even negative reviews draw the attention of consumers. As we've seen, online reviews tend to emphasize playability and cater to people who are reading quickly for clear advice about what to buy. Print reviews, on the other hand, tend to emphasize games' technical aspects and cater to more "hardcore" agent/consumers. Thus these two different venues for game reviews reach two major consumer types.

One consequence of seeing this strategy for market coverage in tandem with the fact that game reviews are essentially prose-heavy advertisements is that it reveals how the meaning-making processes entangled in the art/business contradiction are working. On the artistic side of the struggle, reviewers make it easier for developers to be inattentive to their complicity in big business. By managing a significant component of the marketing of the games, reviewers take on a large share of the responsibility for getting the word out about recent game releases, updates, patches, and add-ons. Unlike authors, who are regularly required to hit the lecture and reading circuit in order to publicize their works, game developers are allowed to remain fairly reclusive.[6] If game review Web sites facilitate the expansion of the shared gaming experience, that frees developers from sullying their artistic hands with the dirty business of hawking one's wares to the public. From the business side of this issue, developers are kept from publicly criticizing their own work (as many artists are wont to do), thereby risking sales. For agent/players, such a system means that their work as consumers is easy: self-select into the online or print audience, make a purchase decision, then go and buy. In the case of a print-oriented audience, for example, where the review emphasis is technical, games are essentially demystified so that their mathematical and computational backgrounds emerge as most important. This rhetorical technique also serves to ameliorate consumers' own struggles over the unhealthy/fun contradiction: How bad could the game be, readers might ask, if the sequel to *Hitman* uses twice as many polygons in each character as were in the first game? The logic of this redirection works not syllogistically but affectively. Readers who are moved by technical details will often find it easy to jump logical tracks, making sense of something—like why a particular game should be purchased—that other logics might find inscrutable.

How can an understanding of mass media *help gamework scholars examine how game reviewers work on (and through) industry contradictions?*

It is the very nature of mass media to be shaped by the technical, political, and cultural constraints that make them successful and (over time) to have a hand in shaping those constraints. This phenomenon is as true for computer games as it is for TV, radio, and newspapers, although games currently occupy a less central position in the mass media arena than those older forms.[7] Games are predominantly one-way communication channels that quickly provide specific kinds of knowledge developed by a few people to millions of players (who can, with relative ease, disengage from the games) without allowing much developer-player dialogue. There is a variety of developments in the game industry that is making computer games increasingly similar to their older cousins: interactive movies and anime, edutainment, and games that allow players themselves to become "stars" in the game world through the use of connected video cameras and microphones, for instance, all make the distinctions between old and new mass media forms difficult to discern. Even the ability to evoke emotion—long a staple of TV and film and long the holy grail of game development—is beginning to take hold in the game industry as designers now routinely and justifiably boast that their games terrify, elate, and amuse gamers as never before. Such emotional power, articulated with games' interactive elements and its imbrication with all manner of other mass media, promises soon to put computer games at the very heart of the processes by which mass media influence culture. This emerging articulation is to be seen nowhere more clearly than in game reviews.

The fact that game reviews are delivered through several mass media channels (e.g., TV, print, and online) suggests that the gaming industry is attempting to reach both the early adopters of technology and a more mainstream audience in its efforts to promote and popularize its products. Interestingly, though, the triad of industry contradictions described earlier is rarely addressed in mass media reviews of any type. While this may not seem all that strange for the art/business and unreal realism contradictions, it certainly seems odd that the potential dangers of gaming are rendered invisible. Those rare occasions when the computer game complex's problems do enter into reviews occur only when other news stories in the mass media force the issue, for example when gun-toting computer gamers shoot up a high school. But even when this happens, the response of the print and online game review venues is not simply to report the events; rather, they defend themselves. This protectionism suggests that the interests of the industry are actively influential factors in how reviewers and developers come to terms with contradictions within their profession. When contradictions like "play is good for you even though it is also widely believed to be harmful" threaten reviewers' and developers' livelihoods, ethical choices must be made. Game reviews, both in print and online, tend to make manifest to agent/players how developers have negotiated this particular contradiction by reviewing content in such a way that games seem disengaged from their producers, like ancient artifacts in a museum. This kind of commodity fetishism is especially symptomatic of the mechanisms of mass media under capitalism, where depictions of the conditions under which many games are produced—high stress, low pay, minimal benefits, and in the worst cases, sweatshop conditions—would likely repel rather than attract consumers.

How can an understanding of psychophysiological force *help gamework scholars examine how game reviewers work on (and through) industry contradictions?*

Psychophysiological influences do meaning-making work that directly affects the body and mind. While mass culture and mass media also have psychological and, to a lesser extent, physiological effects on participants in the computer game complex, they are minor in comparison to the intentional or consequential impacts of applied psychophysiological force. This type of work involves devising tactics to engage people's emotions, challenge their intellects, and test their bodies. The variety of psychophysiological responses that computer games can induce, in fact, is quite astounding, ranging from simple changes in one's concentration or heart rate to dangerous levels of addiction and nerve damage. These influences are moderately well understood by game developers, are exploited by marketers, and in varying degrees, are anticipated by players. When games are given meaning (and also make it) through tactile and psychological prompts, they necessarily manifest traces of the dialectical struggles to which they are connected. Gamework scholars who consider the psychophysiological influences designed into a game might ask questions like "what responses are designers trying to elicit from players and by what means?" "If the desired responses are compelled, what effects do they have on players personally and communally?" And "what effects on game developers and the computer game complex does the elicitation of such responses have?" Answers to questions such as these, particularly in relation to one's emerging understanding of agents, functions, other influences, manifestations, and transformative locales, can provide scholars of the computer game complex with compelling evidence for what relationships exist among the specific struggles of game reviewers and broader struggles in the dialectic.

Consider, for instance, the fact that it is common for the mental and physical effects of computer gaming to be proudly confessed in game reviews from various media, especially when the games are deemed excellent. In several of the reviews cited earlier, for example, references to being thoroughly caught up in the game—to the point of ignoring personal hygiene and relationships—mark the developers' success: initial player ambivalence made manifest in skepticism and impatience has been overcome by the subtle suasory arts of the agent/developers. For online sites that emphasize playability, this level of immersion is the pinnacle of game development, because everything fades into the background as gameplay overwhelms the responses of players' minds and bodies. In print venues, excellent gameplay characteristics are mediated through technical descriptions of how the game is affecting players' perceptual centers, eyes, ears, and touch especially.

The reviews themselves, however, encourage psychophysiological responses in agent/players by positioning (or at least reinforcing) them as both gamers and consumers (a psychological effect), and by encouraging gamers to act on these psychological effects by physically engaging in gaming either by playing them or by going out to purchase them (all physiological effects). The very act of playing games, as noted earlier, has its own complex set of psychophysiological responses that game reviews both feed and feed off. The gamework scholar is left, then, with the question of how this host of responses helps to explain how industry contradictions are engaged through game reviews within which the resolutions—which might actually be evasions—to the contradictions are embedded. More than any of the other influences, the psychophysiological forces at work in the contradictions of the computer game complex relate to the more systemic contradictions that lie within the dialectic. Game reviewers often tell the story of these forces' work, with greater and lesser degrees of facility.

For example, like all good artworks, good computer gameworks draw participants in and make them focus their attention on the represented subjects. But like artists who struggle with the compromises sometimes required by economic conditions, game developers, too, struggle to express their creative energies in ways that are both compelling and remunerative. Scholars of the computer game complex will observe, however, that game reviewers often cite only the former phenomenon and overlook or ignore the latter one. It is unlikely that reviewers are ignorant of the high development costs of most computer games today, so the scholar is left to investigate what might motivate reviewers to discount this factor in their write-ups.

The contradiction concerning mental and physical health as related to computer gameplay is similarly disappeared in most game reviews. One possible explanation is that because there exists no definitive scientific evidence that indisputably supports one position over the other (i.e., computer games are/are not harmful), reviewers ignore the issue altogether. It stands to reason, however, that even in the midst of such ambiguity the recent joint decision by several major medical associations to oppose computer game violence would constitute a sufficient exigence to warrant some kind of response by reviewers. Admittedly, even the "Joint Statement on the Impact of Entertainment Violence on Children" drafted by these medical associations is qualified at every turn with phrases such as "*some* children," "*may* be significantly more severe," and "*can* lead to emotional desensitization" (emphasis added); is it possible that game reviewers refuse to acknowledge these ambiguities themselves simply because they are scientifically ambiguous? Although this may be the case for some, a more likely explanation is that reviewers recognize the transformative power that the resolution of this ambiguity—if it supported the position represented in the "Joint Statement"—would have a dramatic impact on the industry that is their livelihood.[8]

Finally, gamework scholars will want to investigate how game reviewers account for psychophysiological forces when they are applied to the contradiction concerning the limits of computer game realism. Almost every game, and especially highly engaging ones, establishes a delicate balance between making players *feel* immersed in a real experience and not having the simulated experience feel so realistic that it isn't fun. This balance changes from genre to genre: flight simulators, which often have more than fifty different controls, require players to have a higher tolerance for realistic experiences than games like *Pokemon* that have only a few controls (but hundreds of content variations). Other factors that influence realism—environment modeling, character animation, and ambient sound effects, for example—must also be carefully balanced for a game to be deemed "good" by reviewers. If the models are too accurate, computers can't process all the graphics smoothly, which affects gameplay—a problem that will surely be noted in game reviews. The same is true of character animations. Ambient sounds and sound effects become problematic when players spend considerable periods of time in one area of a game. The audio designers of the game *Blood Wake*, for example, had to spend many hours designing one of the players' main weapons—a chain gun—so that its rapid firing sound "was powerful and impactful, could be listened to for extended periods without becoming irritating, and when the player used two chain guns was able to support multiple playback instances simultaneously" (Boyd). The psychophysiological forces, then, bear importantly on developers' plans as they work to negotiate the contradictions inherent in the play processes that they work with and work on.

Game reviews show us very little of these particular struggles, because to do so would be highly speculative and, even if it were not, would detract from the gaming ethos. Instead, reviews essentially celebrate or denigrate the decisions of the developers, praising them for beautiful scenery and "realistic" stories or criticizing them for being needlessly violent, too repetitive, or awkward to control. Gamework scholars working to discern the import of psychophysiological effects will be wise, therefore, to question those details in game reviews that praise or blame, asking upon which of the contradictions such epideictic rhetoric might impinge. Similarly, scholars will want to investigate the implications of such judgments for agent/developers and agent/players.

How can an understanding of economic force *help gamework scholars examine how game reviewers work on (and through) industry contradictions?*

The role of economic force in the processes of meaning-making within the computer game complex is such a powerful influence that it is actually one of the simplest to describe and to discover. All three of the industry contradictions are strongly influenced by economic force, and agent/developers and agent/reviewers alike are required to negotiate its effects almost constantly. In the highly competitive game industry, the popularity of games, and not necessarily their technical or narratological accomplishments, determines the success and failure of the companies that make them. Developers who spend too much time making a game into a work of art will likely go broke due to budget overruns and an overreliance on elite, but tiny, markets. Developers who cater too much to one side or the other of the health contradiction will lose access to thousands of potential consumers who refuse on principle to buy games that are too violent/sexual/vulgar or childish/prudish/prim. And developers who take up the challenge of modeling a scenario with a high degree of realism risk shutting out the majority of computer gamers who are casual players and are uninterested in buying a game they know—from reviews—will require several research trips to the Web and the completion of a four-hour tutorial before they can begin playing.

Economic force can be seen at work in game reviews, then, not only in the price listing or "bang for the buck" indices for the games themselves but also in the ways that production issues are addressed. Reviewers who suggest that a producer ought to have "written bigger checks to the art department" (a comment recently overheard at a game developers' conference) clearly have a sense of the business end of the game industry and are taking issue with how the producers and developers *may* have handled a game's financial allocations and design decisions. If game reviewers speak in awed terms about particular development houses (e.g., Lionhead Studios or BioWare), the gamework scholar can see these, too, as manifestations of economic forces having been influential in the discourses that help determine how games mean. In this case, however, both short-term and long-term effects may be discerned: reverence for a development house in a game review both further establishes a brand identity that might eventually become so powerful that reviews become almost irrelevant (long-term) and confers upon any title developed under its imprimatur a judgment of worthiness that translates into turn-around spending (short-term).[9] The dialectic emerges in such reviews as a struggle for marketplace recognition that demands the attention of masses of consumers but needn't show much concern for individual consumers.

This phenomenon founds all three industry contradictions and forces agent/developers to choose between being powerful and profitable or being weak and at risk of bankruptcy; catering to small markets is no longer viable (in the United States at least), because competition is so intense that companies with giant budgets squeeze out small developers as they saturate the market with mainstream titles that homogenize taste and offend no one with the fifty dollars necessary to buy the title. On the other hand, a sufficiently powerful game house can have very successful runs of controversial games—Rockstar Games, for example—a situation that seriously calls into question the nature of the controversy itself: Is such a game controversial because it challenges certain artistic and/or social conventions? Or is it controversial because a mainstream publisher has adopted a pseudo-naughty persona in order to appeal to a particular market that wouldn't ordinarily buy its games? The answer is probably "both," but in any case how economic force influences the development and distribution of games, as well as how they are interpreted as cultural artifacts, are important issues with many implications for the ways in which game reviews are assigned, researched, and written.

How can an understanding of instructional force *help gamework scholars examine how game reviewers work on (and through) industry contradictions?*

Gamework scholars who accept the proposition that all computer games teach will also recognize that game reviews are orientations to this educative experience. Print-based reviews emphasizing a game's technical aspects, for example, teach even casual players much about the minutiae of computer game creation. Discussions of frame rates, physics engines, and dynamic audio teach players that the fun of a game is the sum of its technical parts. This often creates a mentality about games—and other computer-based arts, too, like online literature and computer-enhanced teaching—that "good" can be judged according to quantifiable units: polygons per second, links per page, or *voxels* per centimeter.

But game reviews make visible the struggles over industry contradictions in other instructional contexts as well, particularly as they address what constitutes "playability." Above all, reviews teach players how to respond to games. By documenting the playability of a game that allows players to turn over the bodies of opponents so that they can see the exit wound of their sabot round, reviewers teach (which is to say influence) readers about what is cool, acceptable, and humdrum. The same is true of computer games that encourage players to dance, to clean up oil slicks, or to shoot advancing rows of "aliens." With few exceptions, reviewers routinely refuse this responsibility, adopting instead a stance that requires consumers to make such ethical decisions entirely on their own. This distance is itself instructional about the computer game complex, primarily because consumers are given little instruction about how to engage their ethical frameworks in the context of computer games. As a result, purchasing habits are governed more by attitudes of resignation in the face of the huge selection than they are by informed personal opinion.[10] Such consumer habits quickly feed back to developers, who, seeing a successful market, continue the practice of their development strategies unchanged except perhaps in responding to increased demand with increased supply. This feedback informs the ways that developers negotiate the industry contradictions, often making them more comfortable with mainstream aesthetics but sometimes driving them to create challenging but nonviolent games, or leading them to abandon the industry obsession with realism and accuracy for a wildly creative adventure that stands without precedent.

Reviewing the Meanings of the Computer Game Complex

A considerable part of how games mean as cultural artifacts depends on how agent/reviewers apply a variety of influential forces in the work they do of evaluating titles for agent/consumers. The impact of game reviews on the computer game complex and of the dialectical struggles—those over media violence, globalization and aesthetics, and the ever-expanding culture industry, for example—in which it participates may be invisible in the short term but can have long-term effects: valuing certain modes and genres to the exclusion of others, criticizing particular performance characteristics, and ignoring a variety of industry practices, for example, can (and does) promote a variety of trends among developers, marketers, and consumers that is difficult to identify without a critical historical perspective.

In such a fast-paced industry as game development, few people writing game reviews take the time to attend to such an outlook, bogged down as they are by pressing deadlines, saturated by messages insisting on the universal harmlessness of play, and living under the constant threat of job elimination through downsizing and market volatility. It is this long view, however, that facilitates reflection and enables transformative moments, not simply at the level of one's subject position in a capitalist economy but at a more introspective level that is inextricably linked to the communities of which one is a part. In the next chapter I draw on several heretofore unexplored elements of the grammar of gameworks to provide an extended analysis of a single game, Lionhead Studios' *Black & White*, focusing on how this artifact depends on economic force both to initiate and to participate in transformative locales, that is, moments of ideological shift.

5
The Economies of *Black & White*

The red mesas of the high desert dwarfed the isolated monastery, and the sun beat down hard on the rocky path leading to the guesthouse. Brother Eric, the guest master, hurried to the porch, not wanting to keep the visitors waiting.

"Hello!" he bellowed, startling the dusty young couple who stood on the porch peering through the windows of a small adjoining gift shop.

"Hi. . . . Is the store open?"

"Sure, sure. Just go on in." The three of them crowded into the tiny room where the brothers of the monastery sold a variety of handmade items. Brother Eric explained that they could pay for anything by just putting the money for it in a basket by the door. Seeing the surprised look on their faces, Eric grinned. "This isn't the city, in case you didn't notice. We figure that if you need something bad enough to steal it, then you should have it. Mind you, we don't really encourage this."

As the couple slowly wandered through the shop, mostly to cool off and rejuvenate from the torturous twelve-mile drive down the access road, Brother Eric filled the air with offhand remarks and bits of history about the monastery, the land, and local politics. When he mentioned that his monastic order observed the rule of silence, Rae, the young woman, said with a devilish smile, "I guess you didn't take that particular vow."

Eric grinned. "Yes, yes, I took that vow, hard to believe as it is. But the guest master at a monastery gets a temporary reprieve from that little rule. It'd be hard to welcome strangers if you couldn't greet people warmly, eh?"

Just then, another man opened the rickety screen door and walked in. Brother Eric waved at him and exclaimed, "Look, Father Dan, we have visi-

tors." Turning to the couple, Eric said, "Father is our abbot. He can talk too. One of the perks of being the boss."

The tall man stepped toward the two, shook their hands energetically, and welcomed them to the monastery. Then he turned back to Brother Eric. "Brother, I need your help. I've purchased some two-way radios so that we can keep in touch with the others when they're out in the field. Ever since Brother Aelred got bit by that rattler, I can't stop worrying about them."

"Excellent, excellent. How can I help?"

"I just want to test them out. I'll go down to the chapel and signal you with the call button, like this." Father Dan pressed a button on one radio, and the other emitted a series of quick, high-pitched beeps. "When you hear that, press this button to talk, then let go of it when you're done. Got it?"

"Got it." The expression on his face was less certain than the tone of his voice. The abbot bid the couple Godspeed and left the shop. "Oh, this is exciting, isn't it? You know, we don't even have a phone out here. When Aelred got that snakebite, we had to read in a book from the library what to do. Thank God we had a visitor staying with us who had a cell phone. He called the hospital in town and had an ambulance meet us at the highway. Poor Aelred sat in the front seat of the pickup while Father drove like a maniac down that awful road. Ahh, but he was fine. Now Aelred has a good story, and the snake had a good lunch." Brother Eric had picked up a broom while he spoke and was sweeping the floor with great determination. As he opened the screen door and swept a small pile of rocky dust out onto the porch, his eyes caught someone approaching. "Here comes Brother Xavier. He's new with us."

A compact young man with a deep tan and a Chicago Cubs baseball cap stepped onto the porch and waved to everyone in the shop. Brother Eric took a glass of water in a paper cup out to him, and as he was stepping back inside, the two-way radio beeped in his tunic pocket. "That must be the abbot" he exclaimed as he pulled the device out and searched for the button he was supposed to press. The radio beeped again, and then once more. Finally, Brother Eric found the button and pushed it awkwardly, but not before the abbot rang a fourth time. Suddenly, the young monk on the porch burst in and looked around with a terrifically curious expression on his face. "Es ése un Gameboy?"

~

In the award-winning 2001 game *Black & White,* players adopt the persona of a god.[1] As the game opens, the player watches from above as a lovable heterosexual humanoid family makes its way down to a beach in the midst of a tropical paradise. As they play in the surf, one of the children is suddenly surrounded by ominous-looking sharks. Panic-stricken and helpless, the child's parents kneel in the sand and pray: "Someone help us! We call to the heavens! Hear us!" And so begins the game that claims to allow players to "find out how *your* mind works [and] who you really are" (D. Evans 2). The opening sequence does not give players the option not to save the child—-presumably such inaction would negate the narrative premise that the child's rescue activates, namely, that this miracle is a sign that there is a god who acts in this virtual world. As a result of this miraculous rescue, the thankful villagers invite the player back to their village, where they say the rightfully deserved praise will be bestowed.

In the previous chapter I showed how the nature of the game review industry is averse to offering careful critiques of computer games, partly because the industry is always trying to keep up with the endless stream of new games, and partly because most reviewers seem to have accepted as a fact that computer gameplay is essentially harmless. This critique emerged out of an application of the grammar of gameworks that drew especially on "influences," those external forces that impinge upon the rhetorical events that work to effect transformations in both agents and artifacts. In this chapter I focus primarily on just one of those influences—economic force—to demonstrate how gamework scholars may use particular elements of the grammar to generate deep and broad analyses of the computer game complex. I will show how a concentrated critique of an artifact's meaning-making processes can be facilitated by attending to how a single influence shapes its construction and use. In *Black & White,* agent/developers embedded an economic system that works enthymematically to engage agent/players while it simultaneously reinforces remarkably unimaginative understandings of both in-game and real-life social and political economies. The influence of economic force pervades this popular game (and others like it) and teaches players several economic lessons that are questionable at best.

From the start of *Black & White* an economy is established. In this economy the player's godly acts are rewarded with in-game characters' belief. Players quickly realize that these characters' belief correlates directly with the extent to which the player-as-god is able to act in Eden, the game's virtual world; without their belief, the villagers' god (i.e., the player) is unable to manipulate the landscape and weather, to perform miracles, and ultimately, to expand his or her area of influence. In a sense, this is all that *Black & White*

Fig. 1. Inside Temple with Consciences. © Lionhead Studios Limited.

is about: gaining and wielding influence for the purposes of geographic expansion.[2] There is a story to the game involving the overthrow of other gods, but both the strength and emphasis of the game are clearly in its provision of an appealing environment that players may freely explore. The game has two connected and sophisticated artificial intelligence (AI) engines that make the behaviors of villagers and the creature that comes to embody the player in the land quite surprising, "realistic," and entertaining.[3] Additionally, the game uses dynamic graphics and audio systems that cause the game's land, architecture, interface, and music to change according to the style in which players behave: benevolent gods inspire soothing music and peaceful landscapes, while malevolent gods inspire grim music and desolate landscapes. In short, game players who are interested in more than target practice or strategizing find in *Black & White* a complex world that allows for nearly endless opportunities for play. Gamework scholars will also observe that every opportunity for play carries with it an instructional component.

I concurred in an earlier chapter with Chris Crawford's assessment that games are always educational. On the positive side of this claim, educators have tried to use the engrossing quality of computer games to teach students a variety of skills that could be transferred to the real world, from the flying of aircraft to the identification of certain kinds of molecules. Skeptics of computer games have likewise used the engrossing and educational nature of computer games to challenge the appropriateness of allowing them to go unregulated. Dave Grossman's concern, for example, is that violent computer games—among other forms of mass media—help people overcome their inherent repugnance to killing and thereby make it more likely that such game-conditioned people will be able to kill in real life. While both of these views are frequently debated, it seems undeniable to me that spending hours in front of and interacting with a compelling game system has influential effects on players. These effects may or may not be long-lasting and dramatic, but they are nonetheless caused. Once made, these effects influence other ways the player understands the world—again, perhaps not in a profound or permanent way, but in *some* way. I suspect that what happens most often is that games merely reinforce more established assumptions and ideologies. *Duke Nukem* probably didn't cause anyone to see Los Angeles police officers as brutally unjust donut-eating pigs, for example, if they weren't already familiar with—and possibly amenable to—that stereotype.

But one of the main reasons I believe it's important to closely examine computer games is precisely because they are having *at least* this reinforcing effect on a broad cross-section of the world's population. It is important, therefore, for scholars to ask what ideologies are being reinforced by the computer game complex: What consequences has it already had on cultures and societies around the world? What implications does its work have for the present? What transformative potential does it hold for the future? When meanings are being managed so adroitly that ideologies are shaped or reshaped, the gamework scholar knows that not only is the computer game complex itself being changed but so too is the dialectic. In this final chapter I will use the grammar of gameworks to investigate such transformations as they are facilitated by economic force, but I will also examine how in-game economic issues both impinge and are impinged upon by other elements within the dialectic. I begin by clarifying the concept of "economy" and show how a variety of economies are made manifest in *Black & White.* From there, I focus on how *Black & White*'s internal game economies work in symbiosis with the agent/player and explore how that relationship might itself be working to manage players' understandings of, and attentiveness to, some of the world's real economies. The chapter—and the book—conclude with some observations about how the grammar of gameworks can help gamework scholars to understand better the forms and magnitudes of the transformations their work (and play) can initiate.

Defining Economies

The word "economy," like the word "rhetoric," tends to be used rather loosely in common parlance. Most people use it to designate that which is related to money and finances. But an economy need not have anything to do with money per se. The earliest understanding of "economy" involved the management of a household and included the attention given to everything from home furnishings and landscaping (for the well-to-do) to meal preparation and child care. More modern developments in economy, from a generation or two before Karl Marx for example, understood "economy" to refer to an organizational construct that helped to determine the value of material objects like machines, houses, and coats. By the early twenty-first century, this "something" had evolved such that what it represented was not necessarily material: today, ideas are recognized as important economic elements, as are other immaterialities like race, gender, sexual orientation, and language.[4] Among the points that Marx did contribute to understandings about economies—in addition to his study of the economic role of labor in different kinds of societies—was that traditional economic categories such as "interest," "capital gain," and "trade tariffs" are "only theoretical expressions, the abstractions of the social relations of production" (*Poverty of Philosophy* 109). Understandings about what and to what extent something is valuable, argued Marx, are determined by the ways people have been organized to produce the material necessities for a community. Economies, in other words, always emerge out of human, not abstract monetary, contexts.

Embedded within the game *Black & White*, there is a single economy that is comprised of three microeconomies.[5] The first microeconomy deals specifically with natural resources; the second deals specifically with spiritual resources; and the third microeconomy deals specifically with time. Each of these microeconomies is itself comprised of several categories. The natural resources microeconomy has three such categories: building materials, food, and people. In the game, players watch, help, and/or hinder the AI-controlled villagers and the god-player's creature to lead their lives in relative comfort and safety. This is often done through direct and indirect interventions with natural resources. When villagers or creatures are hungry, they make this need clear both through prayers the player hears and (for villagers) through a banner that they raise at a building called the "village stores." Other banners are raised here as well, including one that tells the god-player that villagers need more wood to build homes, temples, or public buildings, and another that indicates that more babies are desired.[6]

It is up to the player to decide how—or if—the villagers' needs will be met. A benevolent and interceding god-player might answer the prayers for food by collecting a school of fish from the ocean nearby and delivering it miraculously out of the sky and into the village stores. Such an act, if witnessed by the villagers, will generate considerable "belief." A benevolent but more dis-

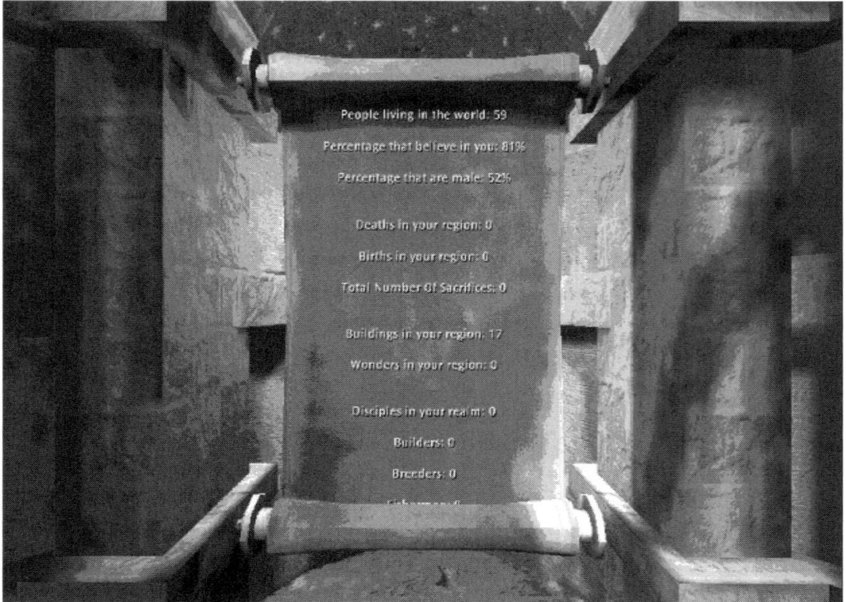

Fig. 2. Temple information scroll (world). © Lionhead Studios Limited.

tant god-player, however, might direct a villager or two to the ocean side and inspire them to fish—which in game parlance would class such characters as "disciple fishermen."[7] Benevolent responses are not the only allowable ones, however. Some players may choose to respond to the prayer for rescue from hunger by throwing half the villagers into the ocean or dropping boulders on them; fewer villagers will allow the limited stores to be stretched further by the survivors. Other players may choose to let the villagers work their problems out by themselves, offering neither help nor hindrance.

Spiritual resources, like natural resources, carry values that have been preassigned by the game developers. Unlike the natural resources, however, resources like "belief," "prayers," "miracles," "discipleship," and "creatures" —the embodiments of god-players in the land—are not so intuitively understood in their economic context. From the perspective of this microeconomy, *Black & White* is the most overtly rhetorical computer game one could imagine: everything in the game revolves around the player's ability to generate "belief" in the villagers, and efforts to gain this belief are referred to in both printed and in-game documentation as "influence."[8] In this sense, *Black & White* is not so much a simulation of being a god as it is a simulation of being

Fig. 3. Initial three creatures. © Lionhead Studios Limited.

a rhetorician: if an agent/player (rhetor) conveys his or her a message (text) effectively to the game's villagers and creature (audience), they will be transformed by it—within the parameters defined by the developers, of course. Spiritual resources provide the player with the means and power to expand his or her sphere of influence in Eden, which in turn gives the player access to more means and more power. Means and power for what? For influencing more people and gaining more power. In this respect, *Black & White* is no different from other god-games in which the ultimate objective is to become as powerful as possible.[9]

The temporal microeconomy of *Black & White* works to make and manage meanings for agent/players by imposing values on how they spend their time. Since the game progresses according to an accelerated solar calendar—days and nights constantly cycle in the world of *Black & White*—management of game time by the player is an important economic skill for players, and gamework scholars, to understand. Every villager in the game is born, ages, and dies, and so the best players will try to keep track of such demographics as median age, average life span, and natality and mortality statistics.[10] Additionally, many of the game's challenges require players to com-

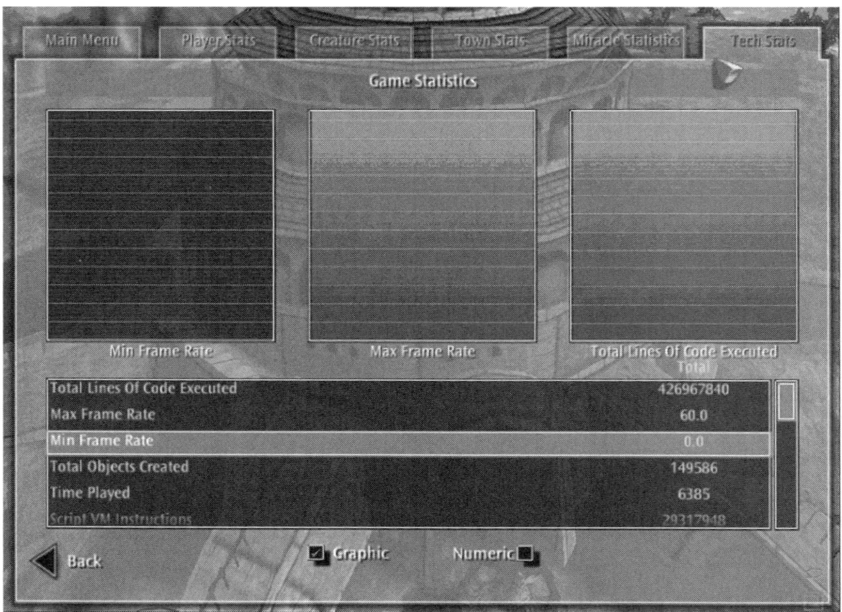

Fig. 4. Game statistics (technical). © Lionhead Studios Limited.

plete certain tasks or to amass certain types of natural and spiritual resources in a specified amount of time. Finally, the game keeps a running tally of how long the player has been playing, a factor that may not have any direct bearing on the game itself but does have consequences in the fan community, where in-game time is often used as an indicator of one's "devotion" or "seriousness."

This chapter will illustrate how gamework scholars can expose much of an artifact's embedded meaning-making process by using a single element from the grammar of gameworks to focus her or his analysis. For example, by examining how the "influence" of economic force can work to facilitate different kinds of transformation—both inside and outside a computer game—the scholar can begin to discover where connections exist between virtual and real economic systems. This kind of demystifying practice—so called because the gamework scholar refuses the developers' and marketers' efforts to mystify the boundary between the virtual and material—uncovers the mechanisms of intense engagement that often make this medium so compelling and instructive. The scholar's demystification of computer games on this level has the effect of bringing into consciousness not only the social

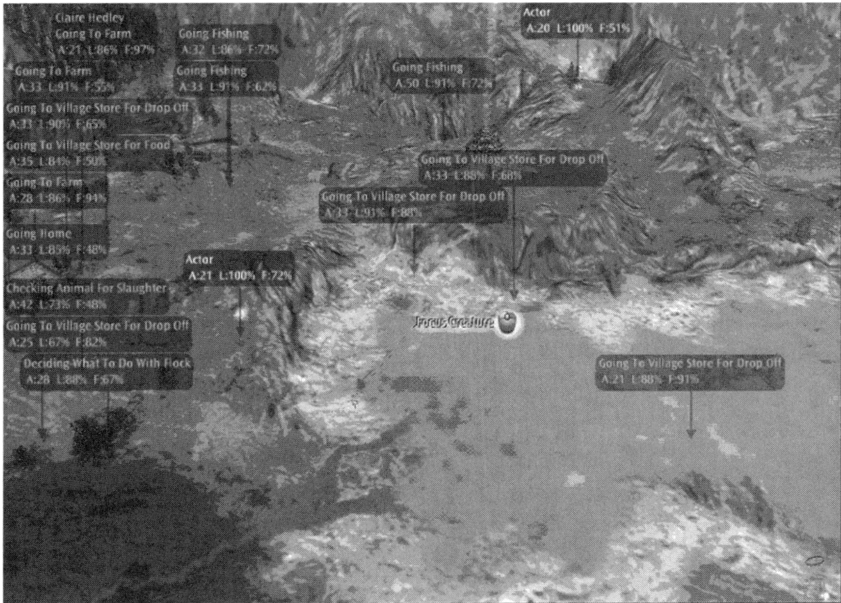

Fig. 5. Villager information bubble. © Lionhead Studios Limited.

relations that are constructed between the agent/player and the game but also those among agent/players, agent/marketers, and agent/developers. At an even broader level, focused analyses of gameworks like *Black & White* help scholars expand their critiques beyond the bounds of the computer game complex; by examining how agent/developers construct the microeconomies of a virtual world, scholars may also come to understand how real economies and real subjects of those economies have been metonymized so that they become (perhaps unintentionally) instructional models for people who thought they were "just playing." I turn now to a more detailed examination of *Black & White*'s microeconomies in order to discover how economic force lends that game substantial meaning-making power.

The "Purchase" of Natural Resources

Trees

In *Black & White*'s Eden, trees are crucial for the functioning of the natural resources economy. There are nine types of trees, each of which is assigned a lumber value. At the top of the list is the oak, worth up to 800 units of wood. Other hardwoods follow, then come softwoods like palm and pine, which are worth up to 350 units each. In an effort to negotiate the realism/tedium contradiction described in previous chapters, the developers have assigned maximum values to these trees, and the game engine keeps track of each tree's age and condition, both of which affect its "worth." A young oak, for example, if harvested and brought to the village stores for processing may be worth only 200 or 300 wood units. A cypress that has been damaged by fire or lightning may be similarly devalued. By harvesting trees and turning them into lumber, villagers and players supply materials for all of Eden's buildings, including huts, civic centers, and places of worship. These buildings in turn influence the satisfaction and desire of the villagers, who in turn have an impact on the ability of the player to make her or his character more powerful.

Left on their own, the villagers will plant, tend, and harvest trees but not very rapidly. Players are encouraged through experience and the in-game counsel of two figures representing "good conscience" and "bad conscience" to help the villagers manage their resources; as gods, players can do such agricultural work much more efficiently than the villagers. With a few sweeps of one's in-game god-hand, a player can water and harvest several large forests—or raze them if one is so inclined—a job that would take the villagers many generations.[11] One of the main advantages of being god in the context of a natural resources economy, then, is the ability to cash in on these resources easily and rapidly.

Trees have other purposes in *Black & White* as well, some of which are linked to their value as spiritual resources (which will be examined later) and some of which are linked to their aesthetic value. In this latter case, players learn that trees planted within a village's borders will not be harvested by the villagers but will instead raise their morale. Trees can also be used as weapons (clubs and missiles) by the god-player and by the creature that embodies the player later in the game. Here again the developers have outdone themselves in terms of their attention to detail: some trees are more aerodynamic than others, a factor that affects their value in the context of a wartime economy.

Food

There are two types of food in *Black & White:* grain and animals. Grain is grown by farmers in plots of land near villages, and even more so than trees it must be carefully tended in order to provide a high yield. Like trees, fields of grain can be harvested early, but at a cost: a fully ripe grain field will yield 350 food units, but less if it is unripe. There is no limit to the number of

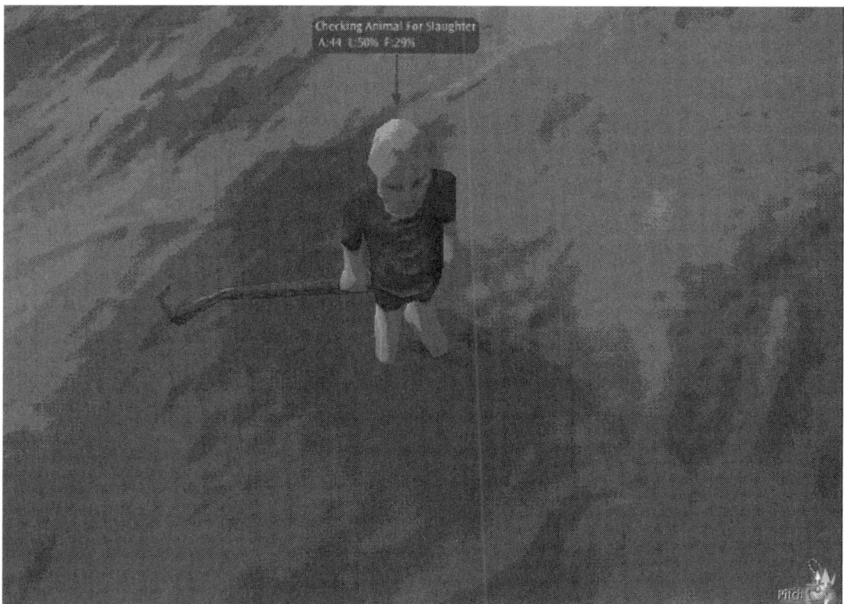

Fig. 6. Male villager information bubble. © Lionhead Studios Limited.

times a field can be replanted—the developers have forgone simulating overcultivation—but the fields do require water, which may be provided by the in-game weather system or by the god-player in the form of a water miracle (discussed below).[12] Without enough water, the crops may not reach full maturity and the grain yield will be poor.

Animals, too, are an important food source. A variety of animals wanders the land of Eden, and some of them are specially domesticated for the purposes of food: fish, sheep, cows, pigs, and even horses may all be processed for meat, and their value in food units is predetermined. Interestingly, players are not required to make animals a part of the villagers' diet, and so it is well within their power to make the villages under their control completely vegetarian. This would mean, of course, that more grain would need to be raised, but that is a relatively small problem provided the god-player is powerful enough to support the water requirements of the fields. As with trees, animals can also be made to serve other functions in the game, acting as weapons (a cow dropped from several hundred feet onto a house will destroy the roof and kill anyone inside), as miracles (players can make any animal "fly" over the village center), and as religious offerings.

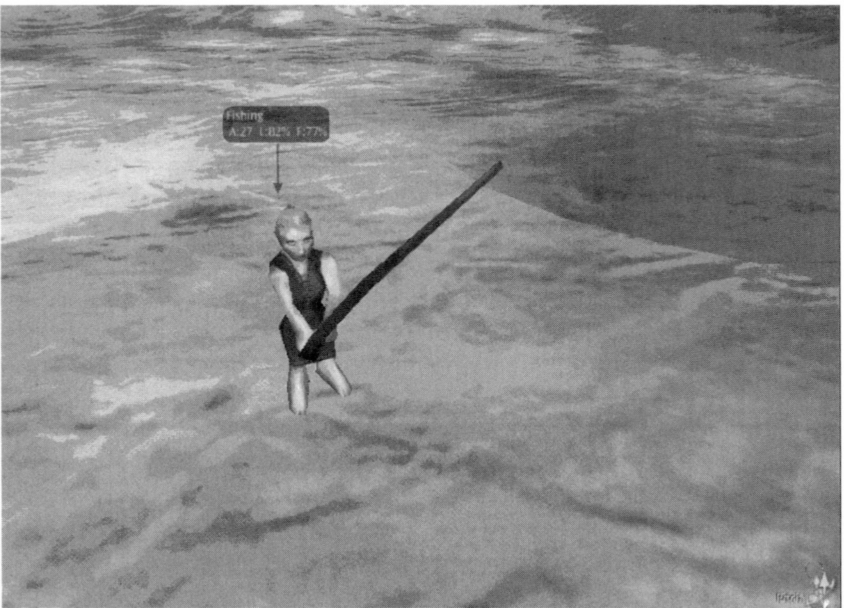

Fig. 7. Female villager information bubble. © Lionhead Studios Limited.

People

In Eden people are themselves a natural resource: they are the managers of the world for the god-player, allowing the player to attend to the less mundane tasks of a deity, such as fending off attacks from neighboring gods, expanding one's sphere of influence, taking on particular challenges that have been designed into the game's narrative, and teaching one's creature/familiar how to behave. Although people cannot be added to the village stores—cannibalism is not an option in the game—the god-player's creature can eat the villagers for food (and fun). People can also be used as weapons by the god-player in the same way that animals can be: drop them from high enough or throw them hard enough and they will do damage to structures, plants, animals, and other people. And since the key to the game is to garner as much belief from villagers as possible, breeding is another important factor in *Black & White*'s natural resource economy; in game terms, strong belief among a few villagers is no better than weak belief among many.

Just as the management of trees and fields might well raise land management issues among some critics (e.g., what are the ethical and agricultural implications of massive deforestation or overcultivation to support a large

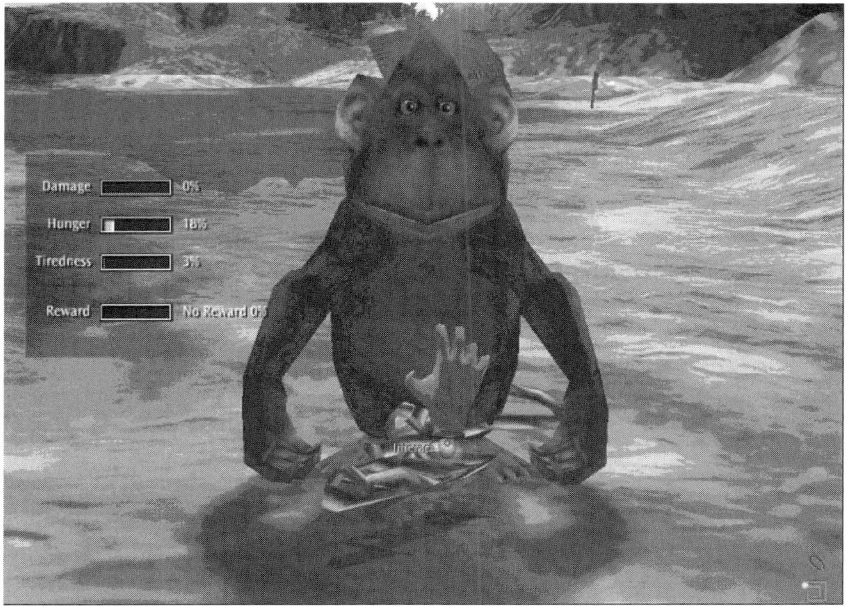

Fig. 8. Creature information box. © Lionhead Studios Limited.

village?), and just as the assumption that animals are to be considered nothing more than foodstuffs might raise issues about the treatment of animals by other critics (e.g., what are the ethical implications of the factory farming mentality encouraged by the game?), the issue of human breeding also raises several problematical issues. So far as I can tell, for example, homosexuality is not an option in *Black & White,* presumably since it offers no overt material advantage to the village.[13] Gender, too, has a sociopolitical role in *Black & White:* while male and female villagers have equal access to all jobs and seem to be able to generate equal amounts of material and "prayer power," at least one published strategy guide (Prima's) suggests that players choose males to be specially designated breeders, since they are not hindered by a nine-month delay of pregnancy. Finally, some degree of eugenics is possible in the game, as each villager can be named and tracked through multiple generations. By selecting certain villagers to breed with certain other villagers, a controlled lineage can be established in the game, the consequences of which are currently unexplored.

People, however, are more important resources than their rather simple role as world managers and populators suggests. Without people, especially people who believe in divine intervention, the god-player would not exist. In this way the people provide the primary contact point between two of the three *Black & White* microeconomies: the god-player must work within a spiritual economy to influence the natural resource economy upon which the people depend. Economic force in this context shapes *Black & White*'s meaning-making potential by giving it the purchase of a familiar fiscal trope: nothing in life is free, not even for gods.

The "Purchase" of Spiritual Resources

Immaterial or spiritual resources in *Black & White* constitute the economy that governs the power of the player within the game. Villagers act as an interface between the material resource economy and this spiritual economy: villagers generate belief, belief coalesces into "prayer power," and prayer power congeals into "miracle power" (D. Evans 17). The greater each of these resources becomes, the more influential the god-player is in Eden. Signs of this increased influence come in the form of enhanced and new godly skills: whereas a weak god may only miraculously water crops and harvest trees for the sawmill, a powerful (i.e., influential) god can spontaneously generate crops and lumber from thin air. The more miraculous the acts of the god-player, the more belief is generated from villagers, which in turn generates more prayer power and miracle power. In this way the player must work for the villagers' belief if he or she has any hope of becoming powerful enough to conquer neighboring tribes and begin to dissuade them of their belief in a different deity. These spiritual resources contribute immensely to the ways *Black & White* catalyzes local meanings as a particular game with an invented economy and as a representative product within the computer game complex that has a considerably more complex economic network.

Belief

Black & White admits that there are varying levels of belief. In the game, any number of actions performed by the god-player may generate "belief points," which, when collected in sufficient quantity, result in villagers (and even entire villages) being committed to worshipping the god-player. Simple godly acts, such as hurling a boulder over a village or uprooting a giant oak and dropping it into the village store, will cause any villager who sees these acts to mildly strengthen her or his belief, thereby generating belief points. Dramatic godly acts, such as raining down lightning bolts or causing an entire forest to spring up overnight, generate many more belief points among those who see them. When enough belief points have been generated—five hundred is the standard number—a village comes under the control of the god-player, allowing the god-player to receive the prayer points the villagers generate during worship.

Prayers

When villagers believe in god, they enact this belief through prayer at a worship site. Prayers generate "prayer power," which the god-player needs to cast miracles; different miracles require different amounts of prayer power. Since prayer points may be generated only by those villagers who are dedicated to worship at a temple, the rapidity with which prayer points are generated is dependent on the number of villagers the god-player has dispatched to his or her temple. This dispatch is indicated to villagers by the height of the god-player's totem, which the player is able to raise and lower at any time. Of course, any villager who is at the temple is not available to farm, construct buildings, or bear and raise children, so the god-player must decide how best to divide the available labor in a given village. Worshippers are also notoriously devoted, and when they are praying at the temple, they will forgo eating even unto death. For this reason, the god-player must take special care to give worshippers a chance to rest and provide them with ample food to keep their energy up. As villages grow, more people can be sent to the worship site, thereby generating increasingly large amounts of prayer power, a power that translates directly into miracle-casting power for the god-player.

Miracles

There are many miracles available to god-players in *Black & White,* and they can be cast for a wide range of purposes: to generate belief, to help or hinder villagers (one's own or one's enemy's), or to accomplish some specific task that may help the god-player expand her or his sphere of influence. Some miracles are destructive (lightning bolt, fireball, megablast), some are defensive (physical and spiritual shields), and some are designed to help villagers or creatures (heal, food, strength). All of these miracles, if seen or experienced by villagers, will generate belief, which again contributes to prayer power. However, miracles also consume prayer power, and so players must carefully budget their use of miracles so that they don't overspend their power reserve and undermine their ability to impress villagers. Miracles are the ultimate tools with which the god-player is able to encroach on and conquer neutral or opposing villages; such triumphs mark the player's overall success. When *Black & White* is being played according to its suggested narrative, an imperialist objective is the game's guiding premise. Miracles, and the commodities that give rise to the power that enables them, are the primary suasory weapons used to accomplish this objective.

The "Purchase" of Temporal Resources

Time itself functions as a third microeconomy in *Black & White*, one that in many respects binds all of the microeconomies into a unified macroeconomy. Unlike many other computer games in which time is an autocrat—for example, games in which a player's race against time serves as the primary inducement into a competitive mode—the *Black & White* developers integrated temporal elements into virtually every aspect of gameplay.[14] As resources and people age, their value fluctuates; as game time passes, the player's performance is judged more or less effective by the "good conscience" and "bad conscience" characters who coach the player throughout the game; tasks undertaken by god-players can often be successfully completed only within given time frames; play time is tracked by the game, lending players credibility among fan groups; and the concept of "god" is notable, among other characteristics, as being unhindered by time (theoretically, anyway).

Although most major developments in the game are triggered by events (e.g., certain tasks completed or game characters met) rather than timers (e.g., after four hours the neighboring village will initiate a raid), there are some points in the game where events cannot proceed if the player has not mastered a host of time-governed game elements: certain gestures performed at the right time, certain resources allocated such that they reach optimal levels at a particular time, or certain villagers and creatures given enough time to traverse the landscape in order to arrive at a given place and time. Even the villagers themselves keep track of time, knowing, for example, when fields are ready for harvest, when their biological clocks are winding up and down, and knowing when children become old enough to be sent from the cradle to the fields, the farmyards, or the construction sites. In all of these ways, time is a contributing factor in how virtually every element of *Black & White* is valued, both among in-game characters and in the players themselves.

The interaction of these three microeconomies—natural, spiritual, and temporal—is what creates so many opportunities for the construction and maintenance of cultural meanings among players. Having used the grammar of gameworks' "economic force" as a generative heuristic to identify the details of *Black & White*'s economic characteristics, I turn now to a discussion of how those details impinge upon the workings of the computer game complex and the dialectic of which it is a part. In this concluding piece of analysis, I draw in other elements of the grammar of gameworks to connect *Black & White*'s economies to the kinds of valuations the game seems to reinforce in players more generally. In particular, I argue that despite the flexibility of the game's play environment, its ability to withstand the seemingly endless creative responses of agent/players is quite dependent on a set of hard-coded rules that most players take as intuitive and intelligent because they also dominate most players' real sociopolitical frameworks.

The Work of Black & White

The macroeconomy that underlies *Black & White*'s playability is arguably the game's most influential component, both within the mechanics of the game itself and in the interactions between the agent/player and game. The graphics and audio of the game are excellent, but they are given vitality through the engine that processes the economic progression of the game and parses it out in millions of graphics and audio instructions per second. The interface is also very elegant—particularly its "gesture recognition system," which tracks the player's mouse movements in order to execute miracles when the cursor is moved in certain patterns—but again the interface would have little impact on the game if it were not linked to the economic system that dictates what data the interface is to present. Without the *Black & White* economy, the game's narrative could not advance, its AI would be quite stupid, and its open design would quickly become tedious. Much of the work of *Black & White*, therefore, is enabled by the complex (by game standards, at least) economic force that influences how the game itself works and how players work with the game.[15] This influence occurs primarily on four levels: the technical, the narratological, the philosophical/theological, and the ideological. Each of these levels of economic force has both direct and indirect effects on how the game works to make or shape players' understandings of how value is assigned to different resources and social relations. *Black & White*'s economic force influences (and is influenced by) the way the game's meaning-making mechanisms function; it helps constitute the ways those functions are made manifest in particular elements of the game; and ultimately the game's economic force influences both the agents (players, marketers, and developers) of the game and the transformative locales in which their ideologies are altered. A closer examination of these four levels of economic force will clarify this process and will reveal how they connect the computer game complex with the broader social and cultural work that it accomplishes in the dialectic.

Economic Force at the Technical Level

Many of *Black & White*'s technical operations are made possible by the ways its agent/developers constructed the economic subsystem of the game. Even with the most powerful desktop computers of 2001 (the year the game was released), the massive number of calculations, statistics, and instructions necessary to make the game as engaging as it is makes it tremendously demanding on hardware resources. One way that developers are able to lower these demands is by designating numerical values for such unquantifiable human experiences as hunger, desire for children, and belief in a god. Indeed, since the medium of the game is a home computer, to do otherwise would be to tax commercially available processing systems to an unworkable degree. By predefining the values of natural, spiritual, and temporal resources within the game—either with hard numbers (e.g., a mature oak is worth three hundred units of lumber) or a simple equation (e.g., units of lumber = value of tree type × age of tree)—the game can work apace to generate a nearly seamless dynamic environment in which the actions of the in-game characters and the player are easily integrated.[16] One important effect of this integration is that players come to feel that their actions—and inactions—are having direct effects on the game world, a rhetorical technique that often makes games highly compelling.

Another technical effect of *Black & White*'s economic system is its ability to make a wealth of information rapidly available to the player and in a form that is easily digestible. When villagers cry out "More food!" players are able to respond more readily than they would if they had to memorize the numerous threshold tables that stand behind such outbursts. Of course, experienced players eventually come to intuit these thresholds, but this is simply an indication of how effectively agent/developers are able to apply the influential effects of economic force within a game system: because players are able to become familiar with the underlying rules so quickly, the economic system becomes essentially transparent. In essence, facts like "villagers always want their communities to expand" and "intelligent creatures learn best when corporal punishments and rewards are meted out to them" become commonsensical. The connection here between ideology and conditionally operative rhetoric will be addressed more fully later; suffice it to say here that economic force influences the technical aspects of *Black & White* primarily by simplifying a wide array of social relations so that they become easily calculable for the game system and easily visualizable for players who have a limited tolerance in the context of "play" for tedious and confusing hyperrealism.[17]

Fig. 9. Belief statistic. © Lionhead Studios Limited.

Economic Force at the Narratological Level

Black & White's economic force also influences the game's narrative. While the game has three styles in which it may be played—single-player, skirmish, and clan competition—it is typically played as a single-player game. In this mode, a rudimentary narrative unfolds, one in which a particularly powerful god is attempting to take over all five lands of Eden (just like the player). Each of the lands constitutes what in standard game parlance would be called a "level," and players must successfully manage and amass the resources of one land before advancing to the next. As players progress, they discover various elements of the game's plot that generally involve the various acts of wickedness and betrayal perpetrated by this super-god. It quickly becomes apparent that the end of the game will somehow involve a confrontation with this god and alliances with other, lesser gods. There are numerous subplots in the game—quests, intelligence gathering, and training projects with one's creature—all of which are in the service of the game economy that ultimately determines a player's chances for survival at the end of the game.[18]

Here again, the meaning-making capacity of economic force—influence that affects the valuations of things—contributes substantially to *Black &*

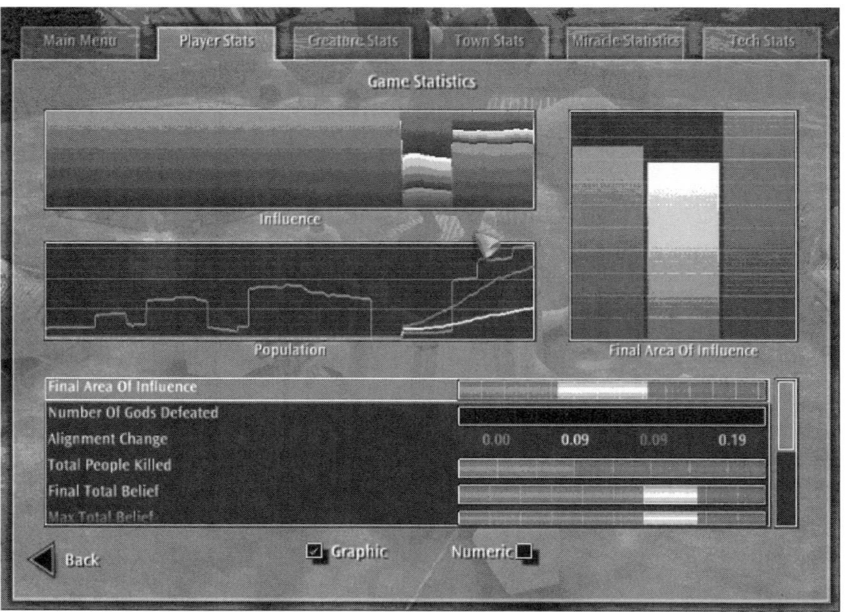

Fig. 10. Game statistics (player). © Lionhead Studios Limited.

White's gameplay. As the story advances, it becomes increasingly important that players be able to manage efficiently all the resources Eden has to offer. Without an ability to inspire the villagers' belief, players won't be able to advance the plot. Despite the complexity of the economic system's integrated microeconomies, however, working through the game's narrative is fairly simple, mostly because the developers have made an effort to make the economic system intuitive (for basic economic elements) and easy to learn (for more complicated elements). It is intuitive to most players, for example, that a village cannot grow if its inhabitants are not producing offspring. It is also intuitive to most players that such production requires a male and a female villager to mate, for the female to become pregnant, and for her to successfully give birth. What is less intuitive, but is easily learned through both the game's documentation and its in-game advisors, is that if the god-player picks up a villager and sets him or her down next to a villager of the opposite sex and of an appropriate age, not only will that couple mate but the villager who was picked up by the god-player will become a "breeder disciple." This special designation results in the villager becoming religiously devoted to breeding, the implications of which I have already noted: male breeders are more effective in this expediency-driven economy than female breeders because males aren't constrained by the physiology of pregnancy.

As players grasp these economic subtleties, their abilities to engage the narrative are enhanced; they are, in other words, being persuaded to think within the constraints of the game. In the disciple-breeder example, for instance, since the game never challenges players to question *Black & White*'s underlying economic structure, it only works to reinforce agent/players' comfort with an economy that grants sexual power—deifically bestowed sexual power no less—to males. The fact that this component of the game is modeled on the sexual economies of many real societies is at once telling and problematic. The issue here is not one that concerns polygamy but rather how the economy is designed to favor some members of the community over others. Certainly a player could choose to make only females into "breeder disciples," but this would be the least expedient way to grow the population in order to advance toward total domination of the game world. Most players, of course, won't trouble over the fact that females in the game take nine months to produce a child. This is because in the real world women also tend to gestate for nine months. Here is a moment, however, in which rhetoric is functioning conditionally. The females of Eden are constructs of the agent/developers, meaning that there is no real necessity for the Edenites' gestation period to be nine months. Why not make it nine days? Or why not make males incapable of procreating while their child is yet unborn? Or why not make males the child bearers? If players are able to suspend their disbelief about myriad other unrealistic elements of the game—giant intelligent cows walking around on two legs and casting magic spells for instance—why not equalize childbearing mechanics? This is one example of how "common sense" is transferred from developers' ideological frameworks into a game's ideology. This capacity for transference is what makes the game itself a medium for ideological reproduction, one that acts on the millions of players who engage with it.

Economic Force at the Philosophical/Theological Level

One of *Black & White*'s most unusual characteristics is its subject matter. Its basic—and to some its controversial—premise is that the player has, to quote the game's packaging, "become supreme god of the land."[19] There are at least two consequences that follow from this scenario: first, it allowed the developers to draw upon certain preestablished and widely accepted notions about what a god can and cannot do; and second, in part because of these preestablished understandings, it creates an immediate ground for disputation. While gamers have long debated the realism of their role-playing games' medieval settings and the truth-to-concept of the numerous games modeled on the *Star Trek* franchise, very few games have provoked the kinds of conversations that *Black & White* does as a matter of course. It is common to find online and face-to-face conversations about the game—long conversations—that discuss the advantages of polytheism, the inherently boring nature of a model of divine love, and the inescapable sinfulness of a god that acts in the world only to have its own needs met. Theologians and philosophers are regularly invoked in these conversations, from Plato, Kant, and Wittgenstein to Augustine, Merton, and Hellwig. Web forums reveal messages in which god-players' creatures are compared to Jesus Christ and Buddha, and players self-identify as being like the God of the Israelites, and Mephistopheles.[20] Nearly all of the online discussions that have followed from these claims are involved, thoughtful, and fairly well informed historically and literarily.

Interwoven in all these discussions, no matter what creeds their interlocutors seem to espouse, are the ethical and moral values that the developers have built into the game and those the players themselves bring to it. This is where the economic force of the game's rhetoric influences, and is influenced by, the players' own real-life values. This is not to say that players always play god as if they really were a god (whatever that might mean), imposing on the villagers and the game land of Eden all of their own real-life values and psychological idiosyncrasies (though it often does mean just that).[21] Rather, *Black & White* in its role as a game essentially requires players to inhabit at least partially the philosophical and theological space of its rule system in order for the game to be entertaining. In games like *Unreal Tournament* or *Hitman,* players typically have to go some distance to suspend their disbelief that they are, for example, a heavily armed cyborg shooting it out in a surreal interstellar landscape or a genetically constructed humanoid created to assassinate politicos around the world. In *Black & White,* however, it is a far less demanding task to imagine that one is responsible for caring for and training humanlike characters so that they behave as one desires. This exercise is similar to being a pet owner, a parent, or a politician—all challenges to be sure, but hardly otherworldly.

For most players, immersion in this familiar-but-simplified game economy will have instructive and transformative effects, particularly on those who have not had the opportunity or inclination to reflect on the systemic consequences of their social actions or inactions. Few players will worry about the developer-initiated elision between the game's built-in values and their own. Gamework scholars, however, will note that *Black & White*'s meaning-making processes engage players philosophically to the degree that if they are to win the game, they are forced to consider how everything in Eden is valued. This rhetoric is enthymematic: the players' valuations of various worldly relations are a major premise, the game's valuations are a minor premise. The conclusions in this logic are unstated, leaving the player to fill them in and make sense of the whole economy. Once this interactive logic has been constructed, the player and the game can coexist in relative harmony, each teaching the other what constitutes good and bad, right and wrong, effective and ineffective. By completing the enthymeme, the player becomes integral to the game itself. The player, in essence, powers (but does not control) the economic force of *Black & White* by reacting to it at a philosophical level.

Economic Force at the Ideological Level

The technical, narratological, and philosophical/theological levels through which economic force contributes to the meaning-making processes of *Black & White* essentially encourage (and even require) agent/players to think and act in predetermined ways. Most agent/developers and agent/players would likely characterize this work as advancing toward one simple goal: to make players have fun.[22] Gamework scholars, however, whose objective is critique, will see other goals in addition to the elicitation of fun. They will see, for instance, that together the technical, narratological, and philosophical/theological levels of economic force inform—and are informed by—ideology. Considered ideologically, *Black & White*'s work changes how players make meaning out of their experiences, not only in the game world of Eden but in the real world as well. Because the game depends on players' preestablished meaning-making frameworks in order to make sense, it is inherently ideological. Because the game challenges some of those ideological conventions—for instance, by presenting players with a fairly unique opportunity to play god, a role most sane people don't often exercise because of its potentially damaging effects on their social relationships—it is also *potentially* ideologically transformative. The work of transforming ideology, of course, is the work of rhetoric.

To the scholar who interrogates the narratological channels through which knowledge of *Black & White*'s economy is conveyed to players, several things are clear. First, the game's subplots are more than just amusing filler; they are moments when various game avatars—the player's good and bad conscience, Sable the creature trainer, and others—teach players how Eden works. Players learn how belief is generated, how to process natural resources, how to raise a creature to behave as the player wishes, and how to expand one's territory. Second, the main plot (conquer all the lands and become the supreme god) is an economic paradigm of archetypal proportions.[23] The utter simplicity of this objective—as a concept, not as a project—makes the game easy to grasp in an instant: get all the power. Third, the game's visual and audio elements give players a wealth of sensory cues that indicate how effectively the work toward supremacy is going: the look and sound of the game actually mutate in order to convey to players the extent of their success. Together, these channels work very efficiently to train each player to become an integral and effective component in *Black & White*'s economy.

The degree to which agent/players cooperate with *Black & White*'s work as a meaning-making artifact—work that is most powerfully conveyed through the mechanisms of economic force—and allow it to intermingle with their own ideologies is ultimately what determines how much "sense" the game makes as a form of entertainment. By most players' accounts, *Black & White* is a nearly perfect game. Hundreds of fan sites, thousands of newsgroup and Web forum messages, and several book-length strategy guides are dedicated to the game and almost uniformly praise its qualities. However, the game has received one rare but consistent criticism. A player who goes by the nickname "Wolfie" summarizes it this way: "You are CONSTANTLY having to micromanage villagers' lives as well as the life of your creature" (emphasis in original). When people complain about *Black & White,* it almost invariably involves how the game forces players to attend to so many tedious details. For these players, the economy of the game—that is, the way the game's valuations are established, transferred to the player, and otherwise manipulated—is problematic and repellent. The "game" makes little sense to these players, because it is not fun: "Teaching something to take care of itself just isn't fun for me," writes Richard Hutnick in the comp.sys.ibm.pc.games.strategic newsgroup. This explains, he says, "why I don't own any pets" and also why he panned the game. Hutnick and Wolfie, among others, resist the ideology of *Black & White* by rejecting the values that are hard-coded into it, both at the level of programming and at the level of design. Both respondents are careful to say that they are fans of the god-game genre but that *Black & White* just doesn't compel them; in other words, this is not a case of first-person shooter fans dismissing an entire game genre they don't appreciate in the first place. These are criticisms by players who wanted to be compelled by the game but weren't.

"Phil," a gamer who evaluates each game he plays on his personal Web site, captures the essence of this resistance to the economy of *Black & White* in an essay titled "Bad Beginnings." Phil's complaint, like others', is that the game requires players to micromanage Eden, including the much-lauded creature. But more than most other players, Phil recognizes that this problem exists in the game only because the developers made it that way:

> I should have obtained my creature elsewhere, however, if at all possible —perhaps at Crazy Bob's Discount Creature Hut on some other island. I say this because Sable, the local creature trainer, soon proved herself to be every bit as persistent and annoying as a group of animal-rights wackos on the warpath. All I wanted to do was watch my creature explore its environment, teaching him what to eat, where to poop and so forth. But my efforts were constantly interrupted by "Sable, the creature trainer, is trying to get our attention!" Things only grew worse as "There is a silver reward scroll down at the beach!" (or something like that) was added to the din. *Let me ask the game designers openly: how much fun do you really think it is, folks, for your player to be nagged every minute or so?* [emphasis added]

Ultimately, Phil becomes so annoyed with the in-game advisors (particularly the good and evil consciences), the needs of the creature, and the demands of the villagers that he is driven to ask, "what kind of god am I? Apparently I'm the kind that can't have a bloody moment's peace without getting dragged around by the ear like a five-year old who doesn't want to take his bath!" In asking this question—"what kind of god am I?"—Phil seems to sense that he not a god at all but rather a single cog among many in a complex rhetorical system that can't work without him, but neither can it work according to his particular desires.

As players intermingle and negotiate their own ideologies with those bound up in the game, they learn that they must submit or be frustrated. Computer games—the ones to date at least—show no quarter. For the vast majority of people who do submit—to refuse, after all, would be to waste fifty dollars—*Black & White*'s economic force works at the ideological level by collaborating with players' initial ideological positions to create, in essence, a virtual test bed wherein they are allowed to enact variations of their ideologies through large- and small-scale exercises of virtual power. In the context of the grammar of gameworks, this is an instance of rhetoric functioning conditionally. The economy of *Black & White* is like any other economy: you give and you get—*it just makes sense.* Because *Black & White* is a game, with all the standard interface features of electronic games, players can save their work prior to different exercises and, if they don't like the consequences, return to the pre-exercise state and try a different approach. In this way, *Black & White* may be described as an ideological heuristic, enabling players to test out different rhetorics in order to find a path to a particular end. For some, the end may be simply to complete the game. For others, the end may be, as the advertising for the game proposes, to "discover who you really are." In either case—or in any number of other possible cases—*Black & White* works ideologically through its imposition of economic force such that agent/players must submit to the rules of the system in order to exercise the power imputed to them by agent/developers for the purpose of having "fun." And the scholar who reflects more widely on the computer game complex will quickly realize that this latter point is at the heart of all game rhetoric: the fun of a game begins with submission to *all* of its rules. As soon as an agent/player tires of this submission, the game's playability drops away.

Transformative Locales: Economic Force as Game Work

The dialectic is the scene of an infinite set of struggles, running from the mundane to the drastic. All of these struggles, however, have in common their foundation on agents' use of meaning-making practices to shift the struggles toward particular resolutions. Such transformations are hard work, both to accomplish and to recuperate from. Using suasory techniques that build on existing ideologies—for instance, assumptions about how things are valued—is one way to make transformative work a bit easier. Agent/developers know this technique well (though most would frame it in marketing terms rather than those of the grammar of gameworks or the academic disciplines of rhetoric, cultural and media studies, and communications) and frequently exploit it; one role of scholars is to draw attention to the use of such techniques, not necessarily to prevent transformations but rather to help people make more informed decisions about the limits of their participation in them. The arts of making and managing meaning—rhetoric—function from all angles to drive the dialectic and the struggles that comprise it this way and that. These arts are not disembodied. People and corporations work to make meanings with greater and lesser degrees of facility, slowly changing the world we all inhabit. Computer games, including *Black & White,* are an increasingly powerful force in the dialectic, and the rhetorics they embody and reproduce are unquestionably capable of eliciting small and great transformations: of people's lives, of institutions, and of cultures and societies.

Players by the millions—boys and girls, women and men, young and old, of many cultures, and across a broad socioeconomic spectrum—now play games for hours at a time, every day. They build Web sites about them. They send messages about them. They read, write, think, and talk about them. Their habits have changed. They watch less TV, fewer movies, and take their entertainment outside less frequently than was once the case. These other, now deprived industries change as a consequence: TV producers create spin-off programs and commercials that feature computer game themes; the movie industry teams up with the game industry to create films like *Final Fantasy* and *Resident Evil;* and the toy industry puts out Duke Nukem action figures and Lara Croft Halloween costumes in order to draw back income lost to Nintendo, Sony, and Electronic Arts.

As these transformative locales develop, massive regulation schemes are advanced in an attempt to contain the transformations. Game rating systems are instituted in order to control access to individuals' personal and idiosyncratic ideological frameworks. By rating a game "For Mature Audiences Only," the potentially powerful rhetorics of graphic violence or sex, harsh language, or drug use contained in that game are restricted to players willing to engage the influences that such rhetorics are capable of; as a consequence, game ratings both quell and command desire.

Similarly, by passing corporate policies that restrict games, communities work to control access to the homological transformative locales: arcades are shut down or have curfews imposed on them; computer stores are prohibited from previewing certain games in their windows; schools forbid game playing in their computer rooms. These restrictions are instituted to control the influences on and transformations of groups of people who share geographic and perhaps cultural values.

Federal legislation—bills prohibiting what can get sold to whom, for example—works to control access to inclusive transformative locales. Restrictions at this level are intended to prevent particular, but still very broad, audiences from being subjected to influences judged (correctly or not) "unhealthy." Societal gestures like these demonstrate the force of law over industry, community, and individual. From a dialectical perspective, transformations enacted at this level are driven by powerful meaning-making processes backed by huge amounts of money and the law (powerful meaning-making constructions in their own right); few are the counter-rhetorics powerful enough to stand in opposition to them. Dialectical struggles engaged at this level—a level far more influential than those in the computer game complex—cease to be characterized by evenhanded resistance and transform into struggles that are characterized by ominous threats and anxious negotiation. Self-surveillance is proposed instead of federal oversight. Consumer action groups are formed and funded with federal and industry dollars. The mass media report government, professional organization, and industry press releases as if they were the work of independent journalists rather than of marketing departments and spin-doctoring.

And so trends shift. People who have never played a single computer game suddenly have deeply held convictions about them. People who play games all the time lose sight of the fact that games are products of a huge industry that ultimately cares more about quarterly financial statements than about interactive storytelling or increased polygon counts. Meaning-making processes operating at the deepest levels—conditionally functioning rhetorics working toward society-wide transformations—slowly circulate and move people to care more about electronic entertainment (for instance) than their families, their communities, and the lives of other people from all over the world to whom they are connected through the commodities they consume: artifacts such as console game systems, video cards, joysticks, and the packages in which these products are enclosed—all assembled by people who cannot afford to buy the very items on which they expend their labor. Economic force facilitates how games mean here, too, masking vast and interconnected systems of production, marketing, and consumption from people, many of whom do not *want* to know the rules of the game at this level, perhaps out of the understandable fear of discovering how decidedly unsafe and unfun is the "game of capitalism," as business historian John Steele Gordon has called it. The economies of *Black & White* illustrate these processes and work to reproduce their attendant anxieties always in the context of play. To the gamework scholar such mass-media driven ideological and cultural work warrants considerable attention, particularly because of the artfulness with which the game's developers accomplish it.

Epilogue

Computer games do real work in the world. They change lives, not just those of game players, marketers, and developers, but increasingly those of everyone. There are sweatshops in Thailand and Hong Kong where computer games are assembled and packaged. Remote villages in Cambodia have been inundated with tourists wanting to see where Lara Croft (Angelina Jolie) prayed with Buddhist monks in the movie *Tomb Raider.* The computer game complex changes national economies. Social structures are altered. Cultures intermingle, are dominated, and homogenized. As globalization—an economic force par excellence—pries open international borders in order to capture new markets, radical social transformations follow close behind. Gratuitous and graphic representations of violence in computer games are disturbing, there is no doubt. The hypersexualization and objectification of the human form in games is similarly problematical, as are the multitude of racial and cultural stereotypes that are designed into them (which, incidentally, *Black & White* has in abundance).[1] But as long as those agents who participate in the processes of how games mean—developers, marketers, and players—ignore the long-range implications of their work and fail to ask about the interests being served by the making, selling, and playing of artifacts like computer games, then the small redresses that are made to lend credibility to the computer game complex—rating systems, "political correctness," and joint industry-academy summits, for example—will accomplish little in the way of enabling a spirit of play to flourish in the lives of *everyone* who works within it. The project of gamework scholars, I propose, is to advance this spirit of play by investigating and disrupting those meaning-making processes that restrict play to a privileged few.

Social transformation on this order is not, of course, the sole responsibility of those involved in computer gaming. The grammar of gameworks detailed in *Game Work,* however, is a method specifically designed to help people in the computer game complex to investigate, describe, and accept responsibility for how games work to inspire transformations, from the personal to the communal and from the cultural to the global. The critiques that emerge from these investigations will, I hope, address the consequences of past gameworks, the implications of present gameworks, and the transformative potential of gameworks yet to come.

Appendix A
A Grammar of Computer Gamework

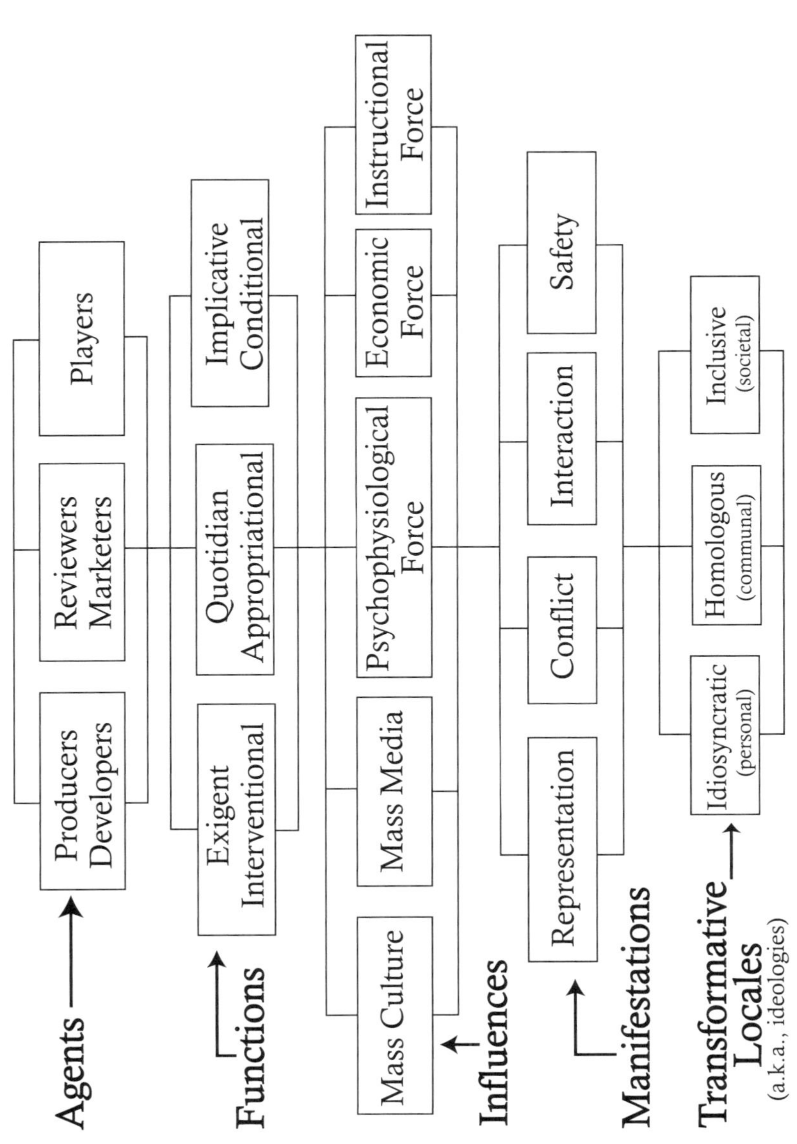

Appendix B
The Relationships Among Dialectic, Rhetoric, Ideology, and Metanoia

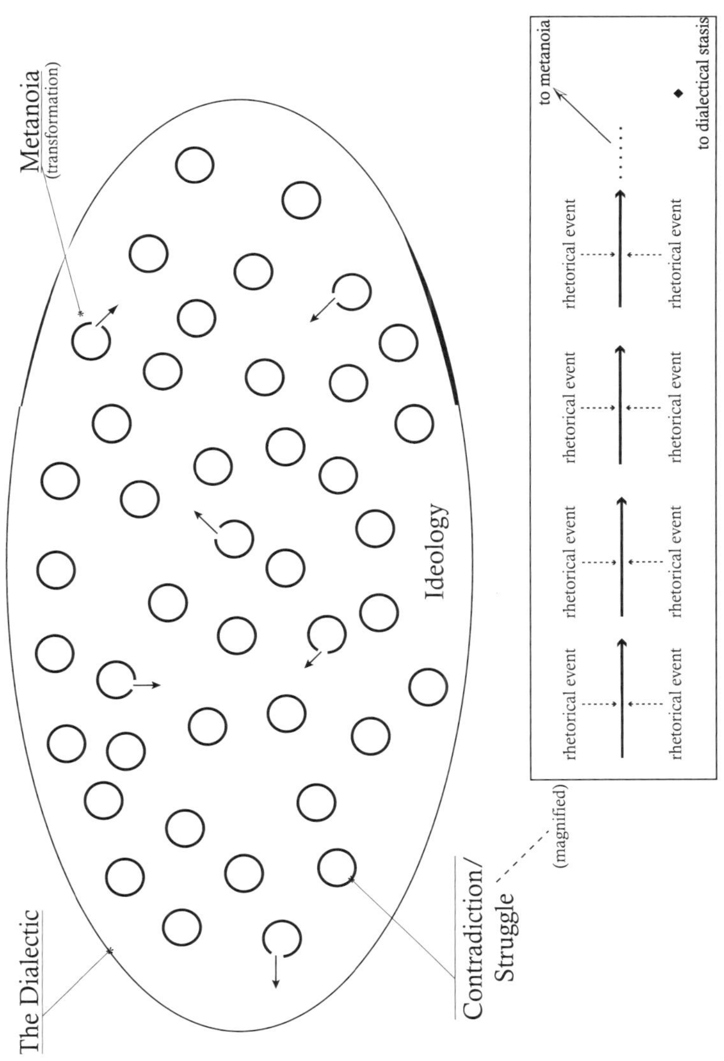

Appendix C
Game Titles Mentioned

Title	Developer	Publisher	Date
Age of Empires II	Ensemble Studios	Microsoft	1999
Air Traffic Control Simulator	Aerosoft	PC Aviator	2001
B17 Flying Fortress	Wayward Simulations	MicroProse	2000
Black & White	Lionhead Studios	Electronic Arts	2001
Blood Wake	Stormfront Studios	Microsoft	2001
Daikatana	Ion Storm	Eidos Interactive	2000
Dance, Dance Revolution	Konami	Konami	2001
Deer Hunter	Sun Storm	WizardWorks	1997
Deus Ex	Ion Storm	Eidos Interactive	2000
Diablo	Blizzard Entertainment	Blizzard Entertainment	1996
Dino Crisis	Capcom	Capcom	2000
Doom	id Software	id Software	1993
Driver 2	Reflections	Infogrames	2000
Duke Nukem	3D Realms	GT Interactive	1996
Escape from Monkey Island	Lucas Arts & Entertainment	Lucas Arts & Entertainment	2000

Title	Developer	Publisher	Date
EverQuest	Verant Interactive	Sony Online Entertainment	1999
Final Fantasy	Square Soft	Nintendo	1990
Gabriel Knight	Sierra	Sierra	1993
Grand Theft Auto: Vice City	Rockstar North	Rockstar Games	2002
Grim Fandango	Lucas Arts & Entertainment	Lucas Arts & Entertainment	1998
Half-Life	Valve	Sierra Entertainment, Inc.	1998
Halo: Combat Evolved	Bungie Studios	Microsoft Game Studios	2001
Heavy Gear	Activision	Activision	1997
Hitman: Codename 47	IO Interactive	Eidos Interactive	2000
Homeworld: Cataclysm	Barking Dog	Sierra Studios	2000
Imperialism	Frog City Software	SSI	1997
Jack Attack	Commodore	Commodore	1983
Jack Attack 2	Series Applications	Series Applications	2000
Jane's USAF	Pixel Multimedia	Jane's Combat Simulations/ Electronic Arts	1999
Jeopardy	Hasbro Interactive	Hasbro Interactive	1998
Jordan vs. Bird: One-on-One	Electronic Arts	Electronic Arts	1988
Madden NFL 2001	EA Sports	EA Sports	2000
Mario Bros.	Nintendo	Nintendo	1983
Max Payne	Remedy Entertainment	Gathering of Developers	2001
Mortal Kombat	Williams	Midway	1992
Myst	Cyan Productions	Brøderbund	1993

Title	Developer	Publisher	Date
Neverwinter Nights	Bioware	Atari Games	2002
Oddworld: Munch's Oddysee	Art Co.	THQ, Inc.	2003
Pacman	Namco	Namco	1980
Phantasmagoria	Sierra	Sierra	1995
Pharaoh	Impression	Sierra Entertainment, Inc.	1999
Pikmin	Nintendo	Nintendo	2001
Pokemon	Nintendo	Nintendo	1996
Pokemon Gold	Game Freak	Nintendo	2000
Pokemon Silver	Game Freak	Nintendo	2000
Pokemon Stadium	HAL Labs	Nintendo	2000
Pokemon Yellow	Game Freak	Nintendo	1998
Populous	Bullfrog Productions	Electronic Arts	1989
Powermonger	Bullfrog Productions	Electronic Arts	1990
P.Y.S.T.	Parroty Interactive	Palladium	1996
Quake	id Software	id Software	1996
Quest for Glory	Sierra	Sierra	1992
Railroad Tycoon	MicroProse	MicroProse	1990
Rainbow Six	Redstorm Entertainment	Redstorm Entertainment	1998
Red Faction	Volition Incorporated	THQ, Inc.	2001
Redneck Rampage	Xatrix	Interplay	1997
Resident Evil	Capcom Entertainment	Virgin Interactive Entertainment	1996
Rogue Spear	Redstorm Entertainment	Redstorm Entertainment	1999
Roller Coaster Tycoon	Chris Sawyer Productions	Hasbro Interactive/Micro-Prose	1999

Title	Developer	Publisher	Date
SimCity	Maxis	Brøderbund	1989
SimEarth	Maxis	Maxis	1990
SimFarm	Maxis	Mindscape	1993
The Sims	Maxis	Electronic Arts	2000
Soldier of Fortune I	Raven Software	Loki Games	2000
Soldier of Fortune II	Raven Software	Activision	2002
Sonic the Hedgehog	Sonic Team	Sega of America	1991
Space Wars	Cinematronics	Cinematronics	1978
Splinter Cell (Tom Clancy's)	Ubi Soft Montreal Studios	Ubi Soft Entertainment	2003
StarCraft	Blizzard Entertainment	Blizzard Entertainment	1998
Star Trek Armada	Activision, Inc.	Activision, Inc.	2000
Star Trek: Starfleet Academy	Interplay	Interplay	1995
Star Wars: Jedi Knight	Lucas Arts	Lucas Arts	1997
State of Emergency	Vis	Rockstar Games	2002
Street Fighter	Capcom	Capcom	1987
Survivor	Magic Lantern	Infogrames	2001
Sydney 2000	Attention to Detail Limited	Eidos Interactive	2000
Thief	Looking Glass Studios	Eidos Interactive	1998
Tomb Raider	Core Design Ltd.	Eidos Interactive	1996
Tony Hawk's Pro-Skater 2	Neversoft Entertainment	Activision, Inc.	2000
Twisted Metal Black	Incoq, Inc.	Sony Computer Entertainment	2001
Unreal Tournament	Epic MegaGames, Inc.	GT Interactive	1999
Virtua Fighter	Sega AM2 R&D Division	Sega	1995

Title	Developer	Publisher	Date
Where in the World Is Carmen Sandiego	Brøderbund	Brøderbund	1985
Who Wants to Be a Millionaire	Jellyvision	Buena Vista Interactive	1999
Wing Commander I	Origin Systems	Origin Systems	1990
Wing Commander IV: The Price of Freedom	Origin Systems	Electronic Arts	1995
WWF Smackdown	Yuke's Media Creations	THQ, Inc.	2000

Appendix D
How to Run a Game Night

David Menchaca, Judd Ruggill, and Ken McAllister
Codirectors of the Learning Games Initiative (LGI)

Introduction

Computer games in the early twenty-first century are ubiquitous, at least in industrialized countries, and as they become increasingly influential components of the sociocultural dynamic, scholars from many and various fields are understandably devoting more of their professional time to studying them. If you are reading this appendix (not to mention the book in which it's contained), you are probably one of these scholars, and you may be wondering how you might use computer games in a pedagogical context or do group analyses of games. This appendix offers one model for using computer games in such contexts and suggests some ways you might generate new models that are specific to your own learning communities.

At the University of Arizona we began our first group-based analyses of computer games by forming "The Learning Games Initiative" (LGI), a research collective that we agreed to codirect. LGI's mission is to investigate—in group contexts—questions concerning the relationships among computer games, culture, and pedagogy. We are interested in studying games in groups because we feel that computer games offer scholars and students of all levels and from all disciplines a remarkable opportunity to collaborate on the critique of games as cultural artifacts. By organizing critical sessions in which a variety of people met to examine computer games, we hoped that not only would we spark some local interest in computer game studies but also that some compelling critiques of computer games would emerge as a result of the diversity of our group. When we began LGI in the fall of 1999, we quickly realized that we could not effectively work toward this mission without first establishing a structure for our meetings, a loose method of inquiry. Our project therefore changed from simply asking provocative questions about computer games (e.g., Why are so many games dependent on racist and sexist stereotypes?) to searching for ways to ask thoughtful questions in a semiformal manner that would provide LGI participants with tangible results, either quantitative or qualitative.

In this appendix we share our experiences as explorers delving into this relatively uncharted territory in the hope that you might find it easier to chart your own new courses. In particular, we describe the research process that LGI currently uses, sharing both its advantages and disadvantages as we have discovered them over the past several years; readers will find summaries of these discoveries in sections labeled "TIP." While we encourage readers to consider the contexts surrounding each tip, we have also tried to make this document "skimmable" so that they can review the tips rapidly and immediately begin to think about how they might adapt the ideas contained in it for their own projects. The reason we have designed this appendix for such dual use is to emphasize the fact that our intent here is not to suggest that we have *the* method for all computer game study but rather to explain what we have done so far and to offer some practical ways that new projects might be begun with a minimum number of avoidable complications.

Procedure

LGI's method of inquiry is called "Game Night." Game Night consists of the following six components:

Content Cohosts: These organizers (usually two people) assume primary responsibility for planning what each Game Night will discuss and how.

Technical Cohost: This person assumes primary responsibility for the technical aspects of Game Night.

Participants: These ten to fifteen people from a variety of disciplines are the analysts.

Event Facilities: This component involves the space where Game Night is held and consists of a number of subcomponents: computer systems, projection systems, audio systems, and accessibility systems.

Content: This component includes the computer game(s) that will be discussed during Game Night, as well as other game-related artifacts the Cohosts decide to bring in, such as action figures, soundtracks, fan books and magazines, movies, etc. It may also include secondary material to be used during an evening's events, for example, excerpts from scholarly books or articles.

Observational Techniques: These are the ways data are collected during a Game Night's events.

Since our budget does not permit us to pay our participants for their time, we always provide them with a light meal (pizza or sandwiches) and refreshments. We find that this helps to create a relaxed atmosphere in what might otherwise be perceived as a stressful test of gaming aptitude and analysis. We will discuss below how each of these components works to facilitate the study of computer games, but first a few words about the goal of Game Night.

The Learning Game Initiative's Game Night is primarily concerned with investigations into three areas:

Studying Games: LGI participants use a variety of multidisciplinary analytical techniques to reveal and understand the ways sociocultural and technical tensions are embedded in, imposed upon, and taught through computer games.

Teaching Games: LGI participants work to develop pedagogies that teach these analytical techniques to students from a wide range of disciplines.

Building Games: LGI participants develop new games that draw upon their critique-oriented knowledge of computer games in order to generate new and more complex opportunities for learning through games.

LGI's motto—"Games always teach multiple things to multiple audiences"—reflects our commitment to working in these three areas, and Game Night, in short, emerged from our desire to study games as scholars, teachers, and cultural critics rather than as game developers. We wanted to focus on how the resources of the academic community might be brought to bear on understanding computer games in their broad social context, not on determining how developers' quality assurance techniques might be perfected.[1] With this understanding clearly articulated, we turn now to a detailed discussion of the five components of Game Night.

Content Cohosts

Generally speaking, the Content Cohosts will be the primary investigators in a computer game study project. The authors of this appendix, for example, have been the Content Cohosts of LGI's Game Night since its inception. We use the designation "Host" rather than other, perhaps more institutional terms (e.g., "Director," "Teacher," "Investigator"), because one of the aims of Game Night is to help people feel comfortable, safe, and playful even as they are asked to attend very carefully to a computer game-cum-cultural artifact. Safety is particularly important, because frequently the discussions in Game Night turn to issues of race, gender, and thresholds of comfort concerning the representation of violence and sexuality. These discussions often depend on the voicing of several contrary views, so it is incumbent on the Content Cohosts to create an environment where these differing voices can be heard in the spirit of collaborative research rather than pointless antagonism.

> TIP
> Make Game Nights comfortable, safe, and playful.

It is also important that Game Nights have a playful atmosphere, since games are supposed to be, after all, fun. In our view, examining games as artifacts automatically introduces the problem that the games are being taken out of context: it's not responsible scholarship, nor is it fair to a computer game and its developers, to remove the game from all the conditions that it was designed to be experienced in and critique it. Although the nature of this work does necessitate removing some of those conditions—playing single-player games as a group, or allowing participants to play a game for only short periods of time, for example—the Content Cohosts can work to maintain the most important aspect of gameplay, namely, that it should be fun. Serving food and beverages, encouraging people to be spontaneous in their responses, and even just energetically calling out "Have fun!" all serve to give the research environment a partylike atmosphere. It is no coincidence that our very best Game Nights from a scholarly perspective are also those that are the most fun.

> TIP
> It is important for Content Cohosts to know that this playful atmosphere can occasionally give participants a false impression about the nature of Game Night. New participants in particular are likely to think of Game Night as a party and may begin to act in ways inappropriate for a research project: inviting unscreened guests, carrying on conversations in the midst of the evening, or arriving late, for example. Content Cohosts can reduce the frequency of such misapprehensions by reminding participants at each Game Night that despite appearances it is a research project. They can also take care to introduce new participants to the project's general protocols prior to the first Game Night they attend.

Beyond the construction of a Game Night's atmosphere, the Content Cohosts must also plan each Game Night's events, direction, and purpose; this is a considerable amount of work and is the primary reason why we recommend that there be *two* Cohosts. There are many ways in which these responsibilities may be addressed. In LGI, for instance, we have had success both with choosing all the events of an evening ourselves—from selecting the game to directing the discussions of that game—and with allowing the participants to be somewhat self-directive—allowing them to choose a game or theme on which a Game Night will focus. In general, we suggest that in its earliest stages a Game Night project be firmly directed by the Content Cohosts and as the participants become comfortable with each other and with the protocols of the research, some of the project's direction be ceded to them.

> TIP
> Once a good rapport has been established in the group, occasionally consult with the participants in content decisions.

Technical Cohost

No matter how well-organized the Content Cohosts are, it will be difficult for them to both plan Game Night and handle all the set-up details. LGI is incredibly fortunate to have found an excellent Technical Cohost—Jeffrey Reed—for its very first Game Night, and he has saved Game Night at least once every time we have met. Computer games have always been notoriously idiosyncratic applications that often require a rare combination of a hacker's knowledge of operating systems, an engineer's supremely methodical mind, and the creativity of a wacky inventor in order to get them installed and running. The technical complexity of a Game Night can be complicated even further if the selected game is network based. For all of these reasons, finding a good Technical Cohost is crucial to the success of a Game Night project.

The work of the Technical Cohost primarily involves installing each Game Night's games and uninstalling them when they are no longer needed, as well as consulting with the other Cohosts about the problems and possibilities that may be encountered when trying to examine particular games in a particular event facility. Ideally, the Technical Cohost will have some prior expertise in installing and running computer games, and in the best of all possible worlds will also proudly lay claim to a title like "Game Geek" or "Hardcore Gamer." A Technical Cohost with this range of skills and knowledge will naturally emerge as a co-leader in a Game Night project, because the Content Cohosts and participants alike will frequently want to call upon her or his expertise.[2]

> TIP
> Find a Technical Cohost who is not only knowledgeable about installing and running games that have a variety of system requirements but who also loves to play them.

Participants

The goal of our first few Game Nights was to determine how the analytical tools of disciplines across a university campus could be used for the critique of games. We therefore arranged for the participation of a group of scholars representing a wide range of disciplinary interests from psychology, media arts, rhetoric, comparative and cross-cultural studies, computer science, computer engineering, family studies, anthropology, history, and philosophy to name a few. We also invited several professional software developers from the area to attend so that we would have input from people who had an intimate familiarity with the harsh practicalities of building complex computer applications.

Rapport among participants is as important as interdisciplinarity in a Game Night project. Because in the examination of computer games many issues arise that may be uncomfortable to discuss in an open forum, participants should be selected who are generally comfortable talking openly about subjects that are typically considered controversial, sensitive, provocative, offensive, or emotionally charged. Both the Cohosts and the event facilities will influence how comfortable the participants are able to be during Game Night, but a great deal of a Game Night's success also depends on the "chemistry" of its participants.

It's difficult to provide techniques for engineering such chemistry, but we can offer two pieces of advice that we have found useful ourselves: (1) choose people who are open to the idea that computer games might have some redeeming qualities, and (2) choose people who work well in groups. The first piece of advice should not be construed to mean that only game devotees should be invited—some of our best participants are skeptical about the social value of computer games. Rather, we have found that people who are simply close-minded about computer games (people, for example, who openly profess to "know" that computer games warp players' minds or that, conversely, they are completely harmless) often work to make Game Night discussions argumentative instead of exploratory. The second piece of advice is important for the simple reason that Game Nights tend to be highly collaborative: gameplay often occurs in groups of two or three, and discussions typically emerge out of the entire collective. Loners, in our experience, isolate themselves in the evening's game, resist participating in group activities, refuse (subtly) to share workstations with other participants, and distance themselves from participation in discussions; such behaviors are at least unhelpful and at most disruptive to a Game Night's proceedings.

In addition to these two pointers for selecting participants, we also offer the following list of participant "types," all of which we have found very able to offer intriguing insights at the Game Nights we have run:

Social workers	Religious leaders
Youth leaders	Kids of all ages
Parents/grandparents/guardians	Mental health workers
Teachers from all educational levels	Visual artists (fine and commercial)
Musicians	Law enforcement officers
Military personnel	Animators/illustrators
Medical professionals	Legal professionals
Athletes	Businesspeople
Community/political activists	Politicians

Ideally, the participants should represent, as fully as possible, the diversity of the community where the Game Night is being held. This is not to say that participants should be expected to somehow "represent" a particular trait that they themselves carry (e.g., a seventy-year-old participant should not be expected to speak for all elderly people or to concentrate his or her critical remarks on issues of age in a game); the purpose of having a diverse group of participants is to increase the likelihood that their contributed thoughts will provide a broad analysis of the problems and possibilities of computer games that are circulated in a diverse society.

In the list that follows, we offer some additional observations about Game Night participants that Cohosts may find helpful to think about and plan for.

Things to Know about Game Night Participants

- Participants will have different, and often unpredictable, game preferences, experiences, and responses to the content you provide. You may want to record some of these differences early on so that you can use them to help plan later Game Nights.

- Cliques may form around player ability or familiarity with game genres: beginners will often band together, as will hard-core gamers. You may want to work to break up these cliques, or you may want to use them somehow.
- Participants' commitment levels, comfort, and willingness to contribute to a Game Night's activities may be unequal. You may want to imagine ways of changing or adapting to this.
- The timing and pacing of Game Night is challenging, partly because the technologies aren't predictable, but mainly because participants tend to get very involved in their thoughtful play. While ending interesting analyses and exercises can be a bit awkward and disappointing, this is usually a better alternative than forsaking your plan. Use the feeling of abbreviated eagerness to generate interest in subsequent Game Nights.
- Some participants will immediately grasp the fundamentals of a game's play (its logic, controls, interface, etc.), while others will need to be taught or coached. Try to design exercises around this fact so that all participants will be able to contribute to the discussion equally.
- Due to the engrossing nature of many computer games, it is often difficult for participants to play a game and then to reflect on that experience afterward. Consider using teams in exercises that require such reflection, so that as one person plays, the other person can take notes. Be sure to have team members take turns playing and taking notes, and don't forget to allow for the time it will take for them to switch places, reload the game, etc.
- Related to the item above, observers and note takers have a tendency to help players along. Be sure to let participants know if this is acceptable or not.
- Some participants will find it frustrating to be asked to stop playing in the middle of a game. Consider warning them that you will be doing this, or try to design exercises around this fact.
- Participants who are familiar with each other or with the evening's focus game may be disruptive. Plan ways to address this if necessary. Also, think about whether or not it will be okay for experienced players to advise inexperienced players.
- The amount of time that participants are allowed or required to play a game can make a significant difference in how they respond to it. Try to allow participants enough time, therefore, to develop the kinds

of responses you would like them to discuss. In some cases you may be able to address this challenge by having participants start a game in mid-play or at selected points along the narrative.

- Again, due to the compelling quality of some games, participants may need to be reminded occasionally that the goal of Game Night is critique, not finishing a level or getting the highest score.
- When participants are immersed in a game, they can easily become unaware of their surroundings and forget the instructions you have given them. Consider reminding them periodically during the play time about what you have asked them to be watching for and thinking about.
- Participants tend to get vocal when they get frustrated with a game. This can be a useful sign for Cohosts to attend to.
- Participants familiar with one game genre may try to map that genre's conventions onto other genres. This can have both interesting and confusing consequences.

> TIP
>
> Select participants who will actively and earnestly engage with the Game Night project, who reflect the diversity of the community, and who are willing and able to be flexible about the unusual expectations of semiformal computer game studies.

Event Facilities

The space where Game Night happens can have a dramatic effect on the event's success. There are dozens of factors involving the event facilities that can make or break a Game Night, and while we can't detail them all here, we can point out the most influential ones (in our experience, at least) for your consideration as you organize your own Game Night. We have divided these factors into two general categories: Space Considerations and Setup Considerations. The first category addresses matters that are essentially unchangeable by the Game Night Cohosts because they involve geographic and architectural features. The second category addresses matters that typically can be changed—with enough planning—by the Cohosts.

Space Considerations

When planning a Game Night, imagine your participants' experiences of the evening from the moment they leave their homes to the moment they return. As you imagine these experiences, make notes about possible problems participants may encounter, and work to alleviate as many of them as possible. Below is a list of some of the most common problems we've discovered, but there are many others that may be specific to your community.

- What will traffic be like when participants leave for and depart from Game Night? Can you schedule around high-traffic times and/or help people coordinate ride sharing and public transportation opportunities?
- Will people be able to park their vehicles easily, inexpensively, and safely near the room where Game Night will be held? If you expect some participants to bike to the event, are there bike racks available?
- If your event will be held after dark or in a crime-ridden area, can you work to ensure that people can make it to and from their vehicles safely? For example, can you encourage people to travel in groups and in well-lit areas?
- Will participants need to climb stairs in order to get to Game Night? Some older adults find stairs difficult to navigate, as do people who use crutches, braces, and wheelchairs. Is there a working elevator they can use, and can you provide them with clear directions to it? Is it operable during the hours you have set for Game Night?
- Are there bathrooms near the Game Night space, and are they unlocked during your event's scheduled time? Are they clean and well stocked with tissue and towels?
- If any of your participants will be bringing babies, are there places where diapers may be conveniently changed? If the need arises, is there a private area where a mother may breast-feed her infant?
- If any of your participants are bringing children who will not themselves be participants in Game Night, are there any child-care facilities on the premises? If not, can you arrange for someone to take on some child-care responsibilities in a nearby room?
- Will the room you've selected for Game Night comfortably accommodate all the participants you've invited?
- Will the Game Night room allow all the participants to have their own workstation? If not, how will you design the evening's events so that this obstacle will be overcome?
- If some of your participants use wheelchairs, are there enough ADA-compliant workstations in the space for them to use?
- Some computer labs and computer classrooms—where Game Nights often take place—have considerable levels of ambient noise gener-

ated by computer equipment and HVAC systems. This kind of noise can make hearing difficult for people with excellent hearing and nearly impossible for people with some hearing loss, even if they use some sort of assistive hearing device (e.g., a hearing aid). Do you need to set up and use some type of microphone and loudspeaker system to circumvent this problem?

- Is there adequate furniture in the room given your plans for the evening? For example, are there enough tables and chairs, and are they in good condition? Remember that your participants will likely be seated for much of the evening, so you want them to be as comfortable as possible while they're there, and you don't want to send them home with backaches or sore feet.

Setup Considerations

Once you know that your participants can comfortably arrive, work, and depart from the Game Night site, you are ready to begin imagining how to set up the more flexible elements of the event. The list below, like the one above, is only partial; you will do well to consider those issues that will be specific to your locale and expectations.

- Are you expecting to serve food and beverages at the Game Night (or allow them to be brought in)? Many computer labs and classrooms have prohibitions against this, but these rules are often negotiable. If you do need to negotiate this allowance, be sure to get the final permission in writing.
- Are you sure the room where you will host Game Night will be unlocked at the time you need it to be? Don't forget to allow for setup time (one or two hours before your participants arrive is usually enough), and be sure to consult with your Technical Cohost about when you need to arrive.
- Do you have enough copies of the game(s) you will be using during the evening? Are they legal? Some game companies will allow temporary copies of their games to be installed on machines for educational and research purposes like Game Night, while others offer good educational discounts for their products; it is worth looking into these opportunities. Also, many games may be downloaded from the Internet as free demos, which are often more than sufficient for the purposes of a Game Night.
- Loading games onto campus computers may require special admin-

istrator privileges. Make sure that you or your Technical Cohost have the necessary access to both local and server drive space.

- Be sure that the games you've selected and the systems you want them to run on are compatible; operating systems (Win 95/98/2000/ME/XP/NT, Mac OS 9/X) frequently cause problems with game setup procedures.
- If you will be using a projector to display a game to a group, be aware that many projectors distort colors. If color is to be an important part of your discussion, ask your Technical Cohost to help you adjust the projection system.
- Since many computer labs and classrooms are not designed to project high-quality sound throughout the room, you may find Game Night discussions about the audio elements of games hindered. Check the quality and loudness of the room's computer speakers to make sure they are powerful enough for everyone in a room to hear the subtleties of music and Foley effects.
- If you intend for all of your participants to play at once on individual workstations, headphones will be necessary to keep noise levels down. (We have found that headphones with volume controls on the wire—not just through the operating system—are much appreciated.)
- Reserving computer rooms for "playing games" can be a challenging project. Start early—it sometimes can take a while to persuade administrators that you are doing legitimate research.
- Some games may require extra equipment to play, such as force-feedback joysticks or trackballs, special video cards, emulators, patch cords, 3-D glasses, etc. Make a list of such items early, and work to obtain them well in advance of the scheduled Game Night.
- Participants will be both right- and left-handed. Be prepared to reconfigure game controllers, keyboard layouts, and mouse/joystick buttons accordingly.
- Viewing or playing games on a large screen often invokes different responses from participants than when they play on small screens. Among these different responses are perceptual ones, such as exaggerated attention to particular elements of the screen, and physiological responses, such as increased incidence of nausea (motion sickness) and seizures (epilepsy). In general, it is a good idea to announce the possible existence of these differences and suggest ways that participants can avoid or counteract them.
- Some games may be made more or less effective by the addition of

ambient lighting and audio material in the play space. Playing through horror- or suspense-filled games in a darkened room may enhance the tension of the game, for example, while playing an audio CD of one's own choosing while playing a driving game may enhance one's feeling of immersion. Use whatever means are at your disposal to enhance and control your Game Nights.

> TIP
> Find facilities and staffers who will support you, even if only through the provision of space and intellectual validation of the project. Be forewarned that many administrators are reluctant to endorse computer gaming in campus computer spaces, and know that it might take some memo writing and legwork to get the necessary permissions to hold a Game Night on your campus. Also, be aware that under certain conditions some people can be made physically ill (nausea and seizures) by computer games; announce this fact and provide suggestions for how these situations may be avoided.

Content

There are a variety of ways to choose the content for your Game Nights: themes, genres, popularity, and audience are all viable options. We offer below an extensive list of these and other such options, but we recommend that you make your decision while keeping this very pragmatic question in mind: Will the game run on the technology available in the space where your group will meet? Spending several hours planning a Game Night only to discover that your featured game has requirements in excess of the equipment you have available is sure to be frustrating; this is an excellent reason to include the Technical Cohost in all planning discussions. When the LGI Cohosts deliberate about what content to bring to our Game Nights, we try to have in front of us a list of the available resources in the space where we plan to meet, and we consult that list frequently as we review our options. The list below describes the kinds of themes, topics, and lines of inquiry with which LGI has had success. Each of the list's items could be explored as it relates to the grammar of games described in this book, or it may be treated independently or put into another critical context. The list is by no means comprehensive, and we strongly encourage other Game Night organizers to invent and try out others. When you find ideas that are particularly effective, let us know!

Ways to Examine Computer Games

- Gender
- Violence
    - Through a variety of channels (e.g., images, music, sounds, narrative)
    - Purpose in game
- Perspective
    - 1st/2nd/3rd person
    - Avatar's role type
- Playability
- Addictiveness
- Immersiveness
    - Positive/Negative effects
    - Hypnotic effects
- Realism
- Genre
    - Visual
    - Thematic
    - Technical
    - Producing company's tendencies
- Appeal
    - Mass
    - Cognitive
- Who likes to play the game?
    - Why do these people like to play the game?
- Artificial intelligence
- Theology/philosophy
- Narrative
- Context of the game
    - Socioeconomic/Cultural
- Voyeurism
- Physics
- Ethnic and racial formations
- Brand loyalty
- Pop culture
- Voice
- Audience
- Puzzles/Challenges
- Usability
- Characters who inhabit the game (stereotypes)
- Music and sounds
    - Diegetic/nondiegetic/extradiegetic (See Wolf)
- Input channels
- Novelty
- Representation of the Other/foreigners
- Instructive elements
- What constitutes satisfaction in the game?
- Developmental/psychological models that underpin the game
- Performance characteristics of weapons
- Level of detail
- Interface
- Balance of realism and fun
- Sequencing of the game
- Intertextuality
- Multigenre crossover
- Role of repetition
- Economies
    - Death
    - Time/Space
    - Rewards
    - Success/Failure
    - Material
    - Use and exchange values
- Comparison to different platforms
    - Arcade
    - Console
    - OS
    - Handheld
- Contextualized verisimilitude

Another approach to thematizing Game Night is to group the elements above into larger categories of critique. As an example, we have listed below ten sets of such categories that could contain all of the above elements. These categories could then become foci of individual Game Nights, becoming a sort of curriculum for game study. The above list, of course, can be grouped in any number of ways to create many more than ten categories. We offer these ten solely as examples to indicate how these elements can be grouped to facilitate additional game study approaches. In the table below, the "Examples" column lists some of the features that could be grouped in each category. For example, if we wanted to examine a game according to its "psychological elements," we might look specifically at the ways violent activity in the game impinges upon player psychology, the set of assumptions that seem to comprise the developers' psychological model of players (or of characters in the game), or those features in the game that seem designed to elicit addictive behavior. We also note that many of the "Examples" could become categories themselves.

Item	Category	Examples
1.	The senses	sight/sound/touch/taste/smell
2.	Social and cultural influences	race/ethnicity/class/gender/profession or work/ritual/religion
3.	Physical traits	dress/facial features/hair color/anthropometrics
4.	Technical features	system requirements/frame rates/palette depth/input devices/storage media/AI
5.	Psychological elements	violence/psychological models/addictiveness/ novelty/immersiveness
6.	Game experience	playability/usability/puzzles/objectives/ challenges/perspective/novelty
7.	Disciplinary conventions	literary/film/tv/sociology/psychology/civil engineering/3-D modeling/audio engineering/ Foley art
8.	Realism	history/accuracy of physics/accuracy of weapons/ accuracy of mechanisms/textures/animation
9.	Genre	visual/thematic/technical/corporate identity/ medium
10.	Industry interests	audience appeal/genre/popularity/aesthetics/ profitability/localization/branding

In some cases, the theme(s) you choose will dictate the games you focus on; in other cases the reverse will be true. No matter how you select the games, however, always consider carefully the impact that the content of the games *could* have on your participants. If a game is particularly violent, racist, misogynist, or is in some other way potentially offensive, think about how you will prepare your participants for that material. In some cases you may want to issue a simple warning. In other cases you may want to preserve the game's shock value but allow for thorough debriefing later. And in still other cases you may want to rethink your selection altogether. This matter is particularly important if some of your participants are young people or are known to be particularly sensitive. If some of your participants are underage, you may well want to obtain permission slips from their guardians and keep them apprised of the content with which their charges will be interacting.

> TIP
> Choose content that is appropriate to your project, while being sensitive to your participants' sensitivities. Offer warnings when necessary, and allow participants plenty of time to process the content with which they have interacted.

Observational Techniques

Depending on what you wish to learn about the computer game complex, the setup of Game Night can be altered to better facilitate your research. For instance, if you are looking at the effects of input/output devices on playability, then either the "over the shoulder" method or the "videotape" method might be the best observational techniques for you to use. If you are investigating graphic representations of cultural issues in games, then the "group watch" method may be best. A good general rule is to think about the kind of data you want to get, then determine the best observational technique to get it. Here are some examples:

Sample Objective	Observational Technique	Description
You want to study the ways participants learn how a game's controls work.	Over the shoulder	One participant plays the game while another takes notes.
You want to study the different ways participants react to a game's content through facial expressions.	Videotape	A participant plays the game while she or he is being videotaped.

You want to study how vocal collaborations emerge during gameplay.	Group play	All participants play the same game at the same time. Talk among players can be controlled or encouraged. Players can be videotaped, or observers can take notes.
You want to study how participants negotiate cooperative and competitive opportunities in first-person shooter games.	Group play—Local Area Network (LAN)	The same as above, but players play with/against each other via a LAN.
You want to study which visual elements of a game are particularly striking to observers rather than to players.	Group watch	The group is shown the game on a large screen and asked to make comments as the game is being controlled by a third party.

One final point about observational techniques that is of the utmost importance for the Cohosts to consider is whether or not the work they are doing falls within the category of "human subjects research." Cohosts of Game Night events are strongly encouraged to familiarize themselves with the protocols of human subject protection, which are outlined on many Web sites and in the book *Protecting Volunteers in Research: A Manual for Investigative Sites* by Cynthia Dunn and Gary Chadwick.

Conclusion

Game Night can be an extraordinarily productive and fun way to investigate how computer games work technically, psychologically, physically, rhetorically, and socioculturally. As computer games and the industries that support them become increasingly influential in societies around the world, it is important that scholars take creative and thoughtful steps to investigate the mechanisms of that influence. Game Night is one such step that the participants in the Learning Games Initiative at the University of Arizona have taken, and with considerable success. The number of conferences, journals, and scholarly anthologies concerning computer games is on the rise, and the emerging field of computer game studies is beginning to be recognized even in the most conservative of educational institutions. Game Nights are an excellent way to familiarize reluctant administrators, anxious educators, and skeptical scholars with the import and relevance of computer game study. They also provide unique opportunities for scholars at all levels to think in complex ways about the work that computer games do. And to scholars already committed to computer game research, Game Night provides an opportunity to further their projects in a collaborative and interdisciplinary environment. It is only through research initiatives such as Game Night that computer games will receive the critical attention that they—and the cultural work they do—deserve.

Checklist for Game Night

To Do
Permission to use room
Permission to eat/drink in room
Send out announcements
Access to room
Access to bathrooms
Order food
Obtain legal use of game(s)
Create agenda that's in keeping with research objectives
Divide up leadership responsibilities

To Bring
Game Night agenda
Original game copy
Copies of game
Game documentation and packaging
Notes from previous Game Night (for distribution)
Extra audio equipment (headphones, speakers, etc.)
Required peripherals (controllers, etc.)
Food
Beverages
Plates, cups, napkins, utensils

Follow-up
Transcribe notes
Prepare notes for distribution
Discuss options for the next Game Night

Appendix E
Glossary

Agent: Any person or organization that participates in an exchange of rhetorical events. See also Developer; Reviewer/Marketer; Player; Avatar; Virtual Agent.

Antagonistic Contradiction: A form of struggle that is closed off from the changes that dialectic makes possible and therefore can be resolved only by coercion (i.e., force). See also Contradiction; Nonantagonistic Contradiction.

Avatar: The visual persona that people adopt in electronic environments such as computer games or virtual reality worlds. The word comes from Hinduism, where it refers to an incarnate deity. See also Agent; Virtual Agent.

Computer Game: A form of entertainment that depends on the interactions between players and game designers. These interactions are mediated by computer technology, including a variety of peripheral hardware and software interfaces (joysticks, keyboards, buttons, menus, graphics, music, sound effects, force feedback). Consequently, computer games are sensational and generate pschyophysiological responses in players to game designers' predefined stimuli. These stimuli include the central challenges of the game (e.g., scoring baskets, shooting "enemies," finding treasure, negotiating exchanges of goods, exploring a place) as well as the mood of the video, audio, tactile, and olfactory components of the game. Because responding to stimuli in a strategic manner in order to achieve particular goals constitutes learning, computer games may also be said to teach players—through game rules, protocols, constraints, and representations. Computer games are highly rhetorical artifacts.

Computer Game Complex: The totality of the computer game industry, including games, gamers, developers, marketers, parents and guardians of gamers, manufacturers of game-related paraphernalia, and so forth.

Contradiction: A point of struggle in the dialectic where there exist multiple but competing truths about a particular knowledge domain. See also Antagonistic Contradiction; Nonantagonistic Contradiction.

Developer: Anyone responsible for the construction of a computer game, including all of those involved in the actual production of a computer game: writers and level designers, hardware and software engineers, visual artists, and musicians, as well as producers and their staff, who typically work to fund the game development process. See also Agent.

Dialectic: An existential state in which there exist an infinite number of contradictions and competing interests. It is the nature of all being and materiality marked by an ongoing involvement in an endless process of struggle and change. It is given motion by rhetoric. See also Rhetoric; Metanoia; Transformative Locale.

Dialectical Analysis/Inquiry ("Dialectics"): Any attempt to locate and understand the reasons for specific struggles and changes that are occurring at a particular point within the dialectic. See also Rhetorico-Dialectical Analysis.

Discourse: Any mode of communication, irrespective of its dependence on an alphabet and explicit rules of syntax and grammar. Thus, a gang symbol that tags the side of a building constitutes discourse among the members of the gang to which the symbol belongs (e.g., "you're in home territory"), among rival gang members (e.g., "you're not in home territory"), and among nongang members (e.g., "there are gangs in this neighborhood").

Eluctable Rhetorical Event: A rhetorical event that is offered by its creator in the spirit of ongoing struggle toward the resolution of a contradiction. Eluctable rhetorical events always engage the struggle, unlike ineluctable rhetorical events, which always refuse the struggle. See also Rhetorical Event; Ineluctable Rhetorical Event.

Functions of Rhetoric, Exigent/Interventional: The management of meaning in instances that are explicitly suasory.

Functions of Rhetoric, Implicative/Conditional: The management of meaning at the largely unconscious level of common sense.

Functions of Rhetoric, Quotidian/Appropriational: The management of meaning in instances that affect everyday decisions.

Game: A form of entertainment that relies on engaging in a challenge or competition. Games always teach multiple things to multiple audiences. See also Play; Computer Game.

Gameplay: That quality of a game that derives from the unique combination of (a) the designers' demands on the player that are expressed through the full range of possible actions built into the game, especially its rules, graphics, sounds, and feedback mechanisms; (b) the game's *original* physical interface; (c) the techniques by which the designers implement strategies to capture the attention of players. See also Playability.

Homologous Ideology: The unique set of assumptions, rules, and constraints that determine how a community makes meaning out of its collective experiences. Homologous ideologies (or "homologies") influence both idiosyncratic and inclusive ideologies. See also Metanoia; Ideology; Idiosyncratic Ideology; Inclusive Ideology; Transformative Locale.

Homology: See Homologous Ideology.

Ideology: The set of assumptions, rules, and constraints that determine how meaning is made. See also Dialectic; Rhetoric; Homologous Ideology; Idiosyncratic Ideology; Inclusive Ideology; Transformative Locale.

Idiosyncratic Ideology: The unique set of assumptions, rules, and constraints that determine how an individual makes meaning out of his or her experiences. Idiosyncratic ideology is not completely idiosyncratic; many—perhaps even most—of the assumptions, rules, and constraints that determine meaning-making are learned from others in the community and then naturalized to the point of becoming "common sense." See also Metanoia; Ideology; Homologous Ideology; Inclusive Ideology; Transformative Locale.

Inclusive Ideology: Ideology held at the societal level and that influences idiosyncratic and homologous ideologies. It is comprised of the set of assumptions, rules, and constraints on meaning-making that operate across homological boundaries. See also Metanoia; Ideology; Homologous Ideology; Idiosyncratic Ideology; Transformative Locale.

Ineluctable Rhetorical Event: A rhetorical event that is offered by its creator in the spirit of a conviction in an abiding resolution. Ineluctable rhetorical events always refuse the struggle, even though they are entangled in it. Consequently, ineluctable rhetorical events have the effect of locally stabilizing the dialectic, essentially making dialectic nondialectical—at least from the position of the creator of the ineluctable rhetorical event. See also Rhetorical Event; Eluctable Rhetorical Event.

Influences: Forces that define a rhetorical event's context and content.

Influences, Economic Forces: Influential phenomena within the dialectic that affect how values are assigned, exchanged, and negotiated.

Influences, Instructional Forces: Influential phenomena within the dialectic that have specifically educational effects.

Influences, Mass Culture: Influential voluntary experiences that are generated by a few specialists for consumption by thousands (or more) and at a profit. See also Influences, Mass Media.

Influences, Mass Media: Communication channels acting influentially within the dialectic that tend to be one-way, originate with a few and are distributed to many (millions), offer minimal opportunities for feedback, are easy to disengage compared to a live interlocutor (i.e., it's easier to put down the newspaper or turn off the TV than to switch off a person), reach audiences quickly, and can have the effect of giving or changing knowledge in the audience (Rogers 193). See also Influences, Mass Culture.

Influences, Psychophysiological Forces: Influential phenomena within the dialectic that directly affect the body and mind.

Manifestations: The form that rhetorical events are given in the context of a dialectical struggle. See also Manifestation: Representation, Interaction, Conflict, Safety.

Manifestation, Conflict: The manifestation of rhetorical events in codes designed to establish, maintain, and resolve struggles among contending forces.

Manifestation, Interaction: The manifestation of rhetorical events in codes designed to evoke feedback-driven participation.

Manifestation, Representation: The manifestation of rhetorical events in codes designed to represent "reality," including virtual or fantasy reality.

Manifestation, Safety: The manifestation of rhetorical events in codes designed to ensure, diminish, or mask harmful effects.

Marketer/Reviewer: Anyone responsible for motivating others to consider obtaining and installing games in players' computers. In addition to advertisers who write copy, design packaging, and sell the product on their store shelves, this term also designates those involved in the distribution process, including logistics experts who figure out the best way to get the product from the factory to the store or the customer, all of the people responsible for carrying out the logistics experts' plans—including office staff, truck drivers, and system administrators—and corporate identity consultants who help keep new product developments in line with a (sometimes) well-crafted public image. See also Agent.

Metanoia: A transformation—a changing of the mind, great or small—that occurs when rhetorical events cause someone to see the world in a different way. See also Metanoetic Experience; Transformative Locales; Idiosyncratic Ideology; Homologous Ideology; Inclusive Ideology; Dialectic; Rhetoric.

Metanoetic Experience: The experience of seeing a dialectical contradiction in a different way. A moment when a struggle resolves into something new but with characteristics of the old. Metanoetic experiences take place in three different ideological contexts (transformative locales): idiosyncratic (personal), homologous (communal), and inclusive (societal). See Metanoia; Transformative Locales; Idiosyncratic Ideology; Homologous Ideology; Inclusive Ideology.

Nonantagonistic Contradiction: A form of struggle that is open to the changes of the dialectic. See also Contradiction; Antagonistic Contradiction.

Play: The occupation of one's time by activities generally deemed unproductive, amusing, and enjoyable. Play is often subtly but powerfully instructive. See also Game; Computer Game.

Playability: A subjective evaluation of how engaging a game is. Most fans of first-person shooter games, for example, find *Halo* to have a high level of playability. Players who do not like first-person shooters, however, might rate *Halo*'s playability as very low if they were evaluating it according to criteria more appropriate to strategy games. See also Gameplay.

Player: Anyone who plays computer games, from those who exclusively use one gaming medium (arcade, console, desktop computer, handheld) or who play only one genre of game (shooters, puzzles, strategy, sports), to those who enjoy a variety of genres and will play games anywhere. See also Agent.

RFU adapter: A device that connects a console game system (e.g., PlayStation 2) to a TV that has no external A/V connectors. RFU stands for Radio Frequency Unit.

Rhetoric: That set of ideologically determined meaning-making events that have the consequence or are intended to have the consequence of creating or prohibiting metanoetic (i.e., transformative) experiences.

Rhetorical Analysis: Any attempt to examine and understand how ideologically determined meaning-making events have been articulated such that they come to generate or prohibit metanoetic experiences. See also Rhetorico-Dialectical Analysis.

Rhetorical Event: Any component of an ideologically determined meaning-making phenomenon. A strand in the web of the dialectic. See also Ineluctable Rhetorical Event; Eluctable Rhetorical Event.

Rhetorical Method: A collection of analytical techniques and strategies that are unified by a guiding philosophical principle. For example, the philosophical principle informing *Game Work* is dialectic.

Rhetorico-Dialectical Analysis: Any attempt to facilitate an understanding of the dialectic specifically through the use of rhetorical analysis. See also Dialectical Analysis; Rhetorical Analysis.

Splining: A technique for generating the path that a game's virtual camera follows using only a few static coordinates.

Transformative Locales: The three different ideological contexts within which metanoias occur. These contexts are idiosyncratic (personal), homologous (communal), and inclusive (societal). See also Metanoetic Experience; Metanoia; Idiosyncratic Ideology; Homologous Ideology; Inclusive Ideology.

Virtual Agent: An electronically produced agent that exercises no independent control within the electronic environment themselves, because they are always responding to some combination of the players' directions and the programmers' instructions. See Agent; Avatar.

Voxel: An informational unit describing a point in three-dimensional space. The starting point for any given polygon in a 3-D game, for example, is indicated with *x*, *y*, and *z* coordinates, which together are known as a "voxel." Short for "volume pixel."

Notes

Preface

1. I prefer "computer game" to "video game" as the generic term for the subject of this book because it more accurately describes the central technology that enables the medium. Video is surely important for computer games, but it is not their only defining characteristic. Games also depend on audio, tactile, and other aesthetic elements to give them life, and indeed some computer games—designed for visually impaired people—have no video content at all.

2. Thierry Kuntzel has made similar arguments about "film-work." See also Ruggill, McAllister, and Menchaca.

Chapter 1

1. As will be discussed in chapters 4 and 5, the marketing and consumption of computer games are attended by similarly opaque signs.

2. Perhaps the greatest indicator of Sonic's popularity is that it became the namesake for an important, but relatively obscure, genetic protein that determines, among other things, the orientation of a body's limbs (e.g., the spine runs vertically, not horizontally). See Stix.

3. In reality, dozens of people have usually been involved in getting a game from the designers' workstations to consumers, including packagers, loaders, truckers, and stockers. These people, however, are only marginally involved in the design of the computer applications they handle and so—for Ohmann, at least—do not figure into his understanding of "mass culture." From the point of view of the "work" of game production, however, all the people who have peripheral roles to the game development process are still crucial to the phenomenon of game popularization. See Ruggill, McAllister, and Menchaca.

4. I will discuss these "strangers" at length in chapter 3.

5. Chapters 3 and 5 will deal with these issues in detail.

6. There also exists a small but growing niche market for current events games, such as those produced by Kuma Reality Games (KRG). KRG builds games rapidly and cheaply, drawing their design inspiration from "Headline News" on CNN. For example, recent titles have reproduced the hunt for Saddam Hussein, rescue missions in North Korea, and tactical battles in Afghanistan. See http://www.kumarealitygames.com.

7. There is considerable evidence supporting this claim, although it should be noted that there is a variety of explanations for it. Much of the research done on the question of how the brain processes images versus other types of information input has been done in the interest of education and instructional technology. See Anglin, Towers, and Levie; Chan Lin; and Molitor, Ballstaedt, and Mandl.

8. Jacques Ellul has observed that one of the main functions of propaganda is to make people believe that restrictions on their human and civil rights are justified and reasonable (*Propaganda: The Formation of Men's Attitudes*). Noam Chomsky makes a similar point in his book *Necessary Illusions: Thought Control in Democratic Societies,* observing that the greatest challenge for propagandists is not to persuade people to think in new ways but rather to persuade people to appreciate their bondage. Chomsky writes that one of the great success stories of democratic U.S. propaganda is that it has worked to make many people see doctrines that define the conditions for what is reasonably thinkable not as constraining but as evidence "that freedom reigns" (48). The ways this process plays out in computer games are discussed in later chapters.

9. There is some debate over this claim due to the different ways in which the two industries calculate their net gains. The fact that such debate exists, however, suggests that the two figures are comparable and that arguments over which is higher say more about the interests of the disputers than about the industries themselves.

10. There also exists a micro genre of fiction in the online fan community that puts computer game characters into romantic, which is to say sexual, situations. *Tomb Raider*'s Lara Croft appears in many of these stories, as does Gabriel Knight from the game series of the same name. Several Web sites exist that specialize in archiving computer game fan fiction, including "A Quest for Fanfic" (http://www.socalbrand.com/quest).

11. The desktop themes and screensavers, it may be argued, also allow players to subvert the guiding business metaphor of the most common operating systems into one of fantasy and play.

12. See Palumbo.

13. For example, see the U.S. Army's recruiting game *America's Army.* Available at http://www.goarmy.com/aagame.

14. One particularly notable example of this is the Liemandt Foundation's recent "Hidden Agenda" contest that will award $25,000 to an undergraduate who designs

a game that's "so fun . . . that [kids] don't notice it's also teaching them something." See http://www.hiddenagenda.com.

Chapter 2

1. For an excellent detailed treatment of dialectical inquiry, see Bertell Ollman's *Dialectical Investigations.*

2. Some additional definition is required here, since "eluctable" and "ineluctable" verge on the neologistic. The Latin word *luctare* means "struggle" and today exists most prominently in the word "reluctant"—tending away from struggle. Putting the prefix "e" before it suggests "movement toward": e + *luctare* = moving toward struggle. Adding the movement-stopping prefix "in" before "eluctare" gives us the sense of resisting any motion toward struggle. Unlike "re-luctance," where the struggle is actively avoided, "in-e-luctance" is static. In terms of rhetoric, then, *eluctable rhetorical events* would be those that are offered by their creators in the spirit of ongoing struggle toward the resolution of a contradiction. *Ineluctable rhetorical events,* on the other hand, would be those that are offered by their creators in the spirit of a conviction (con + *vincere* = completely conquered) in an abiding (a + *biden* = solidly remaining) resolution. While eluctable rhetorical events always engage the struggle, ineluctable rhetorical events always refuse the struggle, even though they are entangled in it. Consequently, ineluctable rhetorical events have the effect of locally stabilizing the dialectic, essentially making dialectic nondialectical—at least from the position of the creator of the ineluctable rhetorical event.

3. Examples of such nondialectical rhetorical analyses would include those directed by other guiding concepts or methods, such as ethnographic rhetorical analyses, gender-oriented rhetorical analyses, techno-rhetorical analyses, and visual rhetorical analyses. It is also important to note that a rhetorical analysis not specifically directed toward the clarification of the dialectic does not exclude it from the dialectic, from which nothing is excluded.

4. Although I reduce "consumers" here to "players," this is only shorthand for "players and all those who sustain the game industry in ways other than development and distribution."

5. An additional consequence of such a dialectical inquiry is that in identifying and explaining a particular struggle, the critic simultaneously contributes to the dialectic and creates a metanoetic moment within which the struggle and the critic are both epistemologically changed.

6. In comparison to Johan Huizinga's work in *Homo Ludens,* the examples of "play" offered here just scratch the surface. Huizinga documents hundreds of uses of the term "play" and its many lemmas and derivatives and tracks them through a dozen or more ancient and modern languages from cultures scattered all over the globe.

7. Crawford suggests that this will change as games—specifically computer

games—become more sophisticated and are designed to be more adaptive to players' personalities. The game *Black & White,* which I discuss at length in chapter 5, is an example of this, as are most massively multiplayer online games. It is also interesting to note that computer games are increasingly being packaged with action figures of characters from the game, a phenomenon that creates a blend of play types that is currently unexplored in the scholarly literature.

8. Examples of such games include *Jack Attack, Jack Attack 2,* and *Pikmin.* Paradoxically, Friedl observes that one recent trend in cooperative computer gaming "lies in employing cooperation and negotiation as the conflict itself; more specifically, embedding alternative cooperation in a player's decision-making processes [involves] both an interpersonal conflict and inner one" (248).

9. This definition has also been attributed to Reynolds's coworker at Firaxis Games, Sid Meier. See Rollings and Morris 38.

10. While these dichotomies are debatable (Isn't justice attained through certain victories? Don't these characteristics of what gets privileged over other characteristics only reinforce the stereotypes that boys are one way and girls are the other?), it seems to me relatively pedantic to do so. It's true that computer games are often sexist (even misogynistic), racist, ageist, sizist, homophobic, violent, gratuitously sexually provocative, and encouraging of narcissistic values, including the accumulation of material wealth and power. Just like every other form of mass media, they deserve to be critiqued as such.

11. In his book *The Interpretation of Cultures,* Geertz writes: "Believing, with Max Weber, that man is an animal suspended in webs of significance he himself has spun, I take culture to be those webs, and the analysis of it to be therefore not an experimental science in search of law but an interpretive one in search of meaning" (5).

12. Or as Kellner puts it: "Cultural studies is thus not just another academic fad, but can be a part of a struggle for a better society and a better life" (39).

13. In *A Grammar of Motives,* Kenneth Burke writes: "it is by reason of the pliancy among our terms that philosophic systems can pull one way and another. The margins of overlap provide opportunities whereby a thinker can go without a leap from any one of the terms to any of its fellows" (xxii). Burke exemplifies this pliancy among his grammar's terms with a metaphor: "We have also likened the terms to the fingers, which in their extremities are distinct from one another, but merge in the palm of the hand. If you would go from one finger to another without a leap, you need but trace the tendon down into the palm of the hand, and then trace a new course along another tendon" (xxii).

14. Burke notes that such a "unique path" may fairly be called a "philosophy": "Speaking broadly we could designate as 'philosophies' any statements in which these grammatical resources [i.e., terms] are specifically utilized" (xvi).

15. Burke puts it this way: "what we want is *not terms that avoid ambiguity,* but *terms that clearly reveal the strategic spots at which ambiguities necessarily arise*" (xviii, emphasis in original). Similarly, in his eleventh thesis on Feuerbach, Marx observed

that "The philosophers have only interpreted the world in various ways; the point is to change it" (15).

16. George Kennedy argues that even animals can be rhetorical agents, and some critics ascribe so much influential power to objects that they come to function as agents (e.g., Ellul, *Technological Society;* Winner).

17. This definition is, for example, instrumentalist and doesn't take into consideration the social dynamic that often transforms the acts of agents in unanticipated ways. For technological instances of this, see Edward Tenner's *Why Things Bite Back.*

18. See, for instance, Adorno's essay in *Prisms* titled "Cultural Criticism and Society," where he writes, "The cultural critic . . . forfeits his legitimation by collaborating with culture as its salaried and honoured nuisance" (20).

19. It is easier, for example, to put down the newspaper or turn off the TV than it is to switch off a person.

20. This is, as I noted in the previous chapter, a contentious claim, and equally reputable empirical grounds exist on both sides.

21. In addition to the sources listed in the "Psychophysiological Influences" section of chapter 1, readers may also see for examples Burgoon, Bonito, Bengtsson, et al.; Friedl; and Schank.

22. For examples, see the sources listed in the "Psychophysiological Influences" section of chapter 1.

23. There are many excellent sources that address localization issues. See, for example, Vanka; Dowling.

24. The Gabriel Knight series of computer games is an excellent example of the ability of games to be educational without ever being promoted as such. Players of these games learn a considerable amount of history, for example, of New Orleans, of Germany, and of the folklore about lycanthropy.

25. It is no secret that game designers make all sorts of decisions about what and what not to include in a game world in order to improve its "playability." Crawford observed as early as 1984 that games offer a "subset of reality" that is actually quite unrealistic. He notes, for example, "The inclusion of technical details of flying would distract most players from the other aspects of the [flying] game" (6).

26. Actually, as of late 2003 this trend seems to be dying out, perhaps because the standard picture of game developers still tends to be dominated by young men of European extraction, a fact that holds little currency for marketers eager to expand the demographic of computer games.

27. It is also worth noting that if one were to try to apply this grammar to a subject other than computer games, the types of influences would need to be changed accordingly. While the influences discussed here should be broad enough to use in dialectical rhetorical analyses of a roughly similar vein (i.e., similar to computer gaming), an analysis of, for example, a particular furniture design or architectural style would benefit from examining long-term historical influences and the influential forces of materials science.

28. A "patch" is a small program distributed after the release of a software appli-

cation that corrects newly discovered bugs and, in some instances, adds new features. "Patch priorities" are ranked lists that developers decide upon that dictate which bug fixes and features are added first.

Chapter 3

1. This is the case, at least, in the United States. Other countries, such as England, Scotland, and Korea, still have strong independent computer game development companies.

2. Consider, for example, Ernest Adams's "Dogma 2001: A Challenge to Game Designers," which is based on a 1998 Independent Filmmakers' manifesto.

3. PC Data, Inc., for *Wired* (May 2001), 151. TRSTS Data, another industry analysis firm, ranks the top four games differently: *Pokemon Silver, Pokemon Gold, Pokemon Yellow, Pokemon Stadium* (*Interactive Entertainment Industry Overview* 20). Differences among such companies are common and reflect the different ways in which each market analysis company defines "top-selling."

4. Paul Provenzano, president of the Interactive Entertainment Academy, in a talk at the Electronic Entertainment Expo in Los Angeles, May 16, 2001.

5. Significantly, the sixth best-selling game of 2003 was *Grand Theft Auto: Vice City*, a title that was actually released in 2002 but that received an astonishing amount of publicity—most of it condemnatory—throughout 2003. The game's singular position in the upper reaches of 2003's annual game sales suggests that there is considerable truth in the adage "There's no such thing as bad publicity."

6. For example, the July 26, 2000, edition of the *Arizona Daily Star* announced "4 Health Groups Link Media Mayhem to Violence by Kids." The four groups are the American Medical Association, the American Academy of Pediatrics, the American Psychological Association, and the American Academy of Child and Adolescent Psychiatry (A6). See also the "Joint Statement on the Impact of Entertainment Violence on Children."

7. The question of what constitutes this mask is arguable. It seems likely to me that it involves some combination of conditional rhetoric determining one's reception of the meaning-making answer to a request for help and some psychological response brought on by the anxiety and frustration of not knowing how to resolve a pressing problem for oneself. Imagine the difficulties of someone who, in the face of being completely lost in unfamiliar territory still could not bring him- or herself to trust the directions of a local inhabitant any more than a used car dealer or overly coiffed infomercial host.

8. In August of 1997, for example, at a development meeting for the game *Deus Ex* (Eidos Interactive), members of the preproduction team argued hotly over which game engine to license. Some members argued that the *WorldCraft* engine, though very expensive, was also the most versatile and advanced—factors that would surely cut production time and help the project ship on schedule. Other members argued that *UnrealEd*, an older and less expensive engine, would more than suffice, since

much of the engine's functionality in either case was going to have to be customized for *Deus Ex* anyway. Warren Spector, the project's director, later noted in an essay in *Game Developer* that while he was glad the team had chosen the cheaper engine, it had indeed caused problems when programmers found themselves confused about how the engine actually processed game data (Spector, "Postmortem" 55).

9. In one of many forums for the *Unreal Editor*, for example, a poster writes:

> In UnrealEd 2.0, I am attempting to use the edit vertices mode. While I have no problem moving the vertices around, this always yields BSP holes in my maps, even with relatively simple brushes. All brushes fit perfectly. Additive brushes have been previously deselected, and subtractive brushes intersected, so there is no overlap. I have tried:
> (1) I have set the ORDER of the problem brushes TO LAST.
> (2) Brushes have been TRANSFORMed PERMANENTLY.
> Can anyone recommend another approach?" (Levi)

Four responses were offered, three of which were sent within eight hours.

10. Of course, to those who attend only to the public that voices its opinion through spending, the continued high sales of computer games with "objectionable" content seem to be loud enough to drown out the exigency calling for reform.

11. Game designers keep repetitious sequences "interesting" by making subtle changes to them: opening different doors will sound slightly different, gunshots will echo differently, footsteps will periodically skip a beat. These slight differences are designed to keep the player from becoming annoyed with repetitious sequences and quitting the game, which is to say that these differences are designed not so much to keep players "interested" as to keep them "engaged." See also the glossary entry on *splining*.

12. As I observed in chapter 2, with the exception of the specific ways rhetoric is made manifest in the computer game complex (i.e., the manifestations of rhetoric in representation, interaction, conflict, and safety), all of the other elements of the grammar of gameworks might well be applied to other artifactual analyses.

13. A small percentage of these are duplicate messages that have been sent to several groups simultaneously.

14. About 2 percent of the messages on this list on any given day, for example, are invitations to porn sites.

15. Google.com, an Internet search engine company, recently purchased the newsgroup archive previously owned and managed by Deja.com. This archive contains all newsgroups and all of their messages back to 1981—over 500 million messages. As of this writing, the Google newsgroup archive contained nearly 15,000 messages posted to the comp.games.development.programming.algorithms newsgroup alone.

16. This and all subsequent quotes from Usenet newsgroups are used with the kind permission of their respective authors.

17. This would be the case, for instance, when the gamework analysis is done on discourse that has taken place over a relatively short time span.

18. M. J. Braun astutely observes that very often negotiation and consensus building have the effect of endlessly deferring the resolution of a problem that can be resolved only by the complete replacement of one value system for another. In such instances, when antagonistic rhetoric prevails, the side that wins is often the one that appears the most "rational," a fact that typically puts at a great disadvantage those whose rhetorical tactics are constructed out of generally less respected rationales of emotion, universal equity, and other marginalized logical systems that carry less authority than the Western capitalist values based on enlightenment reasoning.

19. Tharon Howard rightfully observes that despite the recurrence of participants and the principle of helping one's peers that prevails in newsgroups, they are not necessarily "communities." This is due, he says, to another prevailing attitude in newsgroups called by Howard and others "reciprocity," or to put it more colloquially, "you scratch my back and I'll scratch yours." While reciprocity does not necessarily obviate the possibility that a group of people is a community, Howard does note that when remuneration rather than altruism determines people's commitments to each other, the designation "community" is rather questionable (125–30).

20. The insolubility of this antagonism is perhaps why Adams has recently begun to reject the idea of computer game development as an art: "Game design is neither an art nor a science, it is a craft. Computer games are an art form, but they are a collaborative art form in which many people make a contribution. Game design per se is not an art, partly because the designer doesn't really have as much aesthetic freedom as a real artist requires, and partly because it has too many non-aesthetic considerations" (Friedl 399).

21. Some problems may be a part of more than one dialectical struggle, as for instance, when a violent video game is included in the dialectical struggles of the right to freedom of speech and of the impact of media violence on children.

22. Paging through books from each category, one quickly realizes which type is in hand. Amateur books tend to include lots of advice and quotes from famous game developers and contain numerous simple charts describing, for instance, the difference between *xy* and *xyz* space. Professional books tend to contain dozens of mathematical formulae, explanations of state transitions, and diagrams of hardware abstraction layers.

23. Bates writes: "Throughout the book I refer to players, designers, programmers, and everyone else using the pronoun 'he.' I do this strictly for readability of the text. . . . Therefore, with apologies to the many women game-industry professionals and the many more women game-players, I have opted for the less intrusive 'he'" (xxvi). As pathetic as this excuse is, it is to Bates's credit that he even shows cognizance of the problem; none of the other texts even manage that. This, too, is an instance of conditional rhetoric: using the pronoun "he" for girls, boys, men, and women "just makes sense." It is, as Bates says, more "readable" and "less intrusive."

Does this dismissal of the importance of girls and women make it into Bates's games as well as his books? For the most part, yes. Unfortunately, though, this is a criticism that may be leveled at most game developers.

24. *Awesome Game Creation* tempers this advice slightly.

25. The game itself is almost completely devoted to mass culture in that many of the premises for the game's story are taken from currently circulating conspiracy theories, and many of the scenarios are based on visually familiar locations like New York's Battery Park and Hong Kong's shopping district.

26. By noting these design elements, I do not mean to criticize the game; it has one of the most developed and creative narratives in computer games to date. Rather, I mean to show how the art/business contradiction can be worked out in practical business decisions that are calculated to play on preexisting cultural norms in order to influence the publisher's bottom line.

Chapter 4

1. The alt.games newsgroup was created in August 1991. A thread may have multiple messages attached to it.

2. There is a newsgroup for people interested in game art (comp.games.development.art), but even here there are fewer than a dozen threads related to the problems related to being an artist in the industry.

3. A quick review of all the alt.games subgroups (e.g., alt.games.wing-commander, alt.games.quake) shows that the realism/fun issue is frequently discussed among fans and critics of particular games, however.

4. Cheat codes allow players to give themselves advantages in a game. Common codes allow characters to be invincible, to walk through walls, and to have unlimited ammunition. Cheat codes were originally designed for the programmers, who needed ways to test levels and puzzles quickly without bothering with all the game challenges. Later, however, cheats also became a way to manage player frustration, and today there exist many print and online sources where players can download these codes and thus continue their play with relative ease.

5. While the numbers as to how many games are released each year are debatable, the Entertainment Software Association (ESA) and other trade organizations that track computer game sales data all clearly indicate that the number of units sold and the number of titles released are correlative.

6. Consider, for instance, Tom Russo's remark in the editorial column of *Next-Gen* about "the extremely talented, yet widely anonymous game developers" (7). Russo writes: "inside the video game industry, most developers are kept locked away, and many aren't allowed to demo their products to the press or even attend their game's launch party" (7).

7. One element that keeps certain games from becoming as popular as certain movies is that while only thirty to forty movies are released each year, hundreds of

games are released. This means that although the film and game audience numbers are roughly the same, those numbers are spread more thinly over the multitude of games.

8. Henry Jenkins, a media studies professor at MIT and a scholar of the computer game complex, explores these ambiguous research findings in a Salon.com essay and makes the important observation that "Most [studies] found a correlation, not a causal relationship [between media and youth violence], which means they could simply be demonstrating that aggressive people like aggressive entertainment" ("Coming up Next").

9. Another economic force may also loom here: payola. Though rarely spoken of, there are some in the game industry who are "familiar" with the practice of game publishers offering perks to reviewers in exchange for favorable reviews. This topic has been debated energetically at a number of national and international industry conferences.

10. Actually, there are very few innovative games on the market today. The vast majority of recently released games are remakes and rip-offs of previously successful games, usually made on far smaller budgets in far less time than the trend-setting games upon which they are based.

Chapter 5

1. *Black & White* has won dozens of awards in numerous countries, including: Game of the Year (Game Developers' Choice Award), Best Video Game of 2001 (*New York Times* Reviewer's Choice), Best AI of the Year (*PC Gamer*), Game of the Year (Academy of Interactive Arts and Sciences), and was voted "PC Game of the Year" by gamers in Eastern Europe, Italy, Spain, Germany, and Scandinavia. For a more complete list, see http://www2.bwgame.com/bw/AWARDS.

2. This is true insofar as one is able to say that *Black & White* is "about" anything other than playing with a relatively flexible electronic environment. The game can be made to be about a variety of things, in the same way that chess or Go (an ancient Japanese game) may be.

3. To learn more about the details of these AIs, see Richard Evans's "The Future of AI in Games: A Personal View."

4. It is important to note that while economies may be based in immaterialities and abstractions, they always have material consequences.

5. I do not address, in this chapter, consumer-level economies, that is, value assignment systems that impinge upon the price of games, the cost of game development, or the royalty agreements between game authors and publishers. Readers interested in considering economies such as these are directed to chapter 3 and to the numerous Federal Trade Commission and industry reports that have been published on these subjects.

6. Other banners that the villagers can raise indicate their desire for "village expansion," "civic buildings," "protection," and "mercy."

7. Despite the popularity of god-games among people of both genders, Lionhead Studios, like most other computer game companies, persists in the use of sexist terms. See Cassell and Jenkins for an in-depth analysis of this phenomenon.

8. According to the instruction manual that comes packaged with the game: "The key to *Black & White* is taking over the hearts and minds of other tribes and villages. The more believers you have, the more power you get and the greater your Influence will become" (Leach and Lenoël 25).

9. It is worth noting that Peter Molyneux, the lead designer of *Black & White*, is generally credited with inventing the "god-game" genre with his games *Populous* and *Power Monger*, which debuted in the 1980s (cf. deMaria and Wilson 266–67).

10. Keeping track of these statistics is made considerably easier through the use of the game's built-in demographics tool, which keeps a running record of all of these figures.

11. Time in the game passes according to a cycle of days and nights. To the player, one full day passes in about an hour, during which villagers age ten to twelve years. Most villagers "live beyond 75 years of age" (D. Evans 25).

12. A particularly interesting feature of the game is its ability to link to local weather-reporting Web sites. The game will then draw its weather patterns directly from the real world; if it's raining outside the player's house, it will also be raining in the game.

13. In this game, "love" of any sort—eros, agape, philos—among the villagers seems to have been left unvalued. Desire, not love, is the base rule of *Black & White*. Peter Molyneux, *Black & White*'s designer, did talk in the early stages of the game about including the possibility for homosexuality, but it seems not to have made it into the final release (see Baydak). As of this writing, the only contemporary game with a similarly advanced artificial intelligence engine that has modeled and valued these different types of human relationships (including homosexuality) is Maxis' *The Sims*. Even in this game, however, homosexual characters were not part of the original release. Instead, lesbian and gay characters were designed into an add-on module (sold separately) called "Hot Date." This addition to *The Sims* has sparked a horde of new fan sites that detail the often astonishing and controversial activities that take place in the game, as well as new "skins" for the game characters that allow them to look nude, lewd, and tattooed.

14. For a detailed analysis of the different ways time factors into computer game play, see Mark J. P. Wolf's "Time in the Video Game."

15. The term "force" is justified and appropriate here, both as an element of work in the physics sense ("work" is "a force acting through a distance" and "force" is "that which changes, produces, or stops the motion of a body" [Mandel]) and as an element of social coercion. The economy of *Black & White* forces players to move, think, and make sense of reality—computer-mediated and otherwise—in new or different ways.

16. It is unclear if these "values" should be considered "use" values or "exchange" values. On the one hand, the villagers' labor is done for the good of the village and

so cannot be considered a commodity. Because a thing must be a commodity in order to have exchange value, it would seem that the value of natural resources *in the game* should be classified as use value. On the other hand, if villagers engage in worship and discipleship with the expectation that they will somehow be compensated for their effort—in the form of bountiful harvests or divine interventions against marauders—then they are, in effect, working for their god in such a way that their labor has been commodified and would therefore count as having exchange value. Whether the work and labor that agent/players do within the context of a game is use value or exchange value is a question I have investigated elsewhere (see Ruggill, McAllister, and Menchaca).

17. Recall Chris Crawford's claim that too much realism detracts from the fun of a game (5–6), one of the earliest references to an industry contradiction with which developers have to struggle.

18. Survival, of course, is an operative element of how all games mean.

19. Many other games published prior to *Black & White* adopted a godlike stance, some of which were published by major houses like Maxis (the Sim line) and Sierra (*Pharaoh*). But only *Populous,* another Peter Molyneux title from 1989, puts the player specifically in the role of god.

20. A particularly notable example of the research that is beginning to emerge on this subject is Jennifer Diane Reitz's "Playing 'Black & White' from a Historical Theological Perspective."

21. Reitz observes that "game players by and large will not approach *Black & White* as a serious test of themselves, but instead will, like any game, be played to experience every whim of curiosity, and thus ultimately can say little about the player, save that they are playful." While I contend that with careful analysis more can be said about game players than that they are playful, I concur with Reitz's assessment that few players of *Black & White* are likely to approach the game "as a serious test of themselves." At the same time, it seems probable that some players will approach *Black & White* as they do a horoscope: not expecting it to reveal a truth beforehand but lending the artifact veracity when in hindsight its "truths" appear accurate. Some *Black & White* players, that is, may find themselves saying, "Hey, that *is* how I am." While I cannot pursue this line of inquiry here, I would suggest to readers interested in doing so to begin by reading Theodor Adorno's essay on the cultural work of horoscopes titled "The Stars Down to Earth."

22. "Fun," of course, is as fluid and idiosyncratic a term as "play," but for simplicity's sake we can understand it to mean engaging in self-selected challenges that are typically not life-threatening and are considered entertaining.

23. See, by way of comparison, Rebecca R. Tews's essay "Archetypes on Acid: Video Games and Culture."

Epilogue

1. Although *Black & White* takes place in "Eden," it is populated with eight "tribes" that are distinctly non-Semitic: Aztec, Indian, Celtic, Japanese, Egyptian,

Norse, Greek, and Tibetan. These tribes comprise the groups of villagers who must be colonized in order to advance the game.

Appendix D

1. An interesting consequence of this academic focus has been the discovery of a number of precepts that are equally relevant to computer game scholars and professional computer game developers.

2. Although we will not offer a detailed treatment of how to get permission to run a Game Night from the variety of campus administrators who may object to institutional resources being used for playing games—such a guide would require a document twice the size of this one—we are pleased to acknowledge that administrators are increasingly open to persuasion about the merits of computer game research. The authors and all the participants of LGI, for example, are very thankful to Chuck Tatum, Larry Evers, Susan Bouldin, Hale Thomas, and Jeffrey Reed for their support in this work, and particularly for allowing us to use the College of Humanities collaborative computer classroom (COHLab) in ways that broke nearly every rule in the policy manual dictating appropriate use of such a space.

Works Cited

"4 Health Groups Link Media Mayhem to Violence by Kids." *Arizona Daily Star,* July 26, 2000: A6.

Adams, Ernest. "Dogma 2001: A Challenge to Game Designers." February 2, 2001. Available at http://www.gamasutra.com/features/20010129/adams_01.htm (accessed March 20, 2004).

Adorno, Theodor. *Prisms.* Cambridge, MA: MIT Press, 1967.

———. "The Stars Down to Earth." In *The Stars Down to Earth and Other Essays on the Irrational in Culture.* New York: Routledge, 2001.

Aedy, Richard, and Joe Ierano. "Gaming Pains." Radio National broadcast, February 11, 2002. Available at http://www.abc.net.au/rn/science/buzz/stories/s478608.htm (accessed March 20, 2004).

Ahearn, Luke, and Clayton Crooks. *Awesome Game Creation: No Programming Required.* Herndon, VA: Charles River Media, 2000.

Anglin, G. J., R. L. Towers, and W. H. Levie. "Visual Message Design and Learning: The Role of Static and Dynamic Illustrations." In *Handbook of Research for Educational Communications and Technology,* ed. D. H. Jonassen. New York: Macmillan, 1996. 755–91.

Augustine, Saint, Bishop of Hippo. *On Christian Doctrine.* Trans. D. W. Robertson Jr. New York: Liberal Arts Press, 1958.

Bates, Bob. *Game Design: The Art & Business of Creating Games.* Indianapolis, IN: Premier Press, 2001.

Baydak, Konstantin. *B&W.* Newsgroup message, fido7.su.game.news. September 23, 1998. Available at http://groups.google.com/groups?selm=906556644%40p54.f353.n5030.z2.ftn&oe=KOI8-R&output=gplain (accessed March 20, 2004).

Berger, Brett. "Review: *B17 Flying Fortress: The Mighty 8th:* Da Bomb or The Bomb?" *Computer Games* (January 22, 2001): 76–77. Available at http://www.cgonline.com/reviews/b17flyingf-02-r1.html (accessed March 20, 2004).

Boyd, Andrew. "When Worlds Collide: Sound and Music in Film and Games." February 4, 2003. Available at http://www.gamasutra.com/features/20030204/boyd_02.shtml (accessed March 20, 2004).

Braun, M. J. "Sovereignty, Democracy, and the Political Economy of Logos: A Defense of Antagonistic Rhetoric." PhD Diss. University of Arizona, 2002.

Brummett, Barry. *Rhetorical Dimensions of Popular Culture.* Tuscaloosa: U of Alabama P, 1991.

Brunner, C., D. Bennett, and M. Honey. "Girl Games and Technological Desire." *From Barbie to Mortal Kombat: Gender and Computer Games.* Ed. J. Cassell and H. Jenkins. Cambridge, MA: MIT Press, 1998. 72–88.

Burgoon, Judee K., Joseph A. Bonito, Björn Bengtsson, et al. "Testing the Interactivity Model: Communication Processes, Partner Assessments, and the Quality of Collaborative Work." *Journal of Management Information Systems* 16:3 (2000): 33–56.

Burke, Kenneth. *A Grammar of Motives.* Berkeley: U of California P, 1969.

———. *A Rhetoric of Motives.* Berkeley: U of California P, 1969.

Burzynski, Kamil. "Re: Shortest Path Algorithm Needed." Newsgroup message, comp.games.development.programming. August 16, 2001. Available at http://groups.google.com/groups?selm=9lftnh%24bft%241%40sunsite.i cm.edu.pl&output=gplain (accessed March 20, 2004).

Carbaugh, Donal. "Comments on 'Culture' in Communication Inquiry." *Communication Reports* 1 (1988): 38–42.

Carroll, J. M. "The Adventure of Getting to Know a Computer." *IEEE Computer* 15 (1982): 49–58.

Case, Stevie. "Do Game Journalists Play Fair?" *Electronic Entertainment Expo.* Los Angeles, California, May 16, 2001.

Cassell, Justine, and Henry Jenkins, ed. *From Barbie to Mortal Kombat: Gender and Computer Games.* Cambridge, MA: MIT Press, 1998.

Chan Lin, L. J. "A Theoretical Analysis of Learning with Graphics: Implications for Computer Graphics Design." 1994. ERIC NO. ED370526.

Chomsky, Noam. *Necessary Illusions: Thought Control in Democratic Societies.* Boston: South End Press, 1989.

Coffey, Robert. "Do Game Journalists Play Fair?" *Electronic Entertainment Expo.* Los Angeles, California, May 16, 2001.

Cohen, David. *The Development of Play.* 2nd ed. New York: Routledge, 1993.

Crawford, Chris. *The Art of Computer Game Design.* Berkeley, CA: Osborne/McGraw-Hill, 1984.

Davies, Martin. "Talk before the Electronic Entertainment Expo." Los Angeles, CA, May 16, 2001.

deMaria, Rusel, and Johnny L. Wilson. *High Score! The Illustrated History of Electronic Games.* Berkeley, CA: McGraw-Hill/Osborne, 2002.

Dowling, Patrick. "Localizing for Lands Beyond the Wild Frontier." *Gamasutra* 2.34 (1998). Available at http://www.gamasutra.com/features/production/19980828/localization_01.htm (accessed March 20, 2004).

Dreyfus, Stuart, Hubert Dreyfus, and Tom Athanasiou. *Mind Over Machine: The*

Power of Human Intuition and Expertise in the Era of the Computer. New York: Free Press, 1986.

Dunn, Cynthia, and Gary Chadwick. *Protecting Volunteers in Research: A Manual for Investigative Sites.* Boston: CenterWatch, 2002.

Eberly, David H. *3D Game Engine Design: A Practical Approach to Real-time Computer Graphics.* San Francisco: Morgan Kaufmann, 2001.

Eddy, Andy. "Editorial." *Game Weekly* (May 12, 1999): 76.

Ellul, Jacques. *Propaganda: The Formation of Men's Attitudes.* New York: Vintage Books, 1965.

———. *The Technological Society.* New York: Knopf, 1964.

Entertainment Software Association. "2002 Industry Sales Information." Available at http://www.theesa.com/ffbox8.html (accessed March 21, 2004).

Evans, Dean. *Black & White: Prima's Official Strategy Guide.* Roseville, CA: Prima Games UK, 2001.

Evans, Richard. "The Future of AI in Games: A Personal View." *Game Developer* (August 2001): 46–49.

Fischer, Blake. "Review: *Twisted Metal Black.*" *NextGen* 3.2 (2001): 25–26.

Freud, Sigmund. "The Dream-Work." Trans. A. A. Brill. In *The Interpretation of Dreams.* 1911.

Friedl, Markus. *Online Game Interactivity Theory.* Hingham, MA: Charles River Media, 2003.

"Gaming 2001: The Future of Gaming in America." Press release. Fairfield Research, Inc., January 1999.

GameSpot. *About Our Rating System.* GameSpot Web site. Available at http://gamespot.com/gamespot/misc/userreview/explained.html (accessed March 20, 2004).

"Fighting Game Statistics." *GameWEEK* (May 12, 1999): 60.

Geertz, Clifford. *The Interpretation of Cultures.* New York: Basic Books, 1973.

Gerstenzang, James. "Clinton Sees Violent Influence in 3 Video Games." *Los Angeles Times,* April 25, 1999: A12.

Gordon, John Steele. "Can Enron Improve Corporate America?" Guest Commentary, Minnesota Public Radio. November 30, 2002. Audio file available at http://www.soundmoney.org/archive/listings/shows02_11.htm#1130 (accessed March 20, 2004).

Grossman, Dave. *On Killing: The Psychological Cost of Learning to Kill in War and Society.* Boston: Little, Brown, 1995.

Grossman, Dave, and Gloria DeGaetano. *Stop Teaching Our Kids to Kill: A Call to Action against TV, Movie, and Video Game Violence.* 1st ed. New York: Crown, 1999.

Harzel, H. "Shortest Path Algorithm Needed." Newsgroup message, comp.games.development.programming.algorithms. August 14, 2001. Available at http://groups.google.com/groups?selm=9lbur5%24799%241%40news.kolumbus.fi&oe=UTF-8&output=gplain (accessed March 20, 2004).

Howard, Tharon. *A Rhetoric of Electronic Communities.* Greenwich, CT: Ablex, 1997.

Huizinga, Johan. *Homo Ludens: A Study of the Play Element in Culture.* 1938. Boston: Beacon, 1986.

Hutnik, Richard. "Black and White Is the Future of Gaming! (rant mode on)." Newsgroup message, comp.sys.ibm.pc.games.strategic. April 1, 2001. Available at http://groups.google.com/groups?selm=3AC75491.273B850A%40interbulletin.com&output=gplain (accessed March 20, 2004).

Interactive Entertainment Industry Overview: A Clear Path for Growth. Deutsche Banc: Alex Brown, Inc., May 2001.

International Game Developers' Association. *Game Developer's First Annual Salary Survey (for 2000). Game Developer* 8.7 (July 2001). Available at http://www.gamasutra.com/features/20010831/survey_01_htm (accessed March 20, 2004).

———. *Game Developer's Second Annual Salary Survey (for 2001). Game Developer* 9.7 (July 2002): 32–38.

Jeffries, Amos. "Re: Pattern/Gesture Recognition Aka Black and White Mouse Cursor." Newsgroup message, comp.games.development.programming.algorithms. August 6, 2001. Available at http://groups.google.com/groups?selm=8lub7.1300%24fg7.270214%40news.xtra.co.nz&output=gplain (accessed March 20, 2004).

Jenkins, Henry. "Art Form for the Digital Age." *Technology Review* 2000.

———. "Coming Up Next: Ambushed on 'Donahue'!" 2002. Salon.com Web site. Available at http://archive.salon.com/tech/feature/2002/08/20/jenkins_on_donahue (accessed March 20, 2004).

"Joint Statement on the Impact of Entertainment Violence on Children." Congressional Public Health Summit, July 26, 2000.

Kasavin, Greg. "Game Review Techniques . . . " E-mail to author, September 1, 2004.

———. "Re: Game Review Techniques . . . " E-mail to author, September 1, 2004.

———. "Review: *Deus Ex.*" June 27, 2000. GameSpot Web site. Available at http://www.gamespot.com/pc/rpg/deusex/review.html (accessed March 20, 2004).

Keighley, Geoff. "*Half-Life* Review." November 30, 1998. GameSlice Web site. Available at http://www.gameslice.com/editorial/1130hl.shtml (accessed March 20, 2004).

Kellner, Douglas. "Critical Theory and British Cultural Studies: The Missed Articulation." In *Cultural Methodologies,* ed. Jim McGuigan. London: Sage, 1997. 12–41.

Kennedy, George A. "A Hoot in the Dark: The Evolution of General Rhetoric." *Philosophy and Rhetoric* 25 (1992): 1–21.

Klett, Steve. "Review: *Homeworld: Cataclysm.*" *PC Gamer* 2000: 130–31.

Kuntzel, Thierry. "The Film-Work." *Enclitic* 2.1 (1978): 39–62.

———. "The Film-Work, 2." *Camera Obscura: A Journal of Feminism and Film Theory* 5 (Spring 1980): 7–68.

Leach, James, and James Lenoël. *Black & White Instruction Guide.* Ed. Ede Clarke. Redwood City, CA: Electronic Arts UK, 2001.

Lengyel, Eric. *Mathematics for 3D Game Programming and Computer Graphics.* Hingham, MA: Charles River Media, 2002.

Leone, Wayne. "Req: Line Intersection Algorithm." Newsgroup message, comp.games.development.programming.algorithms. July 23, 1998.

Levi, Tod. "Vertex Edit yields BSP holes!" Newsgroup message, alt.games.unreal.ed. March 31, 2003. Available at http://groups.google.com/groups?selm=fa287614.0303310759.1ff1bc4a%40posting.google.com&oe=UTF-8&output=gplain (accessed March 20, 2004).

Liimatta, Jukka. "Re: Windowproc and Setwindowlong." Newsgroup message, comp.games.development.programming. August 12, 2001. Available at http://groups.google.com/groups?selm=9l6ans%24qnl%241%40news.kolumbus.fi&output=gplain (accessed March 20, 2004).

London, Perry. *Behavior Control.* New York: Harper & Row, 1969.

Lundrigon, Jeff. "Review: *Escape from Monkey Island.*" *NextGen* 3.2 (2001): 85.

Mandel, Siegfried. *Dictionary of Science.* New York: Dell, 1969.

Marselas, Herb. "Where'd It Go? It Was Just Here! Managing Assets for the Next Age of Real-Time Strategy Games." *Game Developer* (November 2000). Available at http://www.gamasutra.com/features/20010221/marselas_03.htm (accessed March 20, 2004).

Marx, Karl. *The Poverty of Philosophy.* Trans. H. Quelch. Amherst, NY: Prometheus Books, 1995.

———. "Theses on Feuerbach." Trans. W. Lough. *Marx/Engels Selected Works.* Vol. 1. Moscow: Progress Publishers, 1969. 13–15.

Molitor, S., S. P. Ballstaedt, and H. Mandl. "Problems in Knowledge Acquisition from Text and Pictures." In *Knowledge Acquisition from Text and Pictures,* ed. H. Mandl and J. R. Levin. Amsterdam: North-Holland, 1989. 3–35.

Moses. "Re: Looking for Games for Promotion and Distribution." Newsgroup message, comp.games.development.programming.algorithms. August 12, 2001. Available at http://groups.google.com/groups?selm=9l5tkj%245ac%241%40neptunium.btinternet. com&output=gplain (accessed March 20, 2004).

Norman, Donald A. *The Invisible Computer: Why Good Products Can Fail, the Personal Computer Is So Complex, and Information Appliances Are the Solution.* Cambridge, MA: MIT Press, 1999.

NPD Group, Inc. "Funworld: Industry Trends—Annual 2003 Video Game Best-selling Titles and Console Accessories." March 10, 2004. Available at http://www.npdfunworld.com/funServlet?nextpage=trend_body.html&content_id=780.

Ohmann, Richard. *Selling Culture: Magazines, Markets, and Class at the Turn of the Century.* London: Verso, 1996.

Ollman, Bertell. *Dialectical Investigations.* New York: Routledge, 1993.

Oti, Okorie. "Re: Windowproc and Setwindowlong (Reply)." Newsgroup message, comp.games.development.programming. August 12, 2001. Available at http://groups.google.com/groups?selm=9l6680%244mb%241%40news8.svr .pol.co.uk &output=gplain (accessed March 20, 2004).

———. "Windowproc and Setwindowlong." August 10, 2001. Available at http://

groups.google.com/groups?selm=9l1frh%24im6%241%40newsg2.svr.pol.co.uk&output=gplain (accessed March 20, 2004).

Palumbo, Paul. "Corporate Web Sites Seek Game Developers." December 19, 1997. Available at http://www.gamasutra.com/features/business_and_legal/121997/web_site.htm (accessed March 20, 2004).

PC Data, Inc. "Best Selling Games, 2000." *Wired* (May 2001): 151.

Phil. "Black & White: Bad Beginnings." July 31, 2001. Available at http://www.geocities.com/phileosophos/essays/bwbadbeginnings.html (accessed March 20, 2004).

Plato. *Gorgias and Phaedrus.* Trans. James H. Nichols. Ithaca, NY: Cornell UP, 1998.

Poole, Steven. *Trigger Happy: The Inner Life of Videogames.* London: Fourth Estate, 2000.

Provenzano, Paul. "Talk before the Electronic Entertainment Expo." *Electronic Entertainment Expo,* Los Angeles, CA, May 16, 2001.

Provenzo, Eugene F., Jr. *Video Kids: Making Sense of Nintendo.* Cambridge, MA: Harvard UP, 1991.

Quintilian. *Quintilian on the Teaching of Speaking and Writing: Translations from Books One, Two, and Ten of the Institutio Oratoria.* Ed. James J. Murphy. Carbondale: Southern Illinois UP, 1988.

Reitz, Jennifer Diane. *Playing 'Black & White' from a Historical Theological Perspective.* March 2001. Unicorn Jelly Web site. Available at http://unicornjelly.com/bwgameplaystyles.html (accessed March 20, 2004).

Reuters Newswire. "Colorado Teen Gunmen Liked Computers, War Games." April 22, 1999.

Rockstar Games. *State of Emergency.* http://www.rockstargames.com. February 26, 2004.

Rogers, Everett M. *Communication Technology: The New Media in Society.* New York: Free Press, 1986.

Rollings, Andrew, and Dave Morris. *Game Architecture and Design: Learn the Best Practices for Game Design and Programming.* Scottsdale, AZ: Coriolus Group, 2000.

Roumani, Hamdi. *PC Reader Review: Deus Ex.* August 26, 2001. GameSpot Web site. Available at http://www.gamespot.com/pc/rpg/deusex/reader_review.html?id=543132 (accessed March 20, 2004).

Ruggill, Judd Ethan. "Corporate Cunning and Calculating Congressmen: A Political Economy of the Game Film." *TEXT Technology* 12.2 (2004).

Ruggill, Judd Ethan, Ken S. McAllister, and David Menchaca. "The Gamework." *Communication and Critical/Cultural Studies* 1.4 (December 2004).

Russo, Tom. "Developers First." *NextGen* (January 2001).

Saltzman, Marc, ed. *Game Design: Secrets of the Sages.* Indianapolis, IN: Brady, 1999.

Schank, Roger C. "What We Learn When We Learn by Doing." Technical Report 60, The Institute for the Learning Sciences, Northwestern University, October 1994. Available at http://cogprints.ecs.soton.ac.uk/archive/00000637/00/Learnby Doing _Schank.html (accessed March 20, 2004).

Sosnoski, James J. "Hyper-Readers and Their Reading Engines." *Passions, Pedagogies, and 21st Century Technologies.* Ed. Gail E. Hawisher and Cynthia L. Selfe. Logan: Utah State UP, 1999. 161–77.

Spector, Warren. "Education Committee . . . " E-mail to author, July 14, 2001.

———. "Postmortem: Ion Storm's Deus Ex." *Game Developer* 7.11 (November 2000). Available at http://www.gamasutra.com/features/10001206/spector_01.htm (accessed March 20, 2004).

Stix, Gary. "Sonic Boon." *Scientific American* 288.1 (January 2003): 30.

Stripinis, David. "The (Not So) Dark Art of Scripting for Artists." *Game Developer* (September 2001): 40–44.

Summerhayes, Geoff. "Re: Shortest Path Algorithm Needed (1st Reply)." Newsgroup message, comp.games.development.programming. August 15, 2001. Available at http://groups.google.com/groups?selm=tnku35484belbc%40corp.supernews.com &output=gplain (accessed March 20, 2004).

———. "Re: Shortest Path Algorithm Needed (2nd Reply)." Newsgroup message, comp.games.development.programming. August 16, 2001. Available at http://groups. google.com/groups?selm=tnnndqjr24m201%40corp.supern ews.com&output= gplain (accessed March 20, 2004).

Tenner, Edward. *Why Things Bite Back: Technology and the Revenge of Unintended Consequences.* New York: Knopf, 1996.

Tews, Rebecca R. "Archetypes on Acid: Video Games and Culture." In *The Medium of the Video Game,* ed. Mark J. P. Wolf. Austin: U of Texas P, 2001. 169–82.

Thomas, Karen. "Kids, Online and Off, Feast on Violence." *USA Today,* April 22, 1999.

Todd, Brett. "Review: Dino Crisis." *Computer Games* 125 (April 2001): 85.

Vanka, Surya. "ColorTool: The Cross-Cultural Meanings of Color." Designing for Global Markets: Proceedings of the First International Workshop on Internationalization of Products and Systems. Rochester, NY, May 20–25, 1999. 33–43.

Waits, Stephen. "What's Better . . . " Newsgroup message, comp.games.development. programming.algorithms. July 21, 1998.

Warhawk, Lance. "PC Reader Review: Deus Ex." June 4, 2001. GameSpot Web site. Available at http://www.gamespot.com/pc/rpg/desuex/reader_review.html?id=411765 (accessed March 20, 2004).

Watkins, Ralph. *A Competitive Assessment of the U.S. Video Game Industry: Report on Investigation No. 332–160 under Section 332(B) of the Tariff Act of 1930.* Washington, DC: U.S. International Trade Commission, 1984.

Wessel, Craig. *A Parent's Guide to Computer Games.* Los Angeles: Mars, 2000.

Williams, Raymond. *Keywords: A Vocabulary of Culture and Society.* New York: Oxford UP, 1983.

Williams, Scott. "Re: What's Better . . . " Newsgroup message, comp. games.development. programming.algorithms. July 22, 1998.

Williamson. "Review: *Sydney 2000.*" *PC Gamer* (2000): 151.

Winner, Langdon. *Autonomous Technology: Technics-Out-of-Control as a Theme in Political Thought.* Cambridge, MA: MIT Press, 1977.

Wolf, Mark J. P. "Time in the Video Game." In *The Medium of the Video Game,* ed. Mark J. P. Wolf. Austin: U of Texas P, 2001. 77–91.

Wolfie. *Black & White: Rants and Raves.* 2001. Available at http://www.wolfiesden.com/games/blackandwhite/ (accessed March 20, 2004).

Ze Dong, Mao. "On Contradiction." *Mao Ze Dong Selected Works.* Vol. 1. Peking: Peking Foreign Press, 1967. 311–46.

Index

Adams, Ernest, 101
Adorno, Theodore, 49, 209n18, 216n21
aesthetics, 34, 40, 139
Age of Empires II: The Age of Kings, 107
agents: artists, 19, 24, 45, 73–76, 84–85, 94, 100–101, 106–109, 113, 115, 120–21, 131, 135, 137, 187, 212n20; designers, 11, 22, 23, 35–41, 45–46, 54, 55, 75, 81, 84–85, 90, 94, 101, 109, 112, 116, 120, 124, 132, 134, 136, 209n25, 211n11, 212n20; developers, 13, 20, 23–25, 32, 36, 40, 42, 45–46, 51–58, 60–63, 72–117, 120–21, 124, 129–31, 134–39, 148, 157–58, 161–66, 169, 213n6; marketers, 32, 42–47, 52–62, 73, 81, 115, 130–34, 136–39, 148–49, 157, 167–169, 209n26; players, vii–viii, 7–16, 19–24, 31–33, 36–42, 44–47, 50–60, 62–63, 65, 76–78, 80–81, 84–91, 100, 112–117, 121–139, 144–66, 169, 186, 188, 195, 207n4, 211n11, 215n16
Air Traffic Controller Simulator, 77
Alternative Educational Environments (AEE), 54
ambiguity, 35, 63, 83, 135
anime, 132
antagonism. *See* contradiction; dialectic
arcade game emulators, 32
arcades, 9
artifacts, 3, 10, 12, 41–43, 47, 61–64, 88, 104–105. *See also* computer games
artists. *See* agents
asset management, 106–7
audio, 14, 19, 41, 54, 87, 100, 121, 136, 138, 205n1; in *Black & White*, 143, 157, 164. *See also* music
audio cards, 19, 21. *See also* audio
avatars, 45–47

B17 Flying Fortress, 126
Bates, Bob, 54, 112, 113, 212n23
Black & White, 97, 140–68; natural resources in, 145–46, 149–54, 215n16; spiritual resources in, 146–47, 154–56; temporal resources in, 147–48, 156–57. *See also* audio; computer game complex; economic force; interfaces; music; power; time
Braun, M. J., 212n18
Brummett, Barry, 10, 15, 30, 47–49, 88
Burke, Kenneth, 45, 208n13

Carbaugh, Donal, 10
Case, Stevie, 124
Cassell, Justine, 73
Clancy, Tom, vii
Clinton, William, 7
Coffey, Robert, 124
comics, 6, 53
computer game complex, x, 6–26, 28, 30–34, 41–65, 169–70; and game production, 80–84, 92, 96, 101, 115, 117; and game reviewing, 120, 130–31, 134, 138–

39; in *Black & White,* 144, 149, 154, 157, 167. *See also* agents; functions; influences; manifestations; transformative locales
computer game designers. *See* agents
computer game industry. *See* agents; computer game complex
Computer Games (magazine), 126–28
computer games: as artifacts, viii, 1, 3, 18, 26, 29, 32–34, 50, 54–58, 61–64, 66, 75, 81, 84, 91, 94, 116, 130, 138, 139, 142, 148, 164, 168, 169, 216n21; as works of art, 71–117; as scapegoats, 6–8, 72. *See also* artifacts; agents; functions; influences; manifestations; transformative locales
Computer Gaming World, 118–19, 124
conflict, 9, 31, 37, 55, 57–58, 116, 208n8. *See also* manifestations
consumers, 12, 20, 22, 24, 38, 46, 73, 75, 121, 129, 131, 138, 167
contradiction, 9, 11–12, 14, 15, 24, 25, 29–34, 44, 109, 129–39, 212n18, 212n20. *See also* dialectic
cooperation, 37, 208n8
coopertition, 113
Crawford, Chris, 23, 35–39, 42, 55–58, 76–77, 207n7, 209n25
Croft, Lara, 9, 21, 45, 101, 167, 169, 206n10

Davies, Martin, 75
Deerhunter, 101, 116
Deus Ex, 115, 122, 124, 125
developers. *See* agents
Diablo, 74
dialectic, 1, 25, 29–34, 37, 41, 49–50, 64, 84, 92, 101–102, 108–109, 121, 137, 144, 166, 207n2, 207n3; and antagonistic contradiction, 29, 31, 33, 109, 212n18; and dialectical inquiry, 29–31, 207n5; and non-antagonistic contradiction 29, 30, 33, 109; and rhetoric, xi, 25, 29–32, 43, 50, 64, 92, 101–109, 166, 207n2, 207n3
Dino Crisis, 126
disciplinarity, 92, 98, 103
discipline, 96, 98, 116
Doom, 6–8, 58, 101
Dreamcast. *See* Sega
Driver 2, 74
Duke Nukem (character), 9, 21, 45, 167
Duke Nukem (game), 7, 13, 58

economic force, 18–24, 53, 136–38, 139, 169, 214n9; in *Black & White,* 142–44, 148–49, 154, 157–68; ideological, 163–66; narratological, 159–61; philosophical/theological, 161–63; technical, 158. *See also* influences
Eddy, Andy, 7–8
Eidos, 86, 210n8
Electronic Arts, 86, 120, 167
Electronic Entertainment Expo, 75, 85, 124
ELIZA, 60, 72–72
emotions, ix, 8, 10, 11, 29, 51, 52, 58, 87, 125, 132–33, 135, 212n18, 186
Ensemble Studios, 107
Entertainment Software Ratings Board (ESRB), 119–20
Escape from Monkey Island, 128
ethnography, 88
EverQuest, 65
exigencies, 29, 47, 50, 62, 80–86, 91–92, 94, 96, 106–108, 135. *See also* functions

Fairfield Research Group, 7
fantasy, 8, 36, 206n11
fanzines, 22
feminist game critiques, 39–40, 73, 160–61
film-work, 63, 205n2
Final Fantasy, 21, 22, 167
first-person shooters, 44, 46, 74, 116, 197
flight simulators, 13, 77, 87, 135
fun, 11, 23, 25, 33, 35, 38, 87, 110, 129, 138, 184, 194, 197; and realism, 76–78, 121, 135; and rules, 163–66
functions of rhetoric, 47–50; exigent/interventional, 47, 79–80, 84, 92–105; quotidian/appropriational, 48, 55, 79–80, 84–86, 105–109, 116; implicative/conditional, 15, 48, 55, 79–80, 86–92, 108–114, 158, 161, 165, 168. *See also* exigencies; transformative locales; rhetoric

Game Boy. *See* Nintendo
game films, 10, 53, 61, 167, 169
game night, 181–98
game reviews, 114, 118–39, 142
GameCube. *See* Nintendo
GameSlice.com, 124
GameSpot.com, 121, 122, 124, 127
gameworks, vii-viii, 2–3, 27–65, 93–94, 169–70; five propositions of, 31–32
gender, 25, 37, 39, 48, 50, 61, 73, 87, 112, 118–19, 142, 153, 161, 166, 207n3, 208n10, 212n23, 215n7
globalization, 53, 139, 169
grammar of gameworks, 1–2, 27–65. *See also* agents; functions; influences; manifestations; transformative locales
Grim Fandango, 128
Grossman, Dave, 55, 58, 74
Gulf War, 13

Half-Life, 87, 125
Heavy Gear, 27
hegemony, 12
Hitman, 119, 132, 162
Homeworld: Cataclysm, 127
homologous ideology. *See* transformative locales
homophobia, 153, 208n10, 215n13
homosexuality, 67, 118–19, 215n13
Huizinga, Johan, 35, 36, 59, 207n6

I/O Devices, 195–196. *See also* peripherals
ideology. *See* transformative locales
idiosyncratic ideology. *See* transformative locales
Immersion Studios, 54
Imperialism (game), 13
imperialism, 37, 99
implicative function of rhetoric. *See* functions
inclusive ideology. *See* transformative locales
influences, 43, 50–55. *See also* economic force; instructional force; mass culture; mass media; psychophysiological force
instructional force, 24–25, 50, 54–55, 116, 138–39. *See also* influences
Interactive Digital Software Association (IDSA), 119
Interactive Entertainment Academy (IEA), 210n4
interactivity/interaction, vii, 7, 8, 14, 23, 33, 36, 39, 42, 51–57, 81–84, 123, 129, 132, 163, 168. *See also* manifestations
interdisciplinarity: viii, 17, 28, 41, 43, 166, 181–83, 186, 198. *See also* multiperspectivalism
interfaces, 12, 23, 24, 40, 53, 54, 63, 78, 82, 86, 101; in *Black & White,* 143, 154, 157, 165
International Game Developers' Association (IGDA), 94, 116
International Game Developers' Conference (IGDC), 85
Interplay, 112
Ion Storm, 86

Jenkins, Henry, 73, 214n8
Jeopardy, 12
Joint Statement on the Impact of Entertainment Violence on Children, 135
Jordan, Michael, 57

Kasavin, Greg, 121–23
Keighley, Geoff, 124–26, 128
Kellner, Douglas, x, 3, 41, 208n12

language, vii, ix, 2, 19, 35, 48–49, 54, 63, 64, 79, 82, 87, 89, 96, 98, 104; sexist, 112
Learning Games Initiative (LGI), 181, 183, 197–98
licensing, 18, 23, 109, 210n8
Lieberman, Joseph, 74
Littleton, CO, 6–8, 72
localization, 54
London, Perry, 72
Los Angeles Times, 7

magazines, 12, 51, 53, 58, 90, 126–29. *See also Computer Games* (magazine); *Computer Gaming World;* fanzines; *NextGen; PC Gamer; Time Magazine*

manifestations, 55–59, 64, 116, 130. *See also* conflict; interactivity; representation; safety
Marilyn Manson, 6
Mario, 9, 21
market research, 62, 106, 112, 210n3
marketers. *See* agents
Marselas, Herb, 107, 109
Marx, Karl, x, 1, 41, 145, 208n15
mass culture, 9–12, 23, 50–51, 68, 88, 100, 103, 115, 130, 131, 205n3, 213n25. *See also* popular culture; influences
mass media, 13–14, 17, 41, 44, 51–52, 55, 63, 72, 75, 88, 89, 101, 115, 132–33, 143–44, 167, 208n10; film/cinema, ix, 6, 10, 18, 47, 49, 51, 58–59, 63, 72–73, 93–94, 115, 119, 124–25, 132, 166–67, 213n7; newspapers, 6, 51, 60, 119, 123, 132; radio, 51, 132; television, 6, 8, 12, 13, 14, 19, 51, 52, 58, 59, 81, 115, 116, 119, 132, 166. *See also* influences
massive multi-player games (MMPG), 51, 207n7
Mattel, 18, 73
Max Payne, 74
Maxis Games, 54, 215n13, 216n19
media. *See* mass media
metanoia, 31, 44, 59–61, 173, 207n5
metonymy, 14, 33, 85, 149
Microsoft, vii, 113; Xbox, 9, 128
Moore's Law, 21
Morris, Dave, 40, 54, 113–14, 129
Mortal Kombat, 10, 21
mosaic, 30–31. *See also* rhetoric
multiperspectivalism, x, 1–3, 17, 41–42, 57, 61–63, 68, 93, 130,
music, viii, 6, 21, 22, 39, 40, 45, 87–89, 106, 107, 109, 143. *See also* audio
Myst, 10, 57, 101, 129

N-Gage, 9
Neo-Geo, 9
Neverwinter Nights, 110
New York Times, 119
NextGen, 128
Nintendo, 19, 73, 119; Game Boy, 9; Game Boy Advance, 70–71; GameCube, 9, 128
novelizations, 22, 53

Ohmann, Richard, 10–12, 205n3
One-on-One, 57
online game reviews, 120–26. *See also* game reviews
online gaming, 20. *See also* massive multi-player games

P.Y.S.T., 10
Pac-Man, 9
parenting, 6, 7, 17, 18, 24, 55, 80–81, 116, 119, 187
PC Gamer, 126–28
peripherals, 40, 53, 198; joysticks, 5–6, 19, 40, 127, 168, 192; mice, 19, 97, 157
Phantasmagoria, 57
play. *See* problematic of play
playability, 24, 126–31, 134, 138, 157, 166, 194, 195, 196, 209n25
players. *See* agents
Playstation*See* Sony
Pokemon (character), 21, 70–71
Pokemon (game), 70–71, 135
Pokemon Gold, 74, 210
Pokemon Silver, 74, 210
Poole, Steven, 39, 76
popular culture: versus mass culture, 10–12, 47
power, ix-x, 1–2, 9–18, 24, 33, 41, 42, 46, 50, 59, 62, 64, 67, 80–83, 92, 98–101, 104, 135; in *Black & White,* 147–56, 164–66, 208n10, 209n16
praxis, 9, 29
printed game reviews, 126–29. *See also* game reviews
problematic of play, 34–39, 41, 42
producers, 32, 44, 63, 84–85, 99, 133, 137. *See also* agents
programmers, 11, 19, 22, 46, 56, 75, 79, 81, 84, 86, 95, 97, 100, 108, 113, 115, 120, 213n4. *See also* agents
propaganda, 206n8
psychophysiological force, 14–18, 41, 50,

52, 63, 115–16, 133–36, 209n21. *See also* influences

Quake, ix, 7
quality assurance, 84, 86
quotidian function of rhetoric. *See* functions

racism, 3, 25, 48, 61, 145, 182, 184, 196, 208n10
Railroad Tycoon, 13
Rainbow Six, 63
realism, 76–78, 121, 133, 135, 137, 139, 150, 158, 161
Red Faction, 33
Redneck Rampage, 44
representation, 6, 12, 33, 36, 41, 44, 53–59, 112, 116, 121, 169, 184, 194, 196. *See also* manifestations
Resident Evil, 10, 129, 167
Reuters, 6
rhetoric, vii, xi, 8, 9, 12, 14–18, 25–26, 28–34, 38, 41–50, 54–64, 69, 120, 131–32, 136, 144–45, 147, 158, 161–68, 209n16, 210n7; of game developers, 71–117; eluctable and ineluctable rhetorical events, 30–31, 207n2; rhetorical analysis, 30–33, 207n3. *See also* dialectic, mosaic
Rockstar Games, 137
Rogue Spear, 52, 87
Roller Coaster Tycoon, 74
Rollings, Andrew, 40, 113, 129
Ruggill, Judd Ethan, 119–20

safety, 36, 37, 55, 58, 116, 184. *See also* manifestations
Sega, 73, 119; Dreamcast, 9, 127; Genesis, 74
Sims, 54, 74, 118, 215n13
Sim City, 54
Sim Earth, 54
Sim Farm, 54
Simpson, Toby, 46
simulation, 6–8, 13, 14, 34, 58, 60, 77, 86, 110, 135, 146, 151
Soldier of Fortune, 74, 119
Sonic the Hedgehog, 9, 205n2,
Sony, 119, 167; Playstation, 9, 18, 74, 126; Playstation 2, 128
Space Wars, 110
spin-doctoring, 7, 167
Splinter Cell, vii, 105
Star Trek, 12, 22, 162
Star Trek: Star Fleet Academy, 10,
StarCraft, 36
State of Emergency, 13
stock market, 18
strategy guides, 22, 53, 153, 164
Street Fighter, 10, 58, 73
Survivor, 12, 51
Sydney 2000, 127

Taylor, Chris, 112
theology, 30, 194
Thief, 87
time, 14, 17, 74, 76, 77, 81, 85, 91, 108, 115, 127, 136, 215n14; in *Black & White*, 147, 156–57, 215n11
Time Magazine, 119
Time-Warner, 18
Tomb Raider, 10, 101, 169, 206n10
Tony Hawk's Pro Skater II, 74
transformative locales, 1, 43, 59–61, 62, 64, 67–68, 80, 116–17, 130, 134, 157, 166–68; homologous, xi, 30–32, 48–49, 52–53, 59, 60–61, 65, 94, 98, 116, 134, 167, 170–71; ideology, viii, 1, 9, 30–34, 39, 42, 44, 52, 59–65, 69, 80, 84, 103, 109, 115, 130, 139, 144, 157–58, 161–67; idiosyncratic, ix, 30, 32, 47–48, 52–53, 59–61, 67–68, 94, 134, 167; inclusive, xi, 1, 30–32, 59–61, 64, 67, 116–17, 167. *See also* mosaic
tropes, 3, 14, 34, 43, 51, 87, 89, 154
Twisted Metal, 128

U.S. International Trade Commission, 20
Unreal Tournament, 32, 162; *Unreal Editor*, 210n8, 211n9
USA Today, 6
Usenet newsgroups, 21, 63, 82, 93–104, 121, 164, 211n15, 213n2

video cards, 20–21, 168
Vietnam War, 13
violence, viii, 3, 6–7, 12, 37, 54, 55, 74, 78, 112, 135, 139, 167, 169, 184, 194, 212n21, 214n8
virtual reality, 23, 25, 54

Weizenbaum, Joseph, 60, 72–73
Wessel, Craig, 55
Where in the World is Carmen Sandiego, 24, 54
Who Wants to Be a Millionaire?, 51, 74
Williams, Raymond, 10
Wing Commander, ix, 10, 13, 22, 63
Wolf, Mark J. P., 215n14
women: in game industry, 61, 94, 124, 212n23; as players, 27–28, 50, 61, 73, 118–19, 166
WonderSwan, 9
World-Wide Web, 12, 21, 23, 51, 53, 63, 65, 71, 82, 85, 93, 98, 119, 120–26, 131, 137, 162, 164, 166, 206n10
work. *See* film-work; gameworks; grammar of gameworks

Zodiac, 9